THE SWASHBUCKLERS

THE ***SWASHBUCKLERS***

The Story of Canada's

Battling Broadcasters

KNOWLTON NASH

M&S

National Library of Canada Cataloguing in Publication Data

Nash, Knowlton
Swashbucklers : the story of Canada's battling broadcasters

Includes index.
ISBN 0-7710-6774-7

1. Broadcasting–Canada–History. I. Title.
HE8689.9.C3N384 2001   384.54'0971   C2001-900945-3

We acknowledge the financial support of the Government of Canada through the Book Publishing Industry Development Program for our publishing activities. We further acknowledge the support of the Canada Council for the Arts and the Ontario Arts Council for our publishing program.

Typeset in Minion by M&S, Toronto
Printed and bound in Canada

McClelland & Stewart Ltd.
The Canadian Publishers
481 University Avenue
Toronto, Ontario
M5G 2E9
www.mcclelland.com

1 2 3 4 5   05 04 03 02 01

To those who made broadcasting better

Contents

Introduction

A key challenge in researching the history of private broadcasters in Canada is the reality that they hated to write down anything on paper. "All broadcasters have a singularly deep-rooted aversion to paper," long-time Canadian Association of Broadcasters (CAB) president T. J. "Jim" Allard once said. "Very few broadcasting stations in the so-called 'private sector' have made the least attempt to keep any records other than those strictly required by law."

So, for a writer seeking to tell that story, among other things, it means exploring closets, attics, basements, bottom desk drawers, musty files, and scattered papers where the occasional nugget of information is hiding.

Fortunately, with the encouragement of the CAB, the diligence of Ryerson Polytechnic University, and, most of all, the dedication of private broadcasting veterans Ross McCreath and Lyman Potts, some of that history has been collected and preserved, some has been stored on the Canadian Communications Foundation Web site, and some has been kept by McCreath and Potts. Of particular value to me was an extraordinary collection of oral history tapes that McCreath has accumulated over the years and stored in a closet in his Toronto apartment. Many of the tapes held conversations recorded by University of Western Ontario

Professor Kenneth Bambrick, who travelled across the country collecting the memories of broadcasting old-timers. It proved to be an invaluable inside look at how private radio and television developed in Canada.

Other oral history tapes included those done for Selkirk Communications by Dick Misner, those done for Dennis Duffy and the B.C. Archives, and a large number done for the Canadian Communications Foundation by Phil Stone. Altogether Ross McCreath has in his collection about 270 tapes, ranging in length from fifteen minutes to a couple of hours. There also are tapes recorded by writer and broadcaster Walter Dales, who put his recollections and opinions into an unpublished book.

Tucked away among his memorabilia, Lyman Potts has a priceless scrapbook of broadcast history, including old newspaper clippings, magazine articles, letters from colleagues, reports, long-ago speeches, and fading photographs. A number of biographies, policy books, and detailed studies of broadcasting such as Mary Vipond's *The First Decade of Canadian Broadcasting, 1922–32* also proved rewarding sources.

All of this material has provided me with a rare insight into the development of broadcasting in Canada, which started when the Marconi Wireless Co. began experimental programming in Montreal in 1919. In 1926, the pioneer broadcasters formed the Canadian Association of Broadcasters, which has been the voice of private broadcasting ever since.

I have been given great help in tracing that history by Tom Curzon at CTV, Ian Anthony at Rogers Communications, Anthony Quinn at CITY-TV, retired broadcaster John Twomey, Ian Morrison at the Friends of Canadian Broadcasting, and, at the CAB, Michael Buzzell and Melanie Hughson, who let me spend hours leafing through hundreds of old files, letters, memoirs, statements, annual reports, photographs, and newspaper and magazine clippings.

Elizabeth Bishop at the Ryerson Polytechnic University Library provided extensive research materials, as did Ryerson Professor John Keeble, Michael MacDonald at the National Archives of Canada in Ottawa, and Anne Mercer of the CBC Toronto Reference Library. Don Jacinto, manager of Le Royal Meridien King Edward Hotel in Toronto, pinpointed the original meeting rooms of the CAB in 1926.

I'm deeply grateful to broadcast consultant Pauline Couture, who read though the manuscript with an expert's knowledge and an editor's eye. I'm grateful, too, for the time, background knowledge, and anecdotes provided by those I interviewed who are listed in "Sources" at the end of the book, as well as to those who preferred to remain anonymous.

I've been blessed in having Heather Sangster copy-edit my book. She took my sometimes quixotic punctuation, spelling, split infinitives, and other literary crimes and turned them into correct English. With her extraordinary patience and expertise, my editor, Dinah Forbes, has tolerated my last-minute amendments and helped develop, structure, correct, sharpen, and generally turn a sometimes rambling manuscript into a much more coherent and readable book.

To all who helped in the preparation of this book, I give my everlasting thanks, but most of all I thank my wife, Lorraine Thomson, and our family, who have suffered through my research and writing preoccupations for the last three years.

Preface

Nowhere in the world has the battle over the kind of broadcasting we hear and see been fought with more ferocity than in Canada. In its extremity, it's been a form of class warfare: the élite versus the hoi polloi; the wine drinkers versus the beer drinkers.

For most of the twentieth century, from the age of crystal sets to the era of satellites, idealists have battled swashbucklers in a war for the domination of broadcasting in Canada. The idealists wanted to use the airwaves primarily to educate and enrich Canadians and to strengthen Canadian unity. The swashbucklers wanted to provide entertainment that was popular and, most of all, profitable.

The swashbucklers won because they had the marketplace on their side. Canadians have liked, craved, and demanded American shows. While they preferred Canadian news and public affairs, flocked to the occasional homegrown entertainment program or series, and told pollsters they wanted Canadian programming, what Canadians *really* wanted was Hollywood shows – the more the merrier.

In rhetoric, Canadian governments time and again championed the idealists but failed to provide the funding their words promised. In action, Canadian governments for the last forty-five years aided and abetted the swashbucklers. The result has been the triumph of commerce over culture.

The swashbucklers, of course, are not all avaricious philistines, nor are the idealists all ivory-tower dreamers. The craftsmen of the private broadcasters' victory have been forcefully articulate advocates of unfettered free enterprise who, as the years have gone by, have grown more sophisticated, more eloquent, and more effective. They gave us what we wanted and in the process grew rich.

Eighty-two years ago, broadcasting began in Canada with programs aired by Montreal's Marconi station, XWA. Through the 1920s, entrepreneurs developed radio in Canada, but in the early 1930s, the do-gooders, who wanted to magnify the culture of Canada, won the day. A small group of public broadcasting zealots outclassed and outmanoeuvred the private swashbucklers using their backroom Machiavellian skills, awesome connections, and velvet-gloved brass knuckles. They succeeded by seducing Liberal Leader William Lyon Mackenzie King, who was philosophically inclined to support public broadcasting anyway, and by scaring the living daylights out of Conservative Leader R. B. Bennett over the possibility of an American takeover of Canadian airwaves.

Private broadcasters, the do-gooders argued, if they were to exist at all, were to be barely tolerated, regulated by the public broadcaster and supplementary to it, carrying much of the public network programming and filling in local gaps where the public system was temporarily absent. Hovering over the private broadcasters was the clear threat of total nationalization.

The private station operators fought back with dogged determination against what they characterized as "civil service" broadcasting, which forced onto Canadians programs that were "good for you" or, worse, were propaganda for the Liberal government. What they were offering were American shows that reaped big profits: Hollywood's slick shoot-'em-ups, comedies, musicals, and soap operas.

Increasingly persuasive, aggressive, and persistent, the swashbucklers eventually won the Conservatives to their cause, finding a champion in John Diefenbaker. As prime minister, in 1958 Diefenbaker emasculated the original concept of public broadcasting, eliminated the CBC's regulatory powers, and encouraged the establishment of private TV stations and networks, paving the way for the progress of private broadcasting's role in Canada from supplemental to equal to dominant. This transformation was accelerated by later CBC budget-slashing, a move that not only cut into the bones of the CBC but into its marrow.

The war for our eyes and ears sprang from the obsessions of two left-leaning, Oxford-educated, strongly nationalistic Canadians named Graham Spry and Alan Plaunt. Counterattacking from the right were two free-enterprise proselytizers by the names of Jim Allard and Walter Dales. While Dales worked behind the scenes, Allard played a highly visible role and eventually became head of the Canadian Association of Broadcasters (CAB), the influential lobby group for private radio and television. Also effectively championing the early cause of private broadcasting were a talented, sophisticated man who became known as "Mr. Private Broadcasting," Harry Sedgwick, the inspirational, street-smart boss of Canada's most successful private station, Toronto's CFRB, and his brother Joe Sedgwick, an articulate, suave, well-connected Toronto lawyer.

Hundreds and thousands of others, passionately on one side or the other, joined in the battle throughout the twentieth century, but the warriors who energized the assault against the infidels, as they described each other, were Spry and Plaunt on one side, and Allard, Dales, and the Sedgwicks on the other.

The story of Spry, Plaunt, and the CBC is written in my 1994 book, *Microphone Wars*, and *The Swashbucklers* is, in a sense, a companion volume of our broadcasting history, with the focus on how the private swash-bucklers of the air fought and won the battle over public broadcasting.

Round one in the 1930s, 1940s, and much of the 1950s went to the cultural missionaries of public broadcasting, but round two in the last half of the century went to the knights of commerce and their private system. With a patina of professionalism provided by the Sedgwicks, and later by Newfoundland private broadcaster Don Jamieson, Jim Allard galvanized into action a hitherto sickly CAB that had been ineffectively representing private broadcasters for a decade and a half. It took them about twenty years, but they won the war for broadcast dominance. The mopping up fell to the likes of John Bassett and Murray Chercover in Toronto, Izzy Asper in Winnipeg, the Shaws in Calgary, Ray Peters in Vancouver. They all grew rich and powerful in what started as a "mom and pop" adventure and became a multibillion-dollar business, employ-ing thirty thousand people by the end of the century.

This, then, is the success story of private broadcasting and the triumph of commerce over culture.

1

Pioneer Days

A snow-swirling gale howled along King Street outside the elegant King Edward Hotel in downtown Toronto in January 1926 as five pioneers of Canadian broadcasting trudged past the early-morning crowds of businessmen, secretaries, and office clerks scurrying to work. The turbulence of the storm matched the anxiety the five men felt about the future of broadcasting in Canada. They were on their way to a meeting to discuss a challenge that could kill the infant business of broadcasting.

The threat was a bill that had been introduced in the House of Commons that would amend the Copyright Act to include radio. This would mean radio stations would have to pay copyright fees for the music they broadcast, which would be costly since music was primarily what the stations put on the air. Paying for it seemed outrageous to them. About 90 per cent of what the four Montreal stations aired was music, and about 60 per cent for CFCA in Toronto. And now there was more trouble for Canada's fifty-five private stations. The Canadian Performing Rights Society was formally launching a test-case lawsuit against Toronto's CKNC for payment of copyright fees. Equally worrisome, officials in Ottawa were also talking about ordering stations to reduce the amount of advertising on radio.

Shaking off the snow, the five men strode past the smiling, grandly uniformed doorman and into the King Edward's spacious two-storey lobby. They walked past a glowing fireplace, marble pillars, and huge oil paintings and took the elevator to the third floor, where, in Room 394, they were going to change the history of broadcasting in Canada.

The five were led by thirty-five-year-old Jacques Cartier, the suave, irrepressible, fluently bilingual manager of Montreal's CKAC, which was owned by the influential newspaper *La Presse*. The station had four employees, including Cartier. He was a cousin of Quebec political activist and future premier Maurice Duplessis and a distant descendant of his explorer namesake who had sailed up the St. Lawrence River four hundred years earlier. The twentieth-century Cartier was, in a sense, an explorer himself in the development of broadcasting. His first job had been with radio's inventor, Guglielmo Marconi, in 1908. As one of four original Marconi Wireless Telegraph staff members in New York City, Cartier provided Hearst's *New York American* newspaper with a list of those drowned in the 1912 *Titanic* disaster. He got a $1,000 bonus for his efforts. Later, he worked with American radio pioneer David Sarnoff. During the First World War, Cartier had been in the Signal Corps developing radio espionage for the Allies, eavesdropping on German military messages. After the war, he helped create radio stations in New York and Philadelphia. The *Montreal Herald* ran an interview with Cartier in which he said, "Radio is here to stay. . . . Radio has become a necessity and will be a permanent household fixture."

In 1922, Cartier helped establish Montreal's CKAC, which claimed to be the world's first French-language station. At CKAC, Cartier was a hugely popular announcer as well as manager, and he was well-connected with Quebec's élite.

A couple of weeks before the King Edward Hotel meeting, a dozen or so early broadcasters had met in Montreal to talk about establishing a pressure group that would protect the interests of station owners. At the meeting five men were asked to lead a plan of action, and now they were gathering in Toronto: Jacques Cartier; A. R. McEwen and C. J. Hanratty, representing the Canadian National Railway, which two years earlier had begun Canada's first national broadcasting network; A. L. MacCallum of the Marconi Wireless Co., which in Montreal in late 1919 had put Canada's first radio station, XWA, on the air. (It later became CFCF, the initials standing for Canada's First, Canada's First); and M. K.

Pyke of the Northern Electric Company, which supplied equipment to many of the broadcasters.

Cartier and his colleagues were meeting to confer before a larger meeting of broadcasters, who would hear their recommendation to establish an organization called the Canadian Association of Broadcasters (CAB) to represent radio stations. Cartier had already dipped his toes into lobbying when, in 1925, he had testified before a parliamentary committee in Ottawa, arguing that as station owners were providing free entertainment for everyone from "farmers to aristocrats," they should not have to pay royalties. Radio was, he told the committee, a tool of democracy at the service of governments, helping cultural pluralism in Canada.

Now a year later, after an hour spent refining their proposals, Cartier and his four colleagues went one floor down to the hotel's Parlour G, where they joined a handful of other broadcasting pioneers from stations in Toronto, Montreal, Ottawa, London, Regina, and Saskatoon. They represented thirteen station owners, including the Jehovah's Witnesses, who operated under the name of the International Bible Students Association; a couple of radio clubs in Ottawa and Toronto; a few electronic equipment manufacturers, Marconi Wireless and Northern Electric; newspapers such as the *Toronto Star*, the *Regina Leader*, *The London Free Press*, *La Presse* of Montreal, and a Toronto battery company.

They were an odd group but nevertheless typical of early radio backers: newspapers that thought radio was a good promotional gimmick; churches that believed radio was an ideal way to save souls; companies that hoped broadcasts would help sell their batteries and wireless sets; and radio club members who were simply fascinated by the new medium.

But now they were outraged, fuming about the cost of having to pay copyright fees and determined to protect their dreams and schemes for radio. "We have two reasons for organizing," said R. H. Combs of CKNC Toronto, a station owned by the Canadian National Carbon Co. "One is for the protection of our own skin," he said. "The other is to ensure that the public get what they expect."

Cartier and his colleagues argued that composers were getting free publicity when their music was played on the radio and should be satisfied with that. They also said that if Canadian broadcasters were driven out of business because of having to pay copyright fees, it would open the way for American stations to take over broadcasting in Canada. McEwen and Hanratty declared that, as CNR Radio was not designed to make a profit, it should be exempt from paying any copyright fees. The newspaper-owned stations, especially the *Toronto Star*'s CFCA, took up the same cry since they, too, didn't seek a profit from radio.

The broadcasters' lawyers, however, warned that any defence against paying the copyright fees would, in the end, likely fail. The broadcasters reluctantly accepted their lawyers' advice and soon began making payments.

At the same King Edward Hotel meeting, the broadcasters quickly accepted the recommendation to establish a Canadian Association of Broadcasters, and Cartier was elected as its first president. The birth of the CAB was little noted by the press, which was preoccupied with stories about the Prince of Wales being thrown from his horse and breaking his collarbone, Trotsky getting a new job in Russia, and a large front-page story in the *Toronto Star* headlined, "CANADIANS GOING TO STATES DOOMED TO DISAPPOINTMENT." In a small page-two story with the headline, "BROADCASTERS FORM CRAFT ASSOCIATION," the *Star* said the CAB was designed "to foster and promote the development of radio broadcasting and the interests of those engaged in any business, profession or industry relating to broadcasting [and] to promote a closer cooperation between its members and the owners of receiving sets, the radio public and all others affected. . . ."

The establishment of the CAB was the first shot in the battle to protect private broadcasters from outside intrusion into their business. By the end of the century, the CAB would represent eighty-six TV stations, more than four hundred radio stations, and sixty-one TV specialty channels.

Broadcasting began in an age of scientific magic that saw the invention of horseless carriages, flying machines, the wireless, the telephone, and, as the twentieth century dawned, something called radio that, incredibly, actually sent words and music flying through the air over mountains, oceans, and cities.

The father of radio, Guglielmo Marconi, believed it would be a vital weapon against international misunderstanding, jealousy, and evils of all kinds and a vehicle for peace, harmony, and intellectual enrichment.

Radio pioneer Dr. Lee De Forest in 1907 dreamed of news, music, and "even advertising" going into people's homes via what was then called "radio telephony."

David Sarnoff, in 1915, as a twenty-four-year-old wunderkind of broadcasting, forecast that the "radio music box" would become a "household utility," providing music and allowing listeners the luxury of "receiving lectures at home which can be made perfectly audible; also events of national importance can be simultaneously announced and received. . . . By purchase of a 'Radio Music Box,' they could enjoy concerts, lectures, music, recitals, etc. which might be going on in the nearest city within their radius." Radio's job, Sarnoff felt, was to entertain, inform, and educate. "And [it] should therefore," he said, "be distinctly regarded as a public service." He believed broadcasting was like "libraries, museums and educational institutions."

As time went on, it was the business of advertising that enticed a growing number of broadcasting enthusiasts who saw dollars dancing in their eyes as they viewed the profit possibilities of this new thing called radio.

Canada played an important role in the development of radio with the Canadian government underwriting some of Marconi's key experiments. Taking Marconi's work one step further, but without any subsidy from Ottawa, was a Canadian, Reginald Fessenden. Working with the U.S. Weather Bureau, in 1900 he started to experiment with sending voices through the air. Then on Christmas Eve 1906, he broadcast the world's first radio program to ships at sea transporting bananas for the United Fruit Company. He played Christmas carols, read Bible passages, and wished everyone a Merry Christmas.

Three years later, an engineering and wireless school in San Jose, California, run by Charles David Herrold, began weekly broadcasts of music and news. In 1910, Enrico Caruso sang via radio from the stage of New York's Metropolitan Opera House to a select audience of fifty people. Dr. Lee De Forest brought the first election results to the United States by radio, reporting the 1916 victory of Woodrow Wilson.

In the century's early years, radio clubs began springing up in Europe, the United States, and Canada, where the nation's first one was established in Winnipeg in 1911 – the Canadian Central Wireless Club, which had twelve members who paid fifty cents a year in dues. A year later, similar clubs were established in Saskatoon and Toronto.

Winnipeg was also the scene of one of the world's first public demonstrations of radio. De Forest came to Winnipeg in April 1910 to make a speech and demonstrate his wireless telephony system. He set up a rudimentary studio in the Royal Alexandra Hotel and, a few blocks away at Eaton's department store, hundreds of people gathered one morning around De Forest's listening equipment to hear a human voice flying over the streets and buildings of downtown Winnipeg. One by one, people clamped a set of earphones to their heads to hear De Forest's voice talking about the miracles of radio. A man by the name of Mayo Evans was the first to listen in and told the initially skeptical crowd that every word was understandable. All day, people lined up to put on the earphones. Astonished at the miracle at its store, Eaton's, in a big newspaper advertisement the next day, stated, "Think of the farmer one hundred miles from the nearest town receiving by wireless telephony in his home the world's news every evening and market reports that he is most interested in."

De Forest predicted that soon all Manitobans would be able to hear news reports broadcast by a central wireless station in Winnipeg. Manitoba Premier Sir Rodmond Roblin was clearly impressed. If man could send his voice through the air for miles, it might even be possible in time, he said to a guffawing crowd, to travel through space to another planet.

Citizen involvement in wireless communication dwindled during the First World War when amateur licences were cancelled for security reasons. But the Army's Signal Corps trained many future "hams," Canada's radio pioneers. After the war, amateur licences were revived and wireless clubs and radio clubs were busy once again. The audience for radio signals began to split into hams, who both sent and received voice transmissions, and those who just listened, who were known as BCLS (broadcast listeners).

With headphones jammed on their heads as they listened to homemade crystal sets, Canadians picked up crackling signals from a few senders as far as twenty-five miles away. With more elaborate equipment, they could hear American stations that were beginning to leap across the border. With their high-powered transmitters, American stations thousands of miles away could be clearly heard in Halifax, Toronto, Winnipeg, Vancouver, and elsewhere in Canada, although mostly only at night.

"I remember people sitting around with crystal sets, listening to the World Series, and only one person at a time could hear the thing, and they'd sort of share this little earplug and report it to everybody else," recalls R. H. Hahn, who later became a music industry executive. "I was never important enough to get my own moment with the earplug."

KDKA Pittsburgh was the first station many Canadians heard, including the family of former cabinet minister Pat Carney in the tiny Ontario town of Norwich. Her mother first heard radio in 1919 in a small concert hall where Hezekiah Forsythe, the local undertaker, who also sold records and a few radios, explained the device on stage. In her book *Trade Secrets*, Carney quotes her mother as saying, ". . . He switched it on [and] for a brief time there was silence, then a crackling sound. Soon into the hall ebbed a sound that was recognizeable as music. We heard a voice announcing that we were listening to station KDKA and that the music was that of a group called the Ipana Troubadours. Everyone was vastly impressed." She said the one question on everybody's mind was voiced by hardware store owner Irv Uren, who said, "Where in Hell does the noise come from? . . . How does it get here?" Hezekiah told them, "The sound comes a hurtling through the air, only it's kinda silent sound, and it gets caught in the wire up there on the roof. Then it comes down this here wire, into the box and out again."

Harry Boyle, who half a century later would be the overlord of Canadian broadcasting as chairman of the Canadian Radio-television and Telecommunications Commission (CRTC), had a similar experience. Two brothers by the name of Martin came into his father's general store in the small town of St. Augustine, Ontario, one summer day in the 1920s and persuaded his father to let them demonstrate the new gadget called radio. As the sun set that night, families came in from their farms to witness the event. A big horn was put on the store counter and wires were strung out everywhere. Boyle was sent across the street with a wire he was told was called an "aerial," and he climbed the church steeple to attach it as high up as possible. "The whole community was there for the demonstration of this fantastic thing which, the Martins said, would bring the whole world to our town," Boyle remembered many years later. "They fiddled around from about seven o'clock. They twisted dials, changed wires, but there was nothing. Finally about 10:30 amidst all the squeals and noise, an announcer came on and we heard the words, 'KDKA, Pittsburgh, Pennsylvania.' Everybody cheered and yelled. There were congratulations all around and that was it. We just got more noise after that. Finally everybody went home satisfied. At least we now knew it was possible."

KDKA Pittsburgh is generally credited with being the world's first radio station on the air with regular, daily programs, although stations in Detroit and Madison, Wisconsin, make similar claims. The Marconi station, XWA in Montreal, started experimenting on air just after the war and, as the 1920s began, it became one of the first stations in the world to air regular programs. It joined a few stations in the United States, England, and the Netherlands in offering live concerts, recorded music, and news reports. XWA's initial audience was mainly hams aboard ships in the St. Lawrence River and in the Montreal area, plus young radio enthusiasts trying to separate crackling sounds from actual words.

While XWA was experimenting with sound over the air, the Marconi company's main purpose was selling radios, not broadcasting to the public. It was looking for ways to expand sales, offering radios from as little as $15 for a primitive set to as much as $385 for elaborate ones that included batteries and handsome mahogany cabinets, which were offered at $10 down and $2.50 a week.

Sales were sluggish until early one January morning in 1920, when a Marconi salesman named Max Smith dropped into his manager's office to talk about an idea he had to sell more radios. At the time, radio wasn't of much interest to Montreal listeners other than hams, for all that could be heard were tinny, crackling sounds and engineers counting to one hundred or reciting the alphabet. "The engineers ran out of breath and grew tired of repeating the alphabet and saying 'ninety-nine'," Smith's colleague Darby Coats later recalled. "Engineers would come back at night just for the fun of the thing and get the thing on the air." One of the engineers was Stewart Finlayson, later president of Canadian Marconi. "People soon asked if there might be some periods each week in which they could be sure of hearing something other than code signals," Coats remembered.

The hams were excited by the process, not by the content, but it was the public that would buy the Marconi radios, and Smith persuaded his manager that they could sell more radios if XWA regularly broadcast something more for the public than engineering chit-chat.

With the manager's agreement to give it a try, Smith and Coats planned a weekly program of music, news reports they would "scalp" out of the Montreal papers, weather information, and Smith's sales pitch on the wonders of Marconi radios and their availability in downtown Montreal stores.

He and Coats first aired the new programming on Tuesday nights, but added other evenings in response to popular demand. To save the company money, Smith borrowed in exchange for an on-air credit a gramophone and some records from a music store on Ste. Catherine St. West. Coats loaned the station a small Swiss music box, which provided some of the first music heard on XWA. Within a couple of years, radio stations all across the country were following Smith and Coats' example, borrowing records from music stores in exchange for on-air mentions.

The two men also acquired a piano, and Smith helped produce and announce live music programs in XWA's tiny, wire-strewn studio on the top floor of the Montreal Marconi factory, as well as hosting musical "remotes" from hotel ballrooms. This made Max Smith and Darby Coats the original Canadian program broadcasters, and also the first to air advertising in Canada. Soon, XWA's programs were being aired in Montreal movie theatres before and after the silent movies of the time and were heard in department store demonstrations. Getting more adventuresome than just offering scraps of news and records, Coats played Santa Claus at Christmas 1920, as XWA welcomed the arrival of Old Saint Nick.

In Ottawa, a special demonstration was given at a garden party held by the Governor General. M. V. Chesnut, who helped put on the demonstration, later rued that they only had one record to play: "When My Baby Smiles at Me." But the most dramatic public showing of radio at the time occurred on a sweltering night in May 1920 when XWA put on a special demonstration for an élite Ottawa audience that included Prime Minister Sir Robert Borden. In the Chateau Laurier ballroom, five hundred of Ottawa's finest listened to a lecture that featured records and a soloist broadcast live from XWA's Montreal studio. "A veritable miracle," reported the *Ottawa Citizen* the next day. "Ottawa had the privilege of being the first city in the world to hear the human voice at a distance of 100 miles."

Even more significant than Borden's presence in the audience that night was the attendance of William Lyon Mackenzie King, who later as prime minister would play a pivotal role for the next quarter-century in the fight between public and private radio in Canada. It was here that King first began to consider the impact of radio.

A few months after the success of the Montreal-Ottawa experiment, Coats took his equipment to the Canadian National Exhibition (CNE) in Toronto. During the exhibition, he broadcast from one building to an audience in another, and demonstrated crystal sets and broadcasting paraphernalia. A year later, Coats was back, broadcasting daily from noon to 1:00 P.M. from a downtown studio to loudspeakers in the main bandstand, where hundreds of people sat and listened in awe. By that fall, Canadian Marconi was broadcasting every Tuesday night in Toronto, and another station, CKCE, run by the Canadian Independent Telephone Company (CITCO), was airing concerts on Monday and Thursday nights and offering a lecture every once in a while. Radio pioneer Harry Swabey remembered the primitive equipment at CITCO's CKCE: "Their microphone was an old carbon mike with a wooden horn on it. You'd have to yell down it." Donald Bankhart described the early microphones as "nothing but a telephone with a horn attached to the mouthpiece that gaped at the artist like a cobra waiting for its prey to walk into its mouth."

At the same time, a young man who would become a powerhouse in Canadian broadcasting was fiddling with radio experiments in his second-floor bedroom at the back of his family's large Rosedale home in Toronto. At age eleven, Edward "Teddy" Rogers had been introduced to wireless communication in his science class and a year later joined the newly formed Wireless Association of Canada. At age thirteen, he had won an award for Ontario's best amateur-built radio. The Toronto *Telegram* reported, "Teddy Rogers is an expert operator and is filled with unbounded enthusiasm for the 'wireless' game." His son, cable king Ted Rogers, says, "He just loved technology, and had wires everywhere in the house. He had a huge tower on his parents' roof. When [my father] was twelve or so, my grandfather [who at one point had been president of Imperial Oil], gave up his study so my father could move out of his bedroom, which was overcrowded with technical stuff."

As a summer job when he was sixteen, Teddy Rogers was a wireless operator on Great Lakes passenger ships. Later he worked as an engineer for CITCO and for the new *Toronto Star* station, CFCA, where he became friends with reporter and announcer Foster Hewitt. In his early twenties, Rogers, with his father's financial backing, was trying to invent a home receiver that would not have to use heavy, messy storage batteries that, when they started to wear down, would leak acid. At age twenty-five, he found a way to plug radio sets into electric light sockets – a "batteryless" system that revolutionized the radio receiver business. "I believe it's going to be a winner as there is nothing like it at all on the market so far," he told a friend. "Just plug in, then tune in" was his slogan for the batteryless radios, which ranged in price from $110 to $370, a lot of money in the mid-1920s and much more than the cost of most battery radio sets. But his prices soon came down. In 1927, he won a radio station licence and gave the new Toronto station the call letters CFRB, standing for Canada's First Rogers Batteryless. It would become the richest radio station in Canada, and Ted Rogers would be inducted into Canada's Broadcasting Hall of Fame.

At the beginning of the 1920s, special-events programs started to be aired by an increasing number of American stations. The event that probably got the biggest radio audience of the time was the August 1921 broadcast of the championship boxing match from Boyles Thirty Acres in Jersey City, New Jersey, when the highly popular Jack Dempsey, the "Manassa Mauler," knocked out Georges Carpentier in the fourth round. The Radio Corporation of America (RCA) had sent it out to anybody who could pick it up. Listeners all across the United States and Canada heard the match. In Toronto and Montreal, it was broadcast by the Marconi stations. Dempsey had earlier visited the XWA studio in Montreal and been interviewed on-air, standing up to his full six feet, one inch, speaking into a microphone consisting of a large horn attached to a metal stand.

In the 1920s, Montreal and Toronto weren't the only Canadian cities with radio stations. In Halifax, war veteran Maj. William Borrett was experimenting with radio equipment and set up the Halifax Radio Listeners Club. In Charlottetown, Keith Rogers, a Signal Corps veteran, was similarly convinced radio was going to change the world. He had been testing bits of equipment since he was fifteen in spite of his father's constant admonition that "Nothing good will ever come of this wireless nonsense, Keith!"

He proved his father wrong when in March 1921 he picked up music being broadcast from a college in Schenectady, New York. Rogers was so impressed he quickly arranged a listening party for the premier of

Prince Edward Island, the mayor of Charlottetown, and leading citizens. Amid clouds of cigar smoke, thirty-seven people crowded around Rogers' equipment, which included for the event an improvised loudspeaker. At first only hissing, crackling, and whistling could be heard, but then on came a tinny voice from Schenectady followed by a tinkling but fading piano. The radio age had arrived on Prince Edward Island.

In London, Ontario, *London Free Press* president Arthur Blackburn was bewitched by wireless radio, spending half the night fiddling with his equipment on the third floor of his home. He was determined to turn his radio hobby into a business for the newspaper. Unlike most publishers who regarded radio simply as a way to promote their papers, Blackburn believed that broadcasting could extend and complement his newspaper, an early version of media convergence.

One thousand four hundred miles west of London and a couple of years after Max Smith and Darby Coats began broadcasting music over XWA, radio music also came to Winnipeg, although in a very limited way. A group of students in what was known as the Kelvin Radio Club added music to their voice transmissions over their experimental school station, XEY. An old-fashioned, hand-cranked Victrola was used to play the one record the students had – a scratchy 78 rpm disc of "The March of the Toreadors." One of the students would wind up the Victrola and hold a microphone in front of its horn while the other club members stayed home to listen to the excerpt from Bizet's *Carmen*.

About the same time, in the tiny grain farming community of Kinistino, Saskatchewan, R. J. Humphrey would call in the neighbours whenever he picked up sounds and music on his crystal set. His daughter Catherine told radio historian Wayne Schmaltz, "They would wait their turn to go into the den [where the radio was]. . . . As each one left, my job was to go quickly into the den and, with a bottle of alcohol hidden behind the curtains, I would wipe the earphones with a cotton swab so listeners would not be in danger of an ear infection."

Humphrey's daughter also remembered that, occasionally, when her father had a particularly clear reception on his radio apparatus, he would call the local telephone operator – a Mrs. Shannon – and she would open all the phones on the party lines across town so that everyone could listen in. "Dad would work the dials to get the best [sound] and I would hold the earphone tilted at just the right angle into [a] Limoges cup which amplified the sound."

About the same time, 170 miles south of Kinistino, Andy McDermott was furtively listening to his crystal set in his Regina high school. "We built crystal sets and sneaked them into school," he said. "We would roll wire tightly on round Quaker Oats boxes and then shellac them, which gave a good pick up. We'd hide them in our desks and have a wire running up our sleeve. You could hear stations from all over the continent."

In Edmonton, G. R. A. "Dick" Rice was also caught up in "radio fever" and, because of his wartime wireless experience with the British navy, he was sought out by the Edmonton *Journal* in 1922 to run the newspaper's new station.

Newspapers in Toronto, Winnipeg, Regina, and Vancouver were also suddenly planning stations to use as a promotional device in their circulation wars. George Melrose Bell, publisher of the *Regina Leader*, was organizing radio stations in Winnipeg, Regina, Calgary, and Vancouver. He, along with Rice in Edmonton and A. A. "Pappy" Murphy in Saskatoon, were among the very few in the early 1920s who saw riches in the future commercialization of radio. At the same time, Marconi was also setting up two more stations, in Halifax and Vancouver.

Before 1922, while only a relatively small number of Canadians could listen to radio's primitive offerings, there was excitement in the air. Something big was happening. Newspapers and magazines spread the word of this new phenomenon called radio. "A feat of magic," stated the *Toronto Star*. "The greatest discovery of the 20th century," said *Radio* magazine. "The new wonder . . . the infant prodigy," declared the *Regina Leader*. "The birth of a new world," said Hector Charlesworth, editor of *Saturday Night*, who, a decade later, would be the czar of all Canadian radio as chairman of the Canadian Radio Broadcasting Commission (CRBC).

"The support of newspapers was vital to the success of our efforts just as soon as experimental speech transmissions were augmented by the odd musical number," said Darby Coats. "The newspapers kept close track of us. For better or worse, they spread the news [of radio] into the homes of their readers."

The miracle of radio was by now ready to burst out of its swaddling clothes. The experiments were over, and information and entertainment programs were about to flood the country, giving Canadians a sense of togetherness, immediacy, and awareness of the world that they'd never had before. If the invention of the car at the turn of the century had taken people out of their homes, the radio brought them back, as they gathered in their parlours to listen to a local amateur hour or a music or comedy show from a distant station.

"Radio . . . builds up the happiness of the home," *Maclean's* magazine said. "Radio is an indoor entertainment which can be and is enjoyed by the womenfolk and the children equally with the man of the house." A New York minister said radio was "a Godsent agency to restore and keep intact the family circle."

But radio also came in for criticism. "Broadcasting stations were often blamed for hailstones, for rain or the lack of it," said Jim Allard, a future broadcasting leader in Canada. "Stations received letters and phone calls from indignant ladies protesting that announcers were viewing them 'down the airwaves' in their bathtubs or aggravating their arthritis or had caused pregnancies." Parents worried that children would go deaf listening to radio or never get their homework done. Some commentators warned that radio would cause nervous conditions, keep housewives from their chores, keep people up too late at night, and destroy intelligent conversation.

Radio was the preserve of private entrepreneurs. Most of them were involved for the fun of it, some because they wanted to use radio programming to help sell radios and batteries or promote newspapers or a religion, and a very few who saw the potential for riches in this new adventure.

F. Walter Hyndman, later Prince Edward Island's lieutenant-governor, was a radio-struck youngster in 1920 when, on his homemade wireless equipment, he caught the first radio words ever heard on Prince Edward Island broadcast from a ship in the Atlantic. He told the local newspaper, which ran a story about it the next day. As he walked down a street in Charlottetown that day, he heard a woman whisper to her companion as she passed by, "That's the fellow that thinks he hears the angels singing."

The angels were, indeed, about to sing.

2

Angels in the Sky

In the Roaring Twenties, nothing roared louder than radio. Beginning in 1922, radio signals were cannonading through North American skies. Suddenly, radio was everywhere, and governments stepped in to license and regulate commercial stations. In Canada, the Department of Marine and Fisheries had the responsibility of licensing and regulating the pioneer stations.

By the end of 1921, 28 stations had been licensed in the United States. Within six months, 458 stations were licensed. In Canada, Ottawa decided to issue the first commercial broadcasting licences in April 1922. In the first month, 21 Canadian stations had been licensed. By the end of the year, there were 58. Not all these stations actually went on the air, as enthusiasm sometimes outran financial reality for radio's shoe-string adventurers. But broadcasting surged through the decade, not just in Canada and the United States, but in Britain, too. In 1922, 35,700 radio-listening licences were issued in the United Kingdom. The next year, there were nearly 600,000, and within a couple of years, 2 million.

In Canada, radio listeners paid a licence fee of $1 a year per radio to tune in, later raised to $2. By the end of the decade, about 600,000 house-holds were paying the annual fee for listening to the radio, although as many as a quarter of all Canadians with radios simply refused to pay, delaying the inspector at the front door while they scurried to hide their sets under the bed or in the closet. In the early years, more than 3,000 bootleg listeners were caught by the so-called ether cops and faced fines of as much as $500, although most paid between $5 and $10. Listeners were warned that they should see the credentials of the licence fee collectors because a racket had developed with fake inspectors going door-to-door and pocketing the money.

"Radio-itis" was sweeping the country. XWA in Montreal, soon to be known as CFCF, was broadcasting about seven hours a week, and listeners were demanding more. By 1923, CFCF was up to ten hours a week, while CKAC Montreal, which came on the air in 1922, was broadcasting twelve hours a week.

Sometimes, though, the new broadcasters ran into trouble from disbelieving listeners. When the six-foot, four-inch Dick Rice was starting the Edmonton *Journal* station, CJCA, in 1922, he held radio demonstrations so people could hear programs broadcast from the studio back at the newspaper. "One time in Lacombe," Rice later recalled, "we put our display in a crowded hall. Halfway through, some of the people there decided it was all a hoax and that we were really using a gramophone. They stormed the stage and tried to find it. Radio was so new, they were positive it was just another carnival trick."

When the *Toronto Star*'s CFCA opened about the same time, publisher Joseph Atkinson didn't think the radio phenomenon would last very long. "He thought of it as a novelty that would only last about six months," said *Star* reporter and announcer Foster Hewitt. CFCA also faced audience disbelief. At a special concert in the Masonic Temple in downtown Toronto (today used by CTV as a studio and for offices), eleven hundred people looked on with incredulity as the *Star* put the "talking box" and horn at centre stage and tuned into a music program coming from a studio three miles away. At first, some mumbled about it being a fake, witchcraft, or that the singers and musicians were hidden behind the curtain. But at the end of the concert, the audience rose in cheers and with, as a reporter noted, "a great wondering that such things could be."

While Torontonians were "wondering" about radio, so, too, were people in Regina, where the *Leader*'s station, CKCK, held an opening ceremony in 1922. Pouring rain and thunder didn't deter hundreds of Regina citizens from coming to city hall, where the first official program would be heard. As they settled into their seats, they muttered and pointed to a big horn attached to a receiving box sitting atop a table on a flag-draped stage. Suddenly, mysterious squeaks came out of the horn and then a scratchy, faraway voice was heard, interrupted from time to time by a strange quavering. But it quickly became clear it was Saskatchewan Premier Charles Dunning, who was speaking from the CKCK studio several blocks away on the top floor of the *Leader* building, formally launching the station. It was the first address ever delivered by radio in Saskatchewan. The mayor also welcomed the station and then the music began, including "Rule Britannia," a presentation by the Knox Church choir, a violin solo, and a report on baseball scores and the stock markets. "God Save the King" ended the program, and listeners crowded up to the stage to get a closer look at the strange contraption called radio that was sending out music and voices that, the *Leader* claimed, could be heard a thousand miles away. The next day, sales for crystal sets and more elaborate radios boomed.

For all the fanfare, though, CKCK had only one employee, a former naval wireless operator, Bert Hooper, nicknamed "Sparks" (as most early wireless operators were), who was the station engineer, announcer, program director, manager, secretary, and general sweeper-upper. With his signature sign-on of "Hello there, friends out in radioland," he soon became a celebrity in Saskatchewan and one of the best-known announcers in Western Canada. In early 1922, during a visit to Victoria, B.C., the publisher of the *Regina Leader*, George Bell, had interviewed him for the job of running his new station. Hooper had never heard of Regina, but he leapt at the opportunity as he was fed up with life at sea. For his audition, Bell gave Hooper a nickel and told him to go to a store, buy a newspaper, and telephone him. "I want you to read the New York stocks and bonds to me," said Bell. Hooper did and got the job.

Many battery and radio salesmen got into broadcasting because they needed programs for people to hear if they were going to sell their products. Typical was A. A. "Pappy" Murphy in Saskatoon, who was co-owner of an electric shop. "Some red-headed fella from Eastern Canada took a swing through the West and he came to our place," Murphy remembered in an oral history interview. (The "fella" was Spence Caldwell, who was then selling Marconi radio equipment and who would establish the CTV network about thirty-five years later. "He loaded us up with a lot of cats' whiskers [fine copper wire for crystal sets] and horns and what not and I said, 'What are we going to do with all of it? I guess we'll have to have a radio station to sell this kind of stuff." Thus, CFQC Saskatoon, "The Voice of the Hub City," was born with a staff of one and "Pappy" Murphy was on his way to becoming a western Canadian broadcasting giant.

Radio came to Cape Breton in much the same way. In his Sydney store, Nathan Nathanson was selling gramophones, music sheets, and the new "radio boxes." American radio signals and a few Canadian ones reached Cape Breton at night, but all that could be heard during the day was largely static. "People were going wild," said T. C. "Robbie" Robertson, one of the first to work with Nathanson in his radio station. "It became increasingly clear that if you were going to sell radios, a local station was needed to keep the people happy."

"The only reason I started a radio station was to give people something to hear with the boxes they were buying," Nathanson said. "Sales of radios soared unbelievably. People who still didn't have one would block the streets in front of homes where there was a radio, listening to the sound. And the sidewalk was so congested with people wanting to buy radios that a policeman would make them line up so others could get by." In some cases, the streets were jammed with people who had pulled up their horses and wagons to listen.

In Fredericton in 1923, hardware store merchant James Stewart Neill broadcast to the five households with receiving sets, using his parlour as the studio while his family whispered and tiptoed about to avoid interrupting his broadcasts. At one point while on-air, he collapsed and lay stunned for several minutes. After a phone call from a listener asking what had happened, his family went into the parlour and found him lying on the floor with the microphone beside him. The doctor was called and diagnosed his ailment as an advanced state of nerves. Three years later, after hearing of the wonders of KDKA Pittsburgh, Neill moved the station, now licensed as CFNB, to his store and started soliciting commercials. One of Canada's first professional newscasters, Russ Deakin, was heard on the 8:00 A.M. CFNB news, and Neill also hired Mary Grannan to tell children's stories and act in a three-person soap opera serial called *Aggravating Agatha*. Grannan later became known nationally with her *Just Mary* children's programs.

In Wingham, Ontario, "Doc" Cruickshank, who earned his nickname while driving around a local doctor during the 1918 flu epidemic, had read about radio in 1921 in *Popular Mechanics* and became a one-man station, CKNX. He broadcast church services, and from his living room, he aired local singers and piano players. "We all got such a tremendous kick out of opening up a microphone and speaking into it. On Sunday after church service, we had a little program from my home," Cruickshank said. "I'd carry the transmitter under my arm down to my house and we'd do an hour broadcast from there, a program of music, hymns, and that sort of thing."

In Winnipeg, the *Manitoba Free Press* won the race against the *Tribune* to be first on the air. "Hello. Hello. Hello. Radiophone broadcasting station 4AH *Free Press* broadcast number one!" said Lynn V. Salton as he launched the station at 10:00 P.M., Sunday, April 2, 1922. Music and a talk by Salton's father, the Reverend Dr. George Salton, followed the opening announcement of a hastily organized program. Two weeks later, Salton's rival, the *Winnipeg Tribune* station, CJNC, was on the air with its gala opening. It may have lost the race to be first, but it had a much more powerful signal and therefore a bigger audience than the *Free Press* station.

The *Tribune*'s opening showcased the most impressive radio programming yet heard in Canada, with welcoming statements by Lieutenant-Governor Sir James Aikins, the mayor, and performances by more than two hundred artists, including the Winnipeg Male Voice Choir, the Oratorio Society, the Princess Patricia regimental band, and soloists and musicians galore. It put to shame the more modest programming of the rival *Free Press* station, which the *Tribune* referred to as "a peanut whistle."

The "peanut whistle" set up a high-powered transmitter three months later in July, however, and launched the new equipment with an impressive two-hour program featuring three numbers from the Princess Pat's band, a coronet solo, singers, pianists, and violinists. "A rare galaxy of talent," said the *Free Press*.

Radio also made rivals of two downtown Winnipeg cinemas, both of which had installed radio equipment to entertain moviegoers, as pioneered in Montreal. Before and after the silent movies and during intermissions, the theatres broadcast programs from Boston, Pittsburgh, San Francisco, and other distant American cities, as well as the *Tribune* and *Free Press* stations.

Another pioneer station in 1922 was CKFX Vancouver, which became CJOR in 1926. George Chandler bought the station for $600: $300 down and $25 a month for a year. The station was housed in an apartment where the kitchen was the engineer's office, the living room was the studio, and Chandler slept in the bedroom. But Chandler had big ideas of putting on public forums, historical dramas about West Coast companies such as MacMillan Bloedel, airing major sports events, and showcasing Vancouver bands. Mart Kenney says CJOR got his group started on becoming Canada's number-one big band of the 1930s and 1940s.

Local radio stations liked to have their own special identifying motto such as announcing their call letters by saying: "CFCY Charlottetown – The Friendly Voice of the Maritimes"; "CHNS Halifax, Nova Scotia – The Front Door of Canada – Always Open"; "CKGN Toronto – Canada's Cheerio Station" (which happened to be owned by the Gooderham & Worts distillery); or in Winnipeg, "CKY – Manitoba's Own Radio Station." "Big Jim" Bromley-Browne boomed on the air in 1931 on CKOV Kelowna, B.C., to the sound of "Land of Hope and Glory," calling it "The Voice of the Okanagan Valley." One of the more unusual call signs was CJHS in Saskatoon, a religious station that sometimes identified itself as "CJHS – Christ Jesus Heals and Saves."

Many of these new stations had to share the same frequency with other broadcasters, and some went on the air without any transmission equipment of their own, simply renting time on an existing station and using their own call letters. Sometimes there were conflicts among stations that shared the same frequency. Frank Makepeace, a CJCA Edmonton technical engineer, recalled one such incident: "It was a Dempsey-Tunney fight. There was a lot of interest in it and we were broadcasting it at CJCA. We used to share a frequency among three stations and our time ran out. I think it was eight o'clock. So [we] asked them whether we could have a little extra time. They said, 'No!' And for a few minutes both stations were on together. That created a lot of ill will."

CKCK and CHWC in Regina were typical in how they shared the same frequency. Wilf Collier, a CHWC announcer of the time, remembered, "We'd come on at nine o'clock in the morning and go to ten. Then we would sign off and the other station [CKCK] would come on. And we'd alternate like this throughout the day. Then we would share time at night. We had three nights a week, they had three nights, then we'd split Sundays."

CHWC's studio, which was next door to a toilet, had paper-thin walls. Every time the toilet flushed, it was broadcast all over town, and

CHWC's nickname became "Can Hear the Water Closet." Regina's CKCK also had thin walls, and one night some years later a toilet near the studio was flushed just as announcer Brian Elliott was going on the air. The noise, reverberating through the studio, sounded like Niagara Falls. Elliott was supposed to announce the program *Twilight Echoes in the Fireside Hour*, but, rattled by the gurgles, he intoned, "Ladies and gentlemen, the Canadian Radio Broadcasting Commission presents from Regina: Toilet Echoes in the Twilight Hour."

The most ambitious radio operation in the nation in the mid-1920s was established by Canadian National Railways (CNR) president Sir Henry Thornton, who became the father of network broadcasting in Canada when he set up a chain of CNR stations across the country. It was a wonderful way, he thought, to advertise the services of the railway. Radio receivers were placed aboard CNR trains and in CNR hotel rooms throughout Canada. The first CNR station opened in Ottawa in early 1924, and within a few years, CNR stations were on the air in Moncton and Vancouver. As well, the railway operated so-called phantom stations in Halifax, Quebec City, Montreal, Toronto, London, Winnipeg, Saskatoon, Regina, Edmonton, Calgary, and Red Deer. CNR programs were also heard in Ontario over stations in Chatham, Hamilton, and Waterloo, and in Brandon, Manitoba, and Yorkton, Saskatchewan.

The CNR programming would begin with the ear-splitting ringing of a locomotive bell and sometimes a three-tone train whistle. "Passengers' eyes would pop out when they put on their headphones and listened to these programs coming in," said CNR Radio announcer Herb Roberts. "It was a miracle of the times." Five years after CNR Radio began, the national railway in France also began offering radio aboard trains, but it charged its listeners the equivalent of thirty cents each journey.

While temporary networks were occasionally formed among private stations for special events, nothing matched the scope of the regular CNR Radio network programming. Operas, symphonies, modern music, comedians, Shakespearean drama, contemporary plays, talks on health, the economy, and politics provided an enriching radio diet, albeit limited in the number of hours each day (about three hours in the early years) but unequalled anywhere, save by the British Broadcasting Corporation (BBC). "It was some of the best radio ever done," said pioneering radio operator William Borrett of CHNS Halifax. Thornton believed that the CNR's programming was a powerful, uplifting, and unifying force for Canada. "It is only through nationwide broadcasts that we shall accomplish a feeling of kinship between all parts of the country," he said. He also sought to lessen the presence of advertising on the air. "It is essential," he said, "that broadcasting be surrounded with such safeguards as will prevent the air becoming what might be described as an atmospheric billboard."

The most adventuresome programming done by the CNR was in the field of drama, where it developed a national audience for the CNVR Players based at its station in Vancouver. This talented group of performers had been formed originally in 1922 and first presented drama on the *Vancouver Province*'s station, CKCD. That station laid claim to the first full-length play ever heard on Canadian radio, although CKAC Montreal makes a similar claim with a historical drama based on the political events in Quebec of 1837–38. Both CKCD and CKAC also produced radio operas in the early 1920s, with CKAC's first presentation in 1923 featuring thirty-five musicians, a choir of thirty-eight, and a number of soloists.

In the early years of radio, Vancouver's CNVR Players produced more than a hundred plays, both classical and contemporary, and were a catalyst for future radio drama presentations such as the CNR's much-heralded *The Romance of Canada* series produced by Tyrone Guthrie in the early 1930s.

Their example was followed by another Vancouver station, CKWX, in its presentation of Sunday dramas involving such future luminaries as Fletcher Markle, Barbara Kelly, Bernie Braden, and John Drainie. Markle became a Hollywood writer and producer, Braden and Kelly became BBC stars, and Drainie became recognized as Canada's best radio actor. CKWX's Fred Bass remembered that every show was a last-minute production, however, and often Markle would be typing the final pages of the script and rushing them into the studio while the program was on the air.

Other stations such as CFCA and CKNC in Toronto, CKAC and CFCF in Montreal, and CKY in Winnipeg offered occasional dramas, but the emphasis was on popular music. Because the federal government believed the public wanted live music, not records, it banned records from the air between 7:30 P.M. and midnight. Thus, the night air was filled with the strains of local dance bands and soloists. But during the day, recorded music was king. In 1926, Ottawa relented slightly by allowing some small stations to play records at night.

Pleading for such an exemption from the nighttime record ban, Darby Coats, who had moved from XWA in Montreal to CKY Winnipeg, told Ottawa, "We are serving the public better by providing the good phonograph music rather than inferior human talent." But whether recorded music was aired day or night, not only were the stations not paying any royalties for it, but most of them didn't even want to buy records. CKCK Regina, for instance, owned no more than a dozen records, and borrowed the rest from Cy's Music store nearby. The Moose Jaw station owned ten records.

Records were played by the announcer, who would put the microphone down beside a hand-wound Victrola to pick up the sound, holding the mike there until the song was finished. Sometimes he would forget to wind up the Victrola beforehand, however, and when the music began to slow down to a crawl, the announcer would apologize and quickly crank up the Victrola to full speed. A few years later, Dick Rice and a couple of his colleagues at CFRN in Edmonton designed an electric pickup that made playing records much easier. CFAC in Calgary was one of the first stations to use records in a theme style, building programs of British music-hall tunes, Viennese waltzes, or jazz numbers.

Apart from the CNR and a handful of big-city stations, in the early years of radio, it was amateur hour across the country. Most stations featured an endless procession of local singers, piano players, violinists, trumpet players, drummers, hotel dance bands, and sprinkled between the musical presentations were local advertisements and the occasional interview, weather and market report, news items, sports, church services, and once in a while a local drama. Nobody got paid, but people clamoured for a chance at the thrill and prestige they got from being on-air. "Everybody and their dog wanted to get on the radio," says CKCK Regina veteran Lyman Potts. Marianne Morrow, daughter of Keith Rogers, who ran Charlottetown's CFCY, remembers that their living room was the studio, overflowing with microphones, control boards, batteries, wires, and transmitters. "The old-time fiddlers used to set themselves up," she says. "Mother would play the piano and the fiddlers would saw away. Many, many people took part musically. The thought of being paid didn't really occur to anyone. It was the honour of being on a broadcast that motivated them."

Broadcaster Hugh Mills became a household name when he started reading the comics on-air at CHNS Halifax. He was Uncle Mel, who described the latest adventures of Popeye, Mickey Mouse, Red Rider, and other comic heroes who appeared daily in the *Halifax Herald*'s comic strips. "Kids loved the show and the newspaper's circulation shot up," he recalled. "Pretty soon everyone was talking about Uncle Mel."

Sometimes there were future stars among the anxious amateurs. One of them was country singer Hank Snow. "A hungry-looking fellow . . . pathetic . . . came in one day with a guitar and asked for a chance to sing," said William Borrett, who set up CHNS. "I could tell right off that this fellow really had something [so] I put him on the air." Snow's rival, Wilf Carter, was at the other end of the country, knocking on the door of CJCJ in Calgary. He would drive in from a ranch north of Calgary to perform at the local station. "He'd come into the studio wearing a ten-gallon hat and chewing a big wad of gum," recalled radio comedian Frank Deaville. "He'd put his hat down on the piano, get out his guitar, take the gum out and stick it on the piano, and do his fifteen-minute program. He'd finish, and on would go the hat. He'd pop the gum back in his mouth and away he'd go." Although they sang for free at the beginning, over the next few decades, both Snow and Carter made millions as superstars in the world of country music.

Church services provided much of early programming for many broadcasters, since they were free for the station and the ministers realized the microphones offered them a much larger audience for their sermons than the congregation sitting in the pews. CFRB Toronto was particularly busy broadcasting church services, as veteran Bill Baker explained. "On Sundays, we did seven church services beginning with morning mass at St. Michael's Cathedral and ending up at midnight at the Bond Street evangelical temple for an hour of hymn singing. We had to drag our equipment from church to church."

The first regular broadcast of a church service in Canada – or in the British Empire, for that matter – came from Regina's Carmichael Presbyterian Church in mid-February 1923. "Radio is one of God's most wonderful gifts to man," declared the editor of the *Canadian Churchman*, Rev. A. A. McIntyre. Other church leaders agreed, and soon the Baptists, Roman Catholics, Presbyterians, the United Church, the Jehovah's Witnesses, and several evangelical groups had their own licences to run radio stations. Most of these stations carried little but church services, sermons, and church choirs. One of the first was VOWR, Voice Of Wesley Radio, in St. John's, which opened in July 1924 and is still operating today more than three-quarters of a century later.

Radio turned out to be a bonanza for the churches as, unexpectedly, listeners began sending in donations. In one church service aired by CKCK in Regina, the minister used the word "correction" and some people misheard it as "collection" and sent in donations, including one of $20. After that the minister tried to mention a collection every time he went on the air. Stations also sold time to a large number of Bible thumpers, who used fiery religious oratory to stimulate donations for themselves, not a church.

Whenever church services were heard on CNR Radio receivers in the parlour cars of trains, money would be tossed into a porter's cap. The railway would forward the cash to the church. The first time it happened was when passengers heard the minister in a Saskatoon church announce the collection. A man at the back of the parlour car rose, walked to where the radio operator sat, and dropped $5 into the operator's hat. He then picked up the hat and passed it around and, said one passenger, "without exception every passenger contributed." When the train pulled into Saskatoon a few hours later, the operator sent almost $30 to the church. (To encourage larger donations, ministers sometimes subtly echoed the words of American evangelist Aimee Semple MacPherson, who told her flock, "God likes the sounds of rustling paper rather than the clink of coins.")

Even iconoclastic Toronto broadcaster Gordon Sinclair, who later reviled organized religion, produced church services for the *Toronto Star*'s CFCA. He worked with future hockey broadcaster Foster Hewitt in bringing Sunday church services to Torontonians in the early 1920s. He would lug broadcast equipment to the churches, set it up, and air the services. "One day, I forgot to turn on the button," he recalled, and the sermon wasn't heard. Sinclair was fired.

Stations were always on the lookout for free program material. Bert Hooper of Regina's CKCK opened his studio window one day and heard a Salvation Army band coming down the street. "I put the microphone in the windowsill and you could hear the band getting louder and louder," he said. "They stopped right opposite our studio. They played hymns and one fellow spoke. They only had an audience of about five people on the sidewalk. I gave the fellow a shout and said, 'Come on, play another tune!' So they started up to play." All this, of course, on the air.

In the early days of VOCM in St. John's (Voice Of the Common Man), the station regularly did sidewalk interviews by opening the studio window, dropping a microphone down to the street on a wire, and shouting out questions to passing people. Occasionally, however, microphones were smashed in the lowering, putting the station off the air.

An accident once forced Hooper off the air in Regina when he was broadcasting a jazz orchestra. The piano player was smoking a cigarette and when he put it down, it rolled onto the piano keys. "They caught fire and burned up," Hooper recalled. "Of course, we had to sign off because we had no piano." Hooper had a problem, too, when an accordion player brought along his pet monkey to the studio. It became transfixed with the microphone, leapt at it in mid-broadcast, and it took several minutes to pry the monkey off so the program could continue.

For seven years, Hooper was the only employee at CKCK, and the station simply went off the air whenever he had his meals, slept, or was sick. "HOOPER ILL, CKCK SILENT," headlined the *Leader* on one occasion.

The *Leader* was not the most generous of employers with its radio station, as Hooper discovered in the early days when a tube blew, putting the station off the air. The paper refused to provide the $15 to buy a replacement tube. Hooper appealed to the Marconi representative on the Prairies, Spence Caldwell, who gave him a tube when Hooper promised to pay for it himself over several months. CKCK had been off the air for a week and the newspaper headline the day after it went back on announced, "BROADCASTING RESUMES: RADIO FANS WELCOME CKCK AFTER SILENCE THROUGH BROKEN TUBE." Hooper celebrated by airing a duet by Miss Verna Elson and Miss C. Elvonick, singing "Sittin' in a Corner" and "The Girl That Men Forgot."

Sports were hugely popular on early radio, and in Regina, CKCK beat Foster Hewitt to air by a week or so, arranging a hockey broadcast, announced by Hooper's friend, sportswriter Pete Parker, from rinkside at the Regina stadium where the Edmonton Eskimos defeated the Regina Caps 1-0. The world's first hockey broadcast had happened a month earlier on the *Toronto Star*'s CFCA, announced by reporter Norm Albert. Foster Hewitt was third in line. But it was Hewitt's that became the best-known voice in all of the country for the next half-century.

Hooper also brought baseball to Regina by broadcasting a World Series game between Washington and Pittsburgh, creating his play-by-play account from news agency copy sent to him by telegraph. His commentary not only went out on the radio, but was piped into a downtown Regina street by a loudspeaker.

Early announcers were sometimes prone to profanity in moments of stress, not yet fully used to the idea of live microphones picking up everything that's said. At a western football championship game in Regina, a part-time CKCK announcer by the name of Larry got overly excited when a player broke loose. "Vic Murdoch has the ball and he's going down the field," he shouted feverishly. "He's made ten yards . . . fifteen . . . twenty! He's going to make it! Jesus Christ, he dropped it!"

Protest calls poured in and the local ministerial association tried to get the station licence revoked.

Buck Thomas was doing the play-by-play for a game at Queen's University in Kingston, Ontario, for CNR Radio when his enthusiasm got the better of him. As remembered by radio veteran Bob Bowman, Thomas was describing Queen's outside wing Red McKelvie as he caught a pass deep in his own end. "McKelvie's got the ball on the ten-yard line," Thomas enthused. "He sidesteps two tacklers. He's at the ten. He's at the fifteen. He's at the twenty. He's at the twenty-five. Look at that son of a bitch go!"

A CKOC Hamilton announcer let his mind wander while reading a commercial one night and inadvertently substituted a decidedly impolite word. Instead of saying, "These days when you are shivering by your radiator . . ." he said, "These days when you are shitting by your radiator . . ." At another Hamilton station, CHML, a hastily recruited organist with a limited repertoire was put in charge of a program aimed at comforting terminally ill hospital patients. He played "Please Don't Talk About Me When I'm Gone."

When Saint John announcer De B. Holly, latterly with the CBC, was starting out, he had a hard time extolling the merits of a patent medicine designed to cure psoriasis. He announced, "This is one of the best remedies for sorry asses."

Two stories about swearing on-air are told by almost every early broadcasting raconteur, who identify differing personalities and stations as the culprit. The version related by Nathaniel Nathanson, "Mr. Radio" of Cape Breton for fifty years, has the technician at his station in Sydney putting on a hymn to start off the Sunday-morning radio schedule. He was alone at the station, but while the record was playing he went across the street for a quick sandwich. "[He] dashed back to the station and put on his headphones," Nathanson remembered. And he heard, 'Jesus Christ. Jesus Christ. Jesus Christ' over and over again. The needle was stuck in a groove. We had a lot of complaints about that."

There were complaints, too, about the announcer who ended a Friday-night children's talent program by muttering, when he thought the microphone was off, "That'll hold the little bastards for tonight." "Everywhere you go, you'll hear the story," recalled pioneer Vancouver broadcaster Don Wilson. "But I'm going to tell you the truth. It happened in Vancouver on CKWX. The man's name was Jerry Taggart, who later became an executive with the CBC."

Announcer Geoffrey Bartlett barely restrained himself from cursing on-air when someone threw a twelve-inch steel bolt at him through the studio window of CFQC Saskatoon. Shortly before, he had reported on the air about a stolen car. Apparently, in an effort to escape, the car thief had driven to the station to stop Bartlett from describing the automobile. When the bolt smashed through the window and whizzed just past his head, he let out a startled cry and shouted into the microphone, "Quick, call the police!" The car thief, however, was never caught.

CNR Radio veteran Vic George remembered broadcasting from Moncton, where his studio was in a Knights of Pythias Hall and he would introduce a musical group called The Pythian Sisters. He once introduced them, however, as The Sythian Pisters. In Calgary on CFAC, one of Canada's best announcers, Jack Dennett, got his tongue twisted, and instead of talking about The Calgary Rug and Drape Shop, he enthused about bargains at The Calgary Drug and Rape Shop. Dennett, who had started to work on-air for CFAC at age sixteen for $4 a week, wound up being one of Canada's best-known newscasters, doing the major morning and evening newscasts at CFRB for twenty-six years.

The CNR had a particular problem with its network programming in the 1920s when line repairmen would inadvertently hook into a broadcast line and be heard by radio listeners swearing in frustration at not getting through. "I can't get the bastard to answer me. . . . What the hell's going on here?" was one comment heard by tens of thousands of Canadians during a CNR program. CNR president Sir Henry Thornton, on being advised of the profanity heard across the country, said only, "Reprimand the man, but don't fire him."

Knowing, however, that the government's Radio Branch was listening in for on-air swearing and aware of public reaction, CNR Radio laid down the law to its announcers, declaring in warning signs posted in studios across the country, "It has to be moral, if it's oral."

While women sang, acted in dramas, and played music on radio, there were few women announcers in the early days of broadcasting. This was partly because so many stations were one-man bands, where the announcer was also the engineer and manager, and partly because station owners thought men's deeper voices lent more authority to broadcasting.

Typical of this attitude was the experience of a First World War British war bride and one-time music-hall performer, Jane Gray, one of the first and most successful women broadcasters, who began reading poetry on CJGC in London, Ontario, in 1924. She had a hard time getting into radio, discouraged by her husband, warned by her church minister to "go back and look after your bairns," and admonished by the CJGC station manager, who told her women belonged at home, not on the air. When she insisted, he reluctantly put her in front of a microphone as a test and ordered her to "say something." She recited a schmaltzy Edgar Guest poem, and the manager hired her at once, although he made her change her first name from Elsie to Jane because, he said, Elsie was unlucky. So she began reading poetry on the air with an organ playing in the background. She was never paid in the four years she was on the air in London. She then moved to Toronto, developed a highly popular drama series for CFRB that cost a total of $12.50 for each half-hour program, and became Canada's most prominent female broadcaster of the late 1920s and early 1930s.

In the 1920s, broadcasting facilities were primitive at best, with studios located wherever it was cheap: in garages, tucked away in a corner of a newspaper building, at the rear of electrical stores, department stores, and, in one case, at the back of a drugstore. Fred Hume of CFXC got free rent for his studio in New Westminster, B.C., in exchange for mentioning the name of the building several times a day.

Keith Rogers' first studio at CFCY Charlottetown was located in his living room. Rogers, his eldest daughter Betty remembered, rigged up a loudspeaker – a big black horn – outside their home so those who didn't have radios could stop by and listen. The living-room walls were draped with bedsheets and blankets to minimize noise and vibration, and such ad hoc measures were true of many of the pioneer stations. CKCK Regina lined the walls with bales of hay and hung drapes in front of them. This may have deadened noise, but it also smelled like a stable and provided a comfortable home for mice. Once two sisters were on-air playing a piano duet when a mouse scooted out of the hay, making the women scream and alarming listeners.

Equipment was also primitive. If a singer prolonged a high note or sang too loudly, it could send the station off the air. Bert Hooper in Regina remembered, "I used to put a mark on the floor where they were supposed to stand and sing into the horn. One woman sang as loud as she could and she got her head right inside the horn, and it blew the transmitter right off the air and blew the fuses. I asked her why she did it. She said, 'I've got a sister listening in Ontario and I wanted to be sure she heard me.'"

In Charlottetown, Keith Rogers protected his microphone by advising a well-known soprano named Hermina West Richards, "Hermina, when you are approaching a high note, would you please back slowly away from the microphone, and then when you are about to hit it, please turn your back and sing your note into that far corner."

She smiled and did.

Herb Roberts of the CNR Winnipeg station warned colleagues about the dangers of static electricity. "If you stood too close to the microphone cord, it would shoot sparks up the cord and into the carbon mike. Speech and music were distorted, so you'd lift the mike, shake it a few times, and then continue with the broadcast."

In Winnipeg, Darby Coats would brew a pot of tea before going on the air and then sprinkle the damp tea leaves on the carpet to reduce static.

No one who worked in radio for any length of time in those days would be without a screwdriver to use on microphones that would suddenly go dead. "When that happened," said Vancouver announcer and musician John Avison, "you took the handle of the screwdriver out of your back pocket and pounded the microphone with it."

In Saskatoon, passing streetcars would sometimes shake the CFQC studio so hard the microphone would stop working and the announcer had to whack it to get it going again. In Calgary, the CFAC studio was used as an office as well, and from time to time the office telephone would ring while the station was on the air, prompting the announcer to say, "Oh, pardon me. The phone's ringing. I'll have to answer it." The audience would then hear one side of the phone conversation, and when it was over, the announcer would say on-air, "Well, I'm back," and he'd go on with the program.

At CJOR Vancouver, a neophyte announcer was the victim of a practical joke by his fellow announcers, who had warned him about the possibility of the equipment exploding. They had fitted a long tube to the microphone and when he was on-air they blew smoke up the tube. He had no knowledge of microphones, thought the mike would blow up at any moment, and flapped his hands frantically to get the technician's attention. Perspiration rolled down his cheeks and his voice quavered all through the fifteen-minute program, but he finished the show.

Another challenge for the early broadcasters was carting seventy-five to one hundred pounds of broadcast batteries, amplifiers, and other equipment to churches, hotel ballrooms, sports arenas, and parades. Jack Carlyle of CNR Radio remembered, "We'd carry the equipment up to St. Patrick's Church and we'd do half an hour or an hour from there. Then we'd switch back to the studio for half an hour, and by that time you would have carried the equipment from St. Patrick's Church along to the Press Club and we'd broadcast the dance band."

CFCA Toronto had only one set of equipment for out-of-studio broadcasts, and Foster Hewitt remembered doing programs one night from five different locations, lugging the equipment all over the city to pick up dance bands, churches, and sports events. Western broadcast veteran Bill Speers said, "Hell, at one time, I spent evening after evening running around town packing a great heavy amplifier and great awkward microphones looking for bands to broadcast, or something to broadcast."

It was tougher still when an out-of-town program was scheduled. Robbie Robertson of CJCB Sydney described covering a hockey game in Antigonish, Nova Scotia, "I went up alone by train, got a taxi, lugged all that stuff into the rink, and set it up. I called the game, did the commercials, and all the colour commentary for the whole game and two overtime periods. Then I packed everything up again, loaded it back into a taxi, and caught the midnight train home. I didn't mind that. It was fun."

Not only sports but politics came to radio, too, as stations in Saint John, Montreal, Toronto, and Vancouver carried election results throughout the night during the December 1921 federal election that saw William Lyon Mackenzie King become prime minister. Four years later, the *London Free Press*'s CJGC carried detailed election results throughout the night, thanks to information provided by the newspaper.

Broadcasters were generally leery of carrying much political debate, reasoning that people wanted to be entertained, not lectured. "Few stations would be willing to sacrifice the good will they have so laboriously achieved by flooding the air with political speeches," *Maclean's* magazine stated in 1924. There were exceptions, though, such as CKAC in Montreal, which carried more political speeches and meetings than any other station in the country. "This station has tried to broadcast as many political meetings as possible in order to stimulate the sales of radios to country folk," said CKAC manager and announcer Jacques Cartier. "French Canadians are keen politicians and they will spend anything to hear their pet orators." In the 1925 election, Cartier sent out radio "mobile" trucks to capture political speeches in Trois-Rivières, Saint-Hyacinthe, Granby, and Sorel, as well as Montreal. Mackenzie King's address in the Montreal Forum was a highlight of CKAC's election coverage.

Winnipeg's CKY also carried extensive political speech-making, giving candidates fifteen minutes each at no cost on the day before an election. CNR Radio also gave free, equal time to Liberal and Conservative candidates. In contrast, in the United States at the time, some stations were charging politicians $200 for ten minutes on radio.

Sometimes things got out of hand, as in the radio coverage of speeches at a Conservative party street-corner rally in Montreal in 1926. Liberal rowdies broke up the meeting, the *Montreal Gazette* reported, because they didn't want Conservative speeches being heard on radio. The radio coverage ended mid-riot.

The most successful political use of early radio was carried out by two silver-tongued politicians – one in Alberta and the other in Newfoundland – who used their persuasive voices to get into the premier's seat in both provinces. In 1925, a Calgary high-school teacher and fundamentalist minister, "Bible Bill" Aberhart, began broadcasting

Sunday-afternoon services from a Baptist church. Within a few years, his hypnotic oratory on CFCN's *Calgary Prophetic Bible Institute* hour made him the most talked-about man in Alberta. "I think he realized for the first time, here was a medium that could elect governments," said broadcaster Dick Rice, who often introduced Aberhart on his radio programs. Aberhart also began a Radio Sunday School and soon expanded his sermons from religious to political and economic issues, embracing a Social Credit philosophy and, amid the Depression, winning adherents by promising to give every Albertan $25 a month to buy necessities.

Rice said that Aberhart's confident voice belied his mike fright. "This was the most nervous and completely reduced to a wobbling jelly type of man I've ever known when he went on the air," said Rice. "He poured with perspiration, and saliva poured from his lips." Nevertheless in 1935, thanks to his potent radio voice, he became the Social Credit premier of Alberta in a landslide vote and remained in office until he died in 1943.

In Newfoundland a few years later, Joey Smallwood also recognized radio as the ultimate political tool. For years, he had told tales on radio as "The Barrelman," and in the late 1940s he used his skills and his radio profile to sell Newfoundlanders on the idea of joining Canada. "Radio was the single most important weapon I used in convincing Newfoundlanders to join Confederation," Smallwood said. "Those who didn't have radios went to houses that did, and in every little nook and cove, every little harbour, every little village, there would be three or four or maybe eight or fifteen people that had radios, mostly battery sets, and eight or ten or twelve neighbours who didn't have them would crowd into the kitchens [to listen]."

"I had spent many years broadcasting and I knew the magic of it," Smallwood later said. "Radio, I've always contended, was invented by God especially for Newfoundlanders, and having done it for Newfoundland, He graciously allowed it to be used in other parts of the world. Radio was the great unifying thing. I knew how to use it. I never let my mouth turn away from the microphone. Never."

Not all politicians welcomed radio's microphones, however. When former British prime minister Lloyd George addressed a Montreal meeting in 1924, he refused to speak into a mike on the grounds that it was "scientific witchcraft" and would strain his voice.

Norman Botterill recalled an Albertan politician in the 1930 Canadian federal election who was so nervous in front of a microphone he refused to make his speech over the radio. "I introduced him and nodded for him to go ahead," Botterill said. "But all I got was an agonized stare. The silence was deadly, so I repeated [the introduction], but he still sat silent and morose. 'You do it!' he finally begged. And by golly, I did." The candidate got wide praise for his "speech" and won the election.

Although most stations provided some news reports each day, they were little more than a lick and a promise, since radio reporters were non-existent and newscasts consisted of reading out stories in the newspapers. Newspapers called the stations "news pirates." "They claimed that we were stealing the news," said Saskatchewan broadcaster Harold Crittenden. "And that was exactly what we were doing." Canadian Press, which saw radio as a potential competitor for newspaper advertising, expressly warned its members to prevent stations from pirating the news, except where stations were owned by the papers.

One of the more elaborate newscasts of the early days was on Regina's CKCK, owned by the *Regina Leader-Post*. Four nights a week it carried a fifteen-minute newscast announced by a veteran *Leader-Post* reporter, Gaston "Gee" Johnston, who read from carbon copies of stories that had appeared in the paper. It was a hastily assembled job, and the reporter was introduced with the words, "Ladies and gentlemen, The News Butcher."

Radio news, with few exceptions, remained a slap-dash affair until the mid-1930s. Sid Boyling, who worked at CHAB in Moose Jaw, said, "Our first newscasts were excerpts from the *Moose Jaw Times-Herald*, given twenty-four hours later. We weren't allowed to air it for twenty-four hours. And so, in the evening, around suppertime, we would read the news from the previous day's paper."

While news programs were sketchy at best, some of the pioneer stations offered extensive educational programming. The University of Western Ontario aired fifteen-minute lectures on CJGC London on subjects such as farming, finance, local history, health, and one discussion on "Mars and Its Inhabitants." CKY Winnipeg provided similar programming on everything from architecture to zoology, lessons in French and Esperanto, and a ten-part series on teeth and health provided by the Manitoba Dental Association. CKUA, the University of Alberta station in Edmonton, did more than anyone else, offering twenty hours a week of lectures, advice, conversation, handicraft information, and literary reviews. Queen's University in Kingston also aired lectures and sports on its station, and in Halifax, CHNS pioneered school broadcasts with help from the provincial Department of Education.

For many, early radio was a serious business and whenever "God Save the King" was played, across the country hundreds if not thousands of listeners would leap to their feet to stand at attention. In Antigonish, a listener reported that her neighbour always put on his best clothes before sitting down to listen to the radio. "He was not the only one to do this," said Mrs. Ellie Grant. "All kinds of people would do this. It [radio] was a very special thing, you see, and they wanted to be dressed correctly for it."

The air of formality sometimes affected announcers as well. Dick Claringbull at CNRV in Vancouver, who had been one of the original CNR on-board radio operators, regularly wore his tuxedo to do his in-studio announcing. In Winnipeg, CNRW announcer Herb Roberts went even further, wearing white tie and tails on Saturday nights to introduce the music from the Fort Garry Hotel.

While many stations didn't have to worry about their budgets, because they were established to promote the products of their owners, such as newspapers or electric appliance shops, others began to worry about the rising cost of running radio stations. They looked to advertising to support their programs, and began to feel restive about the advertising constraints imposed by the federal government. They blamed newspapers for having lobbied the government for the restrictions. "We felt most of the regulations were put there to favour newspapers rather than to do any good for broadcasting," said Jim Allard, future head of the Canadian Association of Broadcasters. "It was the newspaper lobby that prevented us from using prices on the air," complained western broadcaster Gerry Quinney. "They were afraid of losing revenue, and did effectively hold broadcasting back for years."

Two kinds of advertising were allowed in the early days: "indirect" or institutional advertising, which did not promote an individual product, and "direct" advertising with specific product mentions. For much of the 1920s, however, direct advertising was banned after 6:30 P.M., or banned altogether.

The government was clearly uneasy about radio advertising, fearing it would damage newspapers. There was also the belief that the public didn't like ads on the air, especially direct ads promoting a specific product. "The proper place for this type of advertising is in the columns of the newspapers," said the head of the government's Radio Branch, C. P. Edwards. Restrictions on direct advertising lasted until the early 1930s, and the government ban on mentioning prices on-air was in effect until the 1940s. One station was told by the CBC that it could broadcast that a store was having an eighty-eight-cent sale so long as there was no mention of what was for sale for eighty-eight cents.

The more imaginative stations tried to get around this restraint. "You would say, 'Northwest Laundry are doing wet wash at the price of an ice cream cone a pound,'" Winnipeg broadcaster A. J. Messenger recalled. Don Laws in Vancouver remembered putting on radio ads saying, "'Buy so-and-so's chocolate bars. They're less than a streetcar ticket.' You could talk for five minutes about how good a suit was and that the price was unbelievable, but you couldn't mention what the price was. It was a lot of baloney!"

Advertising agencies were initially unconvinced that radio was an effective way to sell products, and many recommended that their clients stay away from it, an attitude vigorously encouraged by newspapers. Most merchants felt newspaper ads, being tangible, were more valuable. Robbie Robertson, Cape Breton radio veteran, explained, "If it was printed in the paper, they could look at it time and again and see it. But with radio, when it was said, it was said and that was it."

As a result, prices were low for radio commercials: $1 for a spot announcement lasting about a minute on CHNS Halifax in 1925; six commercials for $5 at CJCB Sydney. You could get spot announcements for between $3 and $6 on Toronto stations. At CKCK Regina, spot advertisements went for $2.40 a minute, and Calgary radio salesman Francis Martin remembered selling spot ads for 50 cents. CKY Winnipeg charged $100 for an hour at night, and CKGW Toronto would get $150 for a night-time hour.

A number of stations made money from a death notice program. CKAC Montreal ran a nightly program at 7:15 of birth and death announcements for a small fee for each notice. Mac McCurdy, who later became president of Standard Broadcasting, remembers selling obituary ads for $2 each on his station in Brantford, Ontario, although there were days when the program was cancelled because, as the announcer would say, "There are no deaths today." "Mostly, though," says McCurdy, "we'd have five minutes of news and five minutes of death notices."

Some announcers found there was profit in lecturing about the evils of drink or the devil. They would buy air time and end their speech with a plea for donations to support the cause. The donations, of course, would go straight into their own pockets. Bill Speers, who started out in radio in Regina in 1931, said, "You could buy a series of fifteen-minute temperance talks for five bucks. I'd go on the air and read these things and then ask for donations to support this worthy work. I made a helluva lot of money." Keith Rogers at CFCY Charlottetown traded mentions on-air for bread, milk, and lumber. When his father saw several cases of strawberry soft drinks on Rogers' verandah, he asked him, "Did you buy that, Keith, or did you talk for it?"

Radio had a profound impact on the lives of Canadians, especially those living on isolated farms, and particularly in the West. It brought the world into their living rooms. "Radio broke the fearsome isolation of prairie life," says broadcast historian Kenneth Bambrick. "Families and neighbours – often travelling many miles for the privilege – gathered around tinny, store-bought, sometimes, or homemade, often, sets passing the earphones from one person to another to hear a few minutes of disembodied music or voice. Or the earphones might be placed in a fish bowl, which provided some modest amplification so they could all hear at once." Jim Allard remembered those days, too. "You would find families in northern Alberta driving fifty miles in forty below weather to visit a family to get perhaps three or four minutes of reception."

Radio was a boon to prairie farmers not only because it brought them news and entertainment from their neighbourhood and from the world, but it also brought them the latest grain prices. Before radio, grain elevator agents got telegrams from their head offices announcing the grain prices to be paid to farmers. Now, with radio, farmers could hear the prices for grain directly and much sooner. Grain traders themselves set up stations in Alberta and Saskatchewan to provide the prices daily to farmers. They had wanted to set up a station in Manitoba, too, but the provincial government vetoed the idea, so the traders broadcast in from Saskatchewan.

The Manitoba government decided in 1923 that radio should be a provincially controlled station run by the Manitoba Telephone System. This meant the *Free Press* and the *Tribune* in Winnipeg would have to give up the stations they'd launched with such fanfare a year earlier. As it happened, neither newspaper minded because both were unhappy with the cost of running radio and neither had seen the increase in circulation they had thought radio would give them. So the two newspaper stations went out of business and the provincial government took over the airwaves with CKY, making it, in effect, Canada's first public broadcaster.

The federal government agreed to give Manitoba a veto over all broadcasting licence requests in the province and agreed to hand over half of the one-dollar listeners' licence fees paid by Manitobans. The rest of the money to run the station would come from advertising. In the act that authorized this deal, the federal government said a similar subsidy was also available for other stations. Jacques Cartier of CKAC Montreal immediately applied, but his request was denied. In fact, no other station got the subsidy.

Darby Coats was hired to run CKY. Like Bert Hooper at CKCK Regina, he was, at the start, the station's only employee, not only acting as manager, but also as announcer, technical operator, and secretary. Coats, who for some unknown reason was nicknamed "Drip," became known throughout Manitoba as "The Man with the Cheerful Voice." Coats scheduled news, sports, market reports, and recorded music from 12:30 P.M. to 2:00 P.M. every day except Sunday and, as with most stations, borrowed records from local music stores in exchange for on-air mentions of the stores' names. He aired two hours of concerts on Tuesday, Thursday, and Friday evenings, and in the afternoons, he was Uncle Peter, reading children's stories to his "Peterkins." On Thursday nights, he broadcast talks by university professors, and on Sunday nights sacred music started at 9:00 P.M. Coats' annual reading of Charles Dickens' *Christmas Carol* became a Manitoban tradition.

A few months after opening the station, Coats set up "listening posts" in the homes of a number of telephone company employees, who tuned in to American stations. If they reported the reception of the U.S. stations was particularly good, Coats would cut off what he had on the air and switch over to the American signal. This "pirating" of different American station signals might happen half a dozen times a night, all quite illegal but nevertheless a common practice of Canadian stations. Sid Boyling remembered that at CHAB Moose Jaw, he and his colleagues pirated American network shows every night. "We would carry *Amos 'n*

Andy, Jack Benny," he said. "We carried every big show that was receivable from the States until the government stepped in and stopped us." In Unity, Saskatchewan, future CRBC and CBC senior executive Horace Stovin would also "pirate" programs from an NBC station in Bismark, North Dakota. CFCN Calgary would carry *Amos 'n Andy*, picked up from a Denver station, while CFCA Toronto would air dance music from stations in Chicago.

There were problems with pirating, however, when the American signal would fade out in mid-broadcast. Keith Rogers at CFCY Charlottetown was pirating the fight between Jack Dempsey and "Wild Bill" Firpo in 1923, but the signal kept fading. Whenever that happened, Rogers, who knew very little about boxing, would cut in on-air and try to recreate the scene from the boxing arena. One man who was listening, J. "Hy" Goodman, told Rogers' daughter that "when the signal strengthened, Rogers would give a deep sigh of relief and leave the rest of the broadcast to the experts."

CKY, the CNR stations, and a few others such as CFRB, CKNC, CFCA in Toronto and CKAC and CFCF in Montreal carried a wide range of programming beyond the amateur-hour efforts of most stations. But as the 1920s progressed, even the small stations began to get a bit more sophisticated when they started to use electrical transcriptions. These were ready-to-air discs, fifteen minutes on each side, of music, drama, or light entertainment, even advertising. Since the discs came mostly from American advertising agencies, however, they promoted the sale of American-made products with such programs as *The Lone Ranger*, *The Shadow*, or *The Green Hornet*. This raised alarm among those worried about the social impact of radio. The federal government responded by imposing restrictions on nighttime use of transcriptions.

The much greater worry, however, was the Americanizing of the Canadian airwaves through the large number of U.S. stations broadcasting into Canada. In many instances, their powerful signals simply swamped the Canadian stations.

As a result, Canadians in, say, Regina were much more aware of what was going on in Salt Lake City, Chicago, or Omaha than they were in Vancouver, Toronto, or Halifax. By 1925, there were about four hundred thousand radio sets in Canada, three-quarters of them were crystal sets, and it was estimated more than 80 per cent of Canadian radio listeners were tuned to American programs. Survey after survey showed Canadians preferred American programming. In Toronto, listeners tuned in to stations in Buffalo, Pittsburgh, New York, and Schenectady. A southern Saskatchewan survey showed 45 per cent preferred listening to KOA in Denver, 17 per cent to KSL Salt Lake City, and 26 per cent to CKCK Regina.

Listeners twiddled the dial at night looking for American stations in part because they liked the more polished programming, and in part simply because it was fun to bring in as many American stations as possible. Inveterate "twiddlers" often kept maps pinpointing the faraway stations they had heard. "It was a great triumph to come into the office the next day and say that last night I heard Tulsa, Oklahoma, or Fresno, California," said Vic George of CFCF Montreal.

The American stations not only could be heard more clearly and had more sophisticated programming, but the bigger ones were on the air continuously, unlike Canadian stations, which regularly went off the air several times a day. By 1927, CFCF in Montreal was on the air for seventeen hours a week and CKAC twenty hours a week. CHNS Halifax broadcast programs for only eight hours a week and CFCY Charlottetown for twenty-two hours. By contrast, stations in New York or Chicago were on the air almost one hundred hours a week. They seemed to be always there. It was well into the 1930s before Canadian stations would come close to matching the Americans' hours on-air.

In a 1925 letter, Alexander Johnston, the deputy minister in charge of broadcasting, responded to a listener complaining about so much American programming coming into Canada by saying, "Do our Canadian listeners turn their dials to the Canadian stations? I am afraid they do not! In the first place, there is the glamour of receiving concerts from a long distance . . . and secondly, I am afraid we must admit that the average programme turned out by the best stations in the United States is superior to the average programme of the best Canadian stations. . . . These are facts . . . which have . . . got to be faced." Johnston's comment was one of the first hints of the government's growing apprehension about the content of radio programs heard by Canadians. "The ether disregards all boundaries," the director of the Radio Branch commented.

Reflecting these worries, *Maclean's* magazine noted in 1924 that radio "is certainly throwing us all the more under United States influence." *Maclean's* also complained that Canadian stations had too much music and not enough substantial programming such as news, commentary, and informative talks on science, politics, religion, history, and literature.

Although their on-air hours were sharply limited, the CNR Radio and a few big-city stations had begun providing more professionally produced and more informative programs. But most of the first wave of Canadian broadcasters were still just offering recorded music and local amateur talent. They were not seeking to enlighten or elevate society. With rare exceptions, they had no high-falutin' ideas about radio.

Like the stunt pilots of the 1920s going from town to town with their aerial tricks, the broadcasting pioneers got their thrills from doing something new and daring. They couldn't hear the mutterings of Canadian nationalists and social engineers who believed broadcasting should be an instrument for public good. They scoffed at the comment by the head of the BBC, John Reith, that, "To have exploited so great a scientific invention for the purpose and pursuit of entertainment alone would have been a prostitution of its powers and an insult to the character and intelligence of the public."

But something of this sentiment was stirring among influential Canadians, which the radio pioneers ignored at their peril.

3

The Battle Begins

While the swashbucklers of early radio were still swept up in their enthusiasm for their new toy, a handful of public-spirited members of Canada's élite began musing in the late 1920s on using this "toy" as a way to encourage cultural enlightenment, social consciousness, and a sense of Canadianism.

CNR president Sir Henry Thornton, who regarded radio as a "national trust," had already put his beliefs into practice with the CNR's high-quality national radio network. Charles Bowman, editor of the *Ottawa Citizen*, began writing influential editorials promoting the idea of a national public broadcasting system. Graham Spry, the new national secretary of the Association of Canadian Clubs, who felt that American programming was a cancer eating into Canadians' sense of nationhood, wanted a BBC-like radio system. Vincent Massey, Canada's minister to Washington, backroom Liberal party powerhouse, future Governor General, and a man rich beyond imagination, privately urged Prime Minister Mackenzie King and his cabinet to adopt a national broadcasting policy. He, too, clearly preferred the British style of broadcasting to the "chaotic" private system in the United States. At the time, Massey was in the midst of difficult negotiations with the Americans to get Canada a bigger share of radio wavelengths. The Americans would pay more attention to the issue, he believed, if Canada had "some form of government control" over broadcasting.

Massey, Spry, Bowman, and a few other like-minded activists believed radio should be more than an electronic billboard and an outlet for popular music and amateur performers. They feared that unless the federal government intervened, Canadian airwaves would be overwhelmed by the torrent of American radio signals pouring across the border. They also knew that the way to achieve their objective was to convince the politicians, especially King. While they discussed how best to persuade King and his cabinet, the private broadcasters were too busy getting programs on the air to think of such political lobbying. They didn't realize it, but advocates of public broadcasting were off and running and they weren't even in the starting gate.

Mackenzie King had been introduced to radio at XWA's 1920 special broadcast to a meeting of the nation's political and social élite held at the Chateau Laurier Hotel in Ottawa. A year and a half later, a few experimental radio stations had aired the results of the federal election that made him prime minister. Over the years, further election results and several of King's speeches had been aired, but it wasn't until 1926 that he began thinking seriously of radio as a valuable political tool. That year he asked *Ottawa Citizen* editor Charles Bowman, a personal friend, to go with him to London as his public relations adviser at the Imperial Conference. Significantly, Vincent Massey also was on this trip, and Bowman and Massey privately discussed their mutual interest in public radio. Bowman, who had become entranced with the possibilities of radio after listening to his son's crystal set, had already come to the conclusion that private broadcasting in Canada should be replaced by a system something like the BBC in Britain. In London, at Bowman's urging, King gave a radio talk on the BBC – written by Bowman – in which he praised the British for "having the air kept largely free from the clangour of discordant noises," by which he meant the commercials and popular music pumped out by private radio. King fully shared BBC head John Reith's disgust with the "vulgar showmanship" of American radio. Bowman later noted that this radio talk "initiated Mackenzie King into the significance of national broadcasting."

Back in Ottawa, Graham Spry, a World War One Signal Corps veteran who had been experimenting with radio since he was ten years old, was now getting local stations to carry Canadian Club luncheon speeches. In 1926, he sent a memo to the King government recommending a national radio hookup to celebrate Canada's sixtieth birthday the following year, broadcasting an elaborate, day-long ceremony in front of the Parliament Buildings. When King got back from London, he endorsed Spry's idea and the program was put together by CNR Radio and heard by five million listeners over a couple of dozen private stations across the country and wwj in Detroit. It was a resounding success, the most grandiose broadcast ever heard in Canada to that time. There was live music performed by bands, choirs, and soloists, poetry readings, and speeches by King and others of the political élite, who talked into a gold-plated microphone. King was delighted with the impact of the broadcast and saw in radio a new and powerful way to reach the public with political messages. Through radio, he said, "all Canada became, for the time being, a single voice." He marvelled that all citizens could hear "the living voice of a single orator," imagining himself as a Demosthenes addressing the Athenian citizenry.

After that broadcast, King gave several radio talks and a couple of years later arranged a link-up of private stations to broadcast the speeches at a state dinner he gave for British Prime Minister Ramsay MacDonald in 1929. King and MacDonald's voices were heard across the country in homes and on street corners, where citizens without radios gathered. "Every word and phrase was clearly understandable," reported the *Regina Leader*. "It was the next best thing to being present at the banquet and gave listeners a vivid idea of the wonders of modern radio, bringing not only a word picture of the banquet hall, 1,500 miles distant, but actual voices and even vocal mannerisms of the speakers."

Charles Bowman had originally thought there should be a radio network monopoly run by the Canadian newspapers, but by the late 1920s, he had changed his mind. Unless there were a public system, he now warned, Canadian radio would be taken over by powerful American radio interests. It was a message he told with increasing stridency to Mackenzie King in private as well as in his editorials that appeared not only in the *Ottawa Citizen*, but in other Southam papers as well. Complaining about "dull advertising parrot talk" by "radio barkers," Bowman wrote, "Radio broadcasting under private enterprise is permanently handicapped by the necessity of having to raise revenue from advertising."

"The public will surely rise up in protest against the crude interruptions by so-called announcers in the middle of an entertainment," he editorialized in the *Ottawa Citizen*. ". . . Get rid of the barker in radio advertising."

Private station owners were quick to point out that the newspapers Bowman worked for would be more profitable if radio did not carry advertising, so, they said, he had a hidden motive for advocating public broadcasting. The newspapers' worry about private radio competing with them for advertising led many of them to throw their support behind a national public broadcasting system, which they assumed would take few or no ads.

There also was unease about radio advertising at senior levels of government. "Broadcasting licences so far issued do not specifically forbid advertising," a senior Radio Branch official said in a telegraph to the *Toronto Star*. "But Department discourages same and if public opinion and the press demand that advertising be limited or cut out altogether, Department is quite prepared to consider establishment of a regulation to that effect."

Some Ottawa mandarins were openly dissatisfied with the programs private stations were airing. Donald Manson, chief inspector in Ottawa's Radio Branch, surveyed western stations and reported to his bosses, "The stations generally are poorly equipped, the personnel inadequate and largely unqualified . . . and untrained to carry programs into the homes of listeners in the dignified and edifying manner to be hoped for. . . . Broadcast listeners in Canada deserve something better than they are now getting from Canada's Broadcasting Stations."

Amid this growing concern about the quality of Canadian broadcasting, the government was hit by a political lightning bolt that brought both peril and opportunity. With fiery oratorical alarms about the imminence of Armageddon and the evils of other religions and of government, the Jehovah's Witnesses were using their radio stations across Canada to proselytize their brand of Christianity. So much so that other Christian churches were up in arms about the use the Witnesses – known as the International Bible Students Association – were making of their stations in Toronto, Saskatoon, Edmonton, and Vancouver. The Roman Catholic Church had been a particular target of the venomous accusations of the Witnesses.

Then a Witnesses station in Toronto got into a fight over the air time it shared with the *Toronto Star*'s CFCA. The frequency was supposed to be handed over to the Witnesses station at 8:30 P.M. on

Sundays, but on several occasions when the popular but long-winded Baptist minister, the Reverend W. A. Cameron, was giving a sermon, his program ran over. The Witnesses simply cut him off and put on their own program. One listener who was outraged by the cut-off was J. H. Cranston, editor of the *Toronto Star*, a devout Baptist and a particular admirer of the Reverend Cameron. Toronto radio pioneer Ernie Bushnell remembered, "Cranston was the editor of the *Star* at the time and he was a great friend of Mackenzie King. He came down to Ottawa, raising Cain about it, what had happened in Toronto. He told King, 'There's got to be a stop put to this bloody nonsense, the Bible Students cutting off the word of God.' And I believe it was he who suggested that radio should be nationalized. Actually, that was the beginning of the idea of the nationalization of radio."

Letters of protest poured in to the government, and P. J. A. Cardin, the minister of Marine and Fisheries who was also in charge of broadcasting, revoked the Witnesses' station licences. Both Cardin and his deputy minister, Alexander Johnston, were devout Catholics and personally offended by the Witnesses' attacks. But no sooner were the licences cancelled than Ottawa was swamped by protests over government censorship of free speech. Acrimonious debate over the matter erupted in the House of Commons, and the government faced a serious political crisis. There were accusations that the *Star* had sought the cancellation of the Witnesses station in Toronto so that it could have exclusive use of the frequency. When the *Star* was later granted its own frequency, the Toronto *Telegram* and the Conservatives suggested this was a reward to the *Star* for its strong support of King's Liberal government.

The arguments in the House of Commons focused on the accusations of free speech infringement, and also on the quality of radio itself. "Most radio programs are rubbish," one MP said. "A blight to the minds and hearts of our generation," said Thomas Bird, a Manitoba MP. J. S. Woodsworth, then a Labour party MP from Winnipeg, told the House, "The government itself should ... decide upon a comprehensive national policy leading to public ownership and control of this new industry."

Like Woodsworth, Charles Bowman saw this fracas as an opportunity to call for a review of overall broadcasting policy, which he hoped would lead to the elimination of private stations in favour of a national public broadcasting system. "With the experience of the United States where chaotic conditions in radio broadcasting were allowed to develop for lack of public control," he wrote in the spring of 1928, "it would seem the height of folly on the part of Canada to allow this great new public service to drift into similar conditions . . . Canada should act without further delay."

Mackenzie King, who was paying attention to Bowman's editorials, asked him to meet with cabinet to discuss his ideas on the future of radio. Bowman also lunched with Vincent Massey, his old friend, to discuss how to get a government review to make such a recommendation.

Influenced by Bowman, Massey, and Cranston, and looking for a way out of the Jehovah's Witnesses contretemps, King set up a royal commission on broadcasting. The newly formed lobby group for private radio, the Canadian Association of Broadcasters, asked for the right to name two of the commissioners. King denied their request but did accept Massey's recommendations for two of the three commissioners: Charles Bowman and Sir John Aird, president of the Canadian Bank of Commerce, a free-enterprise devotee and Toronto imperialist, who would be chairman. The third commissioner was Dr. Augustin Frigon, the Quebec director general of technical education. The commission secretary would be a charming Scot, Donald Manson, the Radio Branch chief inspector who had been so critical of private broadcasters in the West.

Many radio station operators were decidedly uneasy about King's choices for commissioners. "All seemed to the broadcasters to be extremely remote from the radio scene and unlikely to understand its practical aspects and difficulties," radio veteran Walter Dales wrote. "A few sensed sinister forces in the background and feared the worst."

As if to verify that apprehension, P. J. A. Cardin clearly indicated which way the government was leaning. "We have made up our minds that a change must be made in the broadcasting situation in Canada," he told the House of Commons in announcing the commission. "We are inclined to follow that plan which has been established and which is operating at present in England."

There was another indication of government thinking in the order-in-council setting up the commission, which noted the popularity of American programs. The remedy for this, the order stated, would be to establish a number of high-powered public stations across the country and to see "a greater expenditure on programs than the present licencees appear prepared to undertake." The commissioners were told to consider what would be the best way to use radio "in the national interests of Canada." Privately, King made clear his preference for a network of government-owned and -operated stations, replacing the private stations. Officially, though, he said the commissioners could consider three options: the establishment of one or more groups of private enterprise stations, subsidized by the government; the establishment of stations run by a company owned and operated by the federal government; and the establishment of stations run by the provinces.

The first stop on the commissioners' quest for a Canadian broadcasting policy was New York, where they were taken aback by the American network attitude that Canada was part of the U.S. broadcast universe. The American broadcasters were opposed to any national public radio in Canada and wanted to see in Canada an extension of their all-private system. There were a few Americans, however, who had a different view. Newly elected New York Governor Franklin Roosevelt told Vincent Massey at a private lunch, "I don't want to appear to be interfering or intruding, [but] broadcasting in Canada should be nationally owned and controlled and operated." When he had been assistant secretary of the navy in the First World War, he and his boss, Secretary Josephus Daniels, had tried but failed to persuade the U.S. cabinet to make radio a public and not a private enterprise. Massey quickly reported Roosevelt's position to the commissioners.

Similarly, Herbert Hoover, as Republican secretary of commerce in the early 1920s, had condemned "outrageous" radio advertising, maintaining that radio should not be "merely a business carried on for private gain. . . . It is a public concern impressed with the public trust and to be considered primarily from the standpoint of public interest." Like FDR, however, Hoover had failed to convince his colleagues, and private radio continued to rule American airwaves.

After New York, the commissioners sailed to England, where they were much impressed with the BBC. They then visited continental Europe, increasingly attracted as they travelled to a national public system. When they returned to Canada, they began hearings across the country, starting in Vancouver. Encouraging their growing tilt toward a public rather than a private system of broadcasting, the commissioners heard early on from former Conservative prime minister Arthur Meighen, who attacked private radio. "The amount of fodder that is the antithesis of intellectual that comes over our radios is appalling while the selection of material for broadcasting remains in commercial hands," he said.

Meighen's views were echoed by educators testifying before the commission, and more support for public broadcasting came from unions, farm organizations, the Canadian Legion, and others. But the hearings also prompted the private broadcasters and their allies to mount a concerted attack on the idea of a public system that might see the disappearance of all, or most, private stations. But the debate was being conducted on terrain most of them didn't recognize; a hostile world of politicians, social activists, and zealots who wanted to take the radio business away from them.

They were alarmed at letters the government sent out to station owners stating, "As a result of seemingly unsatisfactory conditions in the matter of Canadian broadcasting services, the government may at some future date discontinue the present policy and as an alternative, adopt a policy of national broadcasting. . . . Licensees may govern themselves accordingly." All licence renewals were stamped: "CONTINGENT ON THE REPORT OF THE ROYAL COMMISSION ON RADIO BROADCASTING."

"The broadcasters were stunned," said Walter Dales. "They didn't know what had hit them. Suddenly the threat of expropriation was in the air."

Representing forty-one stations, the Canadian Association of Broadcasters took up the broadcasters' cause, arguing strenuously for a private system. CAB president Jacques Cartier of CKAC Montreal described to the commissioners the "wonder" of radio, saying, "In private hands, radio in Canada . . . has changed from being a thing of squeaks and howls with an occasional bit of beauty, to a thing of beauty with occasional interruptions." He said private radio was "enterprising," "flexible," and "visionary." Cartier saw the hand of communism in the campaign for nationalized public radio. But he did admit that private stations could and should provide more educational and instructive programming and said that the CAB recognized the distaste of listeners for too much radio advertising. In the biggest concession to the do-gooders, the CAB did agree that the government should be responsible for some modest regulation of the broadcast industry.

The CAB was muted in its effectiveness, however, partly because it was poorly financed and had no staff (it would be 1935 before the first staff person was hired, a secretary) and partly because some CAB members, such as the CNR network and CKY Winnipeg, actually favoured nationalization. There also were differences between the more aggressive stations in Toronto and Montreal and the stations in smaller centres. They were divided, too, between the pioneers, who still loved the adventure of radio, and the big-city newcomers, who loved radio's commercial potential. "They had not fused as a group," said Walter Dales, "and very few of them had any political instincts of any kind. They made a pitifully weak presentation. They looked for all the world like special pleaders with greedy motives and shallow minds."

Two particularly outspoken big-city private broadcasters – Ralph Ashcroft of CKGW Toronto and J. Arthur Dupont of CKAC Montreal – told the Aird commission that small, weak stations should be eliminated in favour of a few powerful private stations. Dupont claimed that big private stations could provide much better and more popular programs than would be possible under a public system, and he warned that a public system would open radio to government propaganda and political interference. He and Ashcroft also said Canadian corporations would be unfairly treated if they could not advertise on radio as their American competitors could. But they did not convince the commissioners. Commissioner Frigon speculated that radio advertising would encourage broadcasters to put on the air "whatever they think will please the public, and not what they [the public] should have."

Alec McKenzie of Toronto's CKNC urged that private stations establish networks with the government subsidizing the transmission costs as a way to get higher quality programs. One of the most vocal opponents of public broadcasting was Horace Stovin, who had begun a radio station at the back of his drugstore in Unity, Saskatchewan, and later ran CKCK Regina. Stovin said that local private broadcasters provided the best way to serve local communities and he said the cost of running "civil service" radio would raise the rate for listener licences from $1 to $14 or $17 a year.

H. R. Worden of CJHS Saskatoon agreed, telling the commission that his listeners were more interested in a local dog fight than in the overthrow of a distant empire. Darby Coats told the Aird commissioners when they visited Winnipeg that if Canada went to a public radio system, he would move to the United States. Supporting the private broadcasters, the Canadian Manufacturers' Association argued that the private stations would produce programs more inexpensively than public stations.

But Aird, Bowman, and Frigon were unpersuaded. They felt some form of publicly owned broadcasting system was needed in Canada, and when they finished their three-month tour of twenty-five cities, the only question was what the details of their recommendation would say.

The commissioners issued their nine-page report in 1929. As expected, it said that broadcasting was a public service, not a business, and was to be used for the benefit of the country. The public interest, the Aird report claimed, "can be adequately served only by some form of public ownership, operation and control, behind which is the national power and prestige of the whole public of the Dominion of Canada."

"It must be a public service," Frigon said, "because you cannot mix up the interests of the man who wants to make money . . . and the man who wants to render a public service to his country. . . . If you accept the point of view of broadcasting in the interests of the nation, it cannot be left to private enterprise."

Although there had been a commendable effort to provide entertainment for the public, the report said, private broadcasting had failed. As a result, most Canadians were listening to American programs and absorbing "ideas and opinions that are not Canadian." "One of the strongest arguments against private ownership," said Donald Manson, "is that it will mean eventual control of the air by the powerful United States companies." Furthermore, the report went on, there were too many stations in big cities and not enough in smaller, more remote areas. Also there were too many advertisements on the air. Altogether, the Aird report was a strong indictment of what the private radio pioneers had done.

In what, to private broadcasters, was a nightmare recommendation, the commissioners declared there should be a single national agency that would both run the system and produce the programs, and a network of seven publicly owned, powerful 50,000-watt stations spanning the country. All private stations should be shut down or absorbed by the new national broadcasting company.

A twelve-member governing board would run the new agency, three representing Ottawa and one from each province. Provincial authorities would have full control over programs broadcast by stations in their areas. Time should be made available for school broadcasts and adult education,

and, in a reference to the dispute over the Jehovah's Witnesses' programming, they said, religious programs should not attack other religions.

To finance all this, the commission recommended raising the listener
licence fee from $1 to $3, which would bring in $900,000; allowing indi-
rect advertising, with no specific product or price mention, which would
provide an additional $700,000; and providing a federal subsidy of
$1 million a year for the first five years. They estimated the capital cost
of building the system to be about $3.2 million, a cost to be met by the
federal government.

Significantly, despite their oft-stated distaste for radio advertising
and their admiration for the ad-less BBC, the commissioners would
make the new public broadcasting agency dependent on advertising
revenue for about one-third of its operating costs, a dependency that
would haunt public broadcasting into the new millennium.

Howls of outrage poured out of the private broadcasters, who saw
the Aird report destroying everything they had done since 1919.
"Confiscation!" they said. "Unfair!" "Silly!" "Shameful!" "Communism!"
Nationalized radio would be a political tool of the government, editorialized Montreal's *La Presse*, owner of CKAC. "A steam roller to dig in a
flower pot," the paper added. "The question to decide is this: Shall
private ownership or state ownership – also called state socialism –
dominate our land?"

"There has been advanced no perceivable good reason for taking
such drastic action in driving private broadcasters off the air in order to
allow a doubtful experiment in government ownership and control of
Canadian radio," stated Toronto's *Globe*.

A *Maclean's* article asked, "Has the federal government any moral
right to confiscate the existing broadcasting organizations which represent a business built up through years of experience and toil, and in
which many millions of dollars are invested?"

"If this scheme goes through, our programs are bound to get worse
until nobody will listen to anything but American programs," said R. H.
Combs, former manager of Toronto's CKNC and a director of the
Canadian Radio and Trades Association. CKGW Toronto manager Ralph
Ashcroft said the private stations should set up a popular network

of their own, financed by advertisers. The Canadian Manufacturers' Association and the Association of Canadian Advertisers joined the naysayers.

Despite the protest in *La Presse*, the Toronto *Telegram*, the *Globe*, the *Calgary Albertan*, and a few other newspapers, most of the Canadian press supported the concept of fully nationalized radio.

In the *Ottawa Citizen*, Charles Bowman led the defence of the Aird report, warning that the Americans would soon control Canadian radio if a public system was not undertaken. "There is no likelihood of private stations in Canada being able to raise sufficient revenue annually from Canadian radio advertising to maintain an independent Canadian system," he said. In this, he echoed Aird, who told a *Toronto Star* reporter, "Radio is not an ideal advertising medium and its value as such is decreasing." In a monumental misjudgment, Aird declared, "Radio advertising is a myth. In my opinion, it is going to die out." Thinking somewhat like Aird, Herbert Hoover in the United States had noted, "The American people will never stand for advertising on the radio."

Six weeks after the commission made its report, the question of the future of Canadian broadcasting was swept off the front pages and out of the minds of politicians when the bottom fell out of the stock market. Because of the economic uncertainties and because an election was pending, the ever-cautious King stalled doing anything about translating the Aird report's recommendations into legislation, even though he personally endorsed them.

Cultural nationalists like Bowman and Graham Spry worried that the momentum for nationalizing radio would fade into indifference. Their worst fears seemed to come true when the Conservatives, under diehard Tory R. B. Bennett, won the 1930 federal election, throwing Mackenzie King out of office. Bowman wrote more editorials and Spry searched for ways to stimulate new support and rejuvenate the now-subdued advocates of public broadcasting.

The answer, they found, was to organize a pressure group to lobby politicians on the value of nationalized radio, the Canadian Radio League. Its basic platform, Spry said, was a "distaste for commercialism and apprehension of Americanization." Radio, Spry said, "is more than selling cakes of soap and toothpaste." He argued, "Broadcasting is no more a business than a public school system is a business. ... Broadcasting, primarily, is an instrument of education in its widest significance. . . . It is a choice between commercial interests and the people's interests."

Spry's first recruit for the coming battle was a rich, nationalistic, hard-driving intellectual named Alan Plaunt. With Spry's nationwide contacts through his job as head of the Association of Canadian Clubs and with Plaunt's intimacy with the Ottawa élite, the two of them ran circles around the tepid and disorganized lobbying of the private stations. They were an ideal pairing, Spry as Sir Galahad and Plaunt as Machiavelli.

In addition to relentless evangelicizing in speeches, articles, interviews, letters, presentations to cabinet ministers, meetings with civil servants and the prime minister, Spry orchestrated accidental meetings with Bennett at lunch or dinner at the Rideau Club, at the Chateau Laurier baths where Bennett got his massages, even on the street. Spry also exploited his father's friendship with Bennett and the fact that as a youngster Spry had delivered newspapers to Bennett's Calgary home.

The two men marshalled more newspaper support by issuing a pamphlet entitled *Radio Advertising – A Menace to the Newspapers and a Burden to the Public*. They also targeted Bennett's key advisers, such as William Herridge and R. K. Finlayson, two old friends of Spry and early Radio League supporters, who became allies for Spry and Plaunt inside the Prime Minister's Office. Herridge also just happened to be Bennett's brother-in-law. Spry had frequent meetings with both men and planned the occasional accidental meeting, once taking a train from Ottawa to Montreal so that he could bump into Herridge in the parlour car and bend his ear. "Intrigue there was, and plenty of it," charged Walter Dales.

"In 1930–32," said Spry later, ". . . we had far better connections and knew our way about the government far better than our opponents, the rather small-town boys . . . who were seeking their fortune in private broadcasting. . . . They didn't know what they were doing. They were absolute children."

An example of that was the woebegone efforts of the CPR's publicity manager, John Murray Gibbon, who crowed that with Bennett's election the Aird recommendations were "dead and buried." In a magazine article, he ridiculed Spry and Plaunt's "delusions" about public broadcasting, saying they would deprive most Canadian listeners of the kind of popular programming the public wanted, to give "solace" to a few intellectuals. Saying there was not enough good Canadian talent to do the kind of programming Spry and Plaunt envisioned, Gibbon said their plan "would drive out with inferior talent some of the excellent programs originating in the U.S."

"The Lord has delivered the enemy into our hands," Spry chortled, and the CPR disowned Gibbon.

Spry and Plaunt enlisted to their cause big-name bankers, business-men, civic leaders, educators, churchmen, editors, labour leaders, and social activists. Their close supporters included a couple of future prime ministers – Lester Pearson and Louis St. Laurent – as well as Mackenzie King, several future cabinet ministers, senior diplomats, and public service mandarins. Most of these men were not regular radio listeners themselves, but nevertheless thought that radio could and should be more intellectually enriching and play a powerful role in cementing national unity. They agreed with Spry's comment: "Here is a majestic instrument of national unity and culture. . . . It is the greatest Canadianizing instrument in our hands. . . . Its potentialities are too great, its influence and significance are too vast, to be left to the petty purpose of selling cakes of soap."

Ernie Bushnell, manager of CKNC in Toronto, complained that most of those listed as Radio League supporters in fact knew little about either radio or the league. "The big shots on the letterhead didn't know what its aims were," he said, dismissing the efforts of Spry and Plaunt as "the greatest snow job ever." In speeches, articles, and radio commen-taries, he condemned the government for having "swallowed holus bolus" the public broadcasting arguments of this "nebulous, will-o'-the-wisp" organization. He claimed private station programming was getting higher in quality, and charged that a public system would have programs to please academics and civil servants, not the public. He also warned that a public system would become a pawn of government.

Spry and Plaunt were undeterred and played their American card. "The American broadcaster has command of the Canadian ear," Spry said. Canadians were listening to the black-face buffoonery of *Amos 'n Andy*, Paul Whiteman's jazz orchestra, crooner Rudy Vallee, Ben Bernie's big band, and the dramatic series *The Shadow*, *Sherlock Holmes*, as well as other American shows. In many cities near the U.S. border, American programs dominated Canadian air in the day as well as at night. "Ninety per cent of the people of Hamilton woke up in the morning listening to a Buffalo station," said one-time CKOC Hamilton executive Lyman Potts.

Canadians heard these shows not only on American radio signals flooding across the border, but also from four powerful Canadian stations that had become affiliated with American networks: CFRB Toronto and CKAC Montreal with CBS; and CKGW Toronto and CFCF Montreal with NBC. The American networks hoped to acquire more Canadian affiliates, and Canadian stations were anxious to carry the popular American shows. W. W. Grant, from CFCN in Calgary, believed Canadian stations could only hold their listeners if they filled at least one-third of their air time with U.S. programs. The Toronto *Telegram* enthused about CKGW's NBC affiliation, saying it "is but a forerunner to other Canadian stations being added to the [NBC] list."

In the United States, NBC president Merlin Aylesworth said the American networks wanted to send their programming into more parts of Canada. American programming, he said with pride, makes the Canadian border non-existent. For Spry and Plaunt, that was exactly the problem. There was an unconfirmed but widespread report that NBC had made overtures to buy a larger number of Canadian private stations and form an NBC branch network across Canada.

Aird commissioners Bowman and Frigon argued that they didn't want to prevent American programs from coming into Canada, but did want stations here to offer more and better Canadian programming in competition. Instead of the present 80-20 ratio of Canadian listeners in favour of American programs, they hoped they could make that "at least" a 50-50 split.

If Spry and Plaunt couldn't win over the right-wing Imperialist Bennett with philosophical arguments about nationalized radio, they could and did scare him to death about the American takeover of the Canadian airwaves. Bennett adviser R. K. Finlayson later said that Spry and Plaunt's warnings had "worked Bennett up to such a pitch of fear about American domination, [I thought] the old man would call out the troops."

Cannily reaching into the inner sanctums of government, Spry and Plaunt manoeuvred and manipulated behind the scenes, winning over Bennett's advisers and exploiting the weakness of the private broadcasting advocates. Between 1930 and 1932, Spry and Plaunt, as they admitted privately, "bamboozled" Bennett with the slogan of "Canadian Radio for Canadians." Bennett was swayed. "We'll show the States that Canada is no appendage," he told Spry later at a private lunch, adding, "It may well

be, Graham, that you have saved Canada for the British Commonwealth."
Publicly, the prime minister told the House of Commons, "Radio can be
made a most effective instrument of nation-building."

Ralph Ashcroft, a staunch Tory who had worked for Bennett's 1930
election, felt his leader had betrayed private broadcasters. "We who had
handled the broadcasting campaign of the Conservative party from coast
to coast," he said, "and who were told that if the Liberals went out of
power we could 'forget the Aird report,' actually believed that nationalism
was a dead letter." He complained about Spry and Plaunt's "endless
streams of propaganda" and denounced them as "theorists," "possibly
idealists," and "super Canadians," with no experience in radio. He said
public broadcasting would require a huge government subsidy, perhaps
$15 million a year. Spry retorted that it would cost less than a cent a day per
Canadian. The Toronto *Telegram* chimed in with the comment that public
broadcasting was "a colossal blunder." The *Financial Post* went further,
saying public broadcasting was "another step toward communism."

The CAB's public comments were more subdued, even though many
of its members feared the Aird report was a death sentence. Programs
were getting better, the CAB said in a statement prepared by Ernie
Bushnell, and it was untrue that Canada was threatened by a growing
American control of radio listening. No Canadian stations were owned
by Americans, and American programs heard on Canadian stations
carried Canadian advertising.

The private broadcasters offered to provide more educational programming and proposed no advertising on Sundays other than the
mention of a sponsor's name, restricting commercials to a maximum of
5 per cent of program time after 7:00 P.M. on weekdays and airing no
spot advertisements at all after 7:00 P.M. The CAB also sought a government subsidy of $1 million or more for private stations in order to
improve their programming.

Fighting for its members' livelihoods, the lobby group argued that
private stations already had set up networks and that the larger stations
had adequate facilities to do the kind of programming envisioned
by supporters of a national public system, such as the Imperial
Oil–sponsored ad hoc network of weekly symphonies or *The Vagabonds*
sponsored by Canadian General Electric on twenty-two stations during
the 1931–32 season. The private stations also pointed to a 1931 New Year's
morning broadcast by Prime Minister Bennett from his Palliser Hotel

room in Calgary that, they said, was carried by 171 stations in Canada and the United States. They noted, too, that CKGW's Ralph Ashcroft's Trans-Canada Broadcasting Co., which he set up in 1928, had aired the 1930 opening of Parliament and the first broadcast of the Christmas Day message from Buckingham Palace, as well as musical shows such as *The Canadian Wrigley Hour* and *Jack Frost and His Anti-Freezers*.

In 1930, the Canadian Broadcasting System, using CKNC Toronto as its flagship, aired programs produced for the Imperial Tobacco Co., Bell Telephone, William Nielsen, and other advertisers. Foster Hewitt's Toronto Maple Leafs hockey game coverage also went on a network of stations, sponsored by General Motors at a cost of $500 per game. There also were networks in the Maritimes and on the Prairies. One of the more ambitious networks brought nightly programs to CFRB Toronto, CFCF Montreal, CKOC Hamilton, and CFPL London. In 1931, CFRB became the flagship station of something called the Canadian Radio Corporation Trans-Continental Network, a linkage that brought programs to twenty-six stations from Charlottetown to Vancouver.

The CAB's effectiveness, however, was diluted by mutiny in the ranks. Two of its founding and most powerful members – the *Toronto Star*'s CFCA and CNR Radio – resigned from the CAB because of philosophical differences and for their own financial reasons. Both endorsed the concept of public radio and both soon would go out of the radio business altogether. The Manitoba government's station, CKY, and CFAC, owned by the *Calgary Herald*, also withdrew because they disagreed with the CAB's anti-Aird position and the aggressive comments made by CKGW Toronto and CKAC Montreal. Even some of those who stayed with the CAB felt Ashcroft's pugnacious public attitude and private arm-twisting had damaged the case of the private broadcasters. Unlike Spry and Plaunt, he did not hide his aggressiveness.

Shortly after these resignations, Ashcroft, who was a CAB vice-president, resigned himself, because the association had not fought hard enough in support of private radio.

"The organization lacked a consistent membership or leadership, money, and central direction," says radio historian Mary Vipond. "As a result, the CAB was unable to rally strongly and decisively against the Aird Report and the Canadian Radio League."

One last hurdle before Parliament could consider any broadcasting bill was an appeal to the courts by Quebec, supported by Saskatchewan,

Manitoba, Ontario, and New Brunswick, on the basis that broadcasting was a provincial, not federal, responsibility. The Supreme Court of Canada and the Privy Council in London denied Quebec's petition, and immediately Parliament began considering the proposal for public broadcasting based largely on the Aird report.

The familiar arguments about private versus public radio surfaced again during the broadcasting committee hearings on the new broadcast proposals. In his testimony, Aird explained that he had rejected the idea of a subsidy for private stations because it could lead to untoward political pressures on the stations and become a subsidy for advertisers. "It would be a serious error to burden radio broadcasting in Canada with subsidies whether for land lines or any other form of broadcasting equipment under private ownership," he said. He reiterated his belief that advertising could not support adequate Canadian programming. "One could not close one's eyes to the apparent impossibility of Canadian broadcasting being adequately financed by revenue from private sources such as radio advertising," he said. "An adequate broadcasting service in this country will need more revenue than private enterprise can raise from operating broadcasting stations for gain."

The committee hearing was a tour de force for Spry and Plaunt, who dominated the sessions with their testimony and their back-corridor lobbying. Spry testified five times and Plaunt twice. They brought in other witnesses, including a senior BBC official, Gladstone Murray, a Canadian who was particularly effective in stating the case for public broadcasting. Spry and Plaunt also arranged private meetings for Murray with the prime minister, with Opposition Leader Mackenzie King, and other Ottawa powers. They placed on the committee record a statement of support by former Conservative prime minister Sir Robert Borden, and they made sure the committee knew that another former Conservative prime minister, Arthur Meighen, also favoured public broadcasting. Spry and Plaunt presented committee members with a letter of endorsement from radio pioneer Dr. Lee De Forest, who told the politicians, "We look to you in Canada to lead radio in North America out of the morass in which it is pitiably sunk."

Private broadcasters were furious, feeling that the parliamentary committee was being "drenched in a flash flood of ambiguities, contradictions and misstatements." Vic George, who had been a CNR Radio executive and was now manager of CFCF Montreal, angrily attacked "the myth that

Canadian [private] stations did nothing for Canadian talent," and Jim Allard later said, "No member of the House of Commons Broadcasting Committee had the remotest understanding of the technicalities or practicalities of broadcasting. . . . The atmosphere prevailing throughout the committee hearings was at best hysterical and at times manic."

The private broadcasters' complaints paled beside Spry and Plaunt's efforts. Their lobbying was a textbook example of how to influence government decision-makers, orchestrate public support, massage the government bureaucracy, and sweet-talk politicians. Their real worry was not the CAB, but the president of the CPR, Sir Edward Beatty.

Beatty proudly told the broadcasting committee that CPR Radio had aired, over a couple dozen stations, 108 sponsored programs in 1931, including shows such as *The Canadian Pacific Hour of Music*, *Singing Stars of Tomorrow*, and *Melody Mike's Music Shop*. He proposed a national network that would be owned by both the CPR and the CNR plus other radio interests. It would be a private monopoly operating under federal regulations on advertising, educational programming, and licences, he explained, adding that it would acquire existing stations to form its network and would broadcast ten hours a day. Beatty figured it would cost $2 million a year to run, money that would come half from advertising and half from government subsidy through the listeners' licence fee.

Since Beatty was a close friend of the prime minister and Bennett had been the CPR's lawyer, many observers of this battle royal thought the CPR proposal had a real chance of being approved. It gave Spry and Plaunt sleepless nights and hard-working days. "We kept telephoning, seeing powerful people, shaking our heads in horror, and so on," Spry said later. But in the end, the committee rejected the CPR's proposal along with the concerns of private stations, and accepted the principle of public broadcasting. In its findings, the committee criticized private broadcasters, saying, "The present system, excellent as it is in certain respects, does not meet the requirement in quality and scope of broadcasting to ensure its maximum benefits."

To the alarm of the private broadcasters, the bill the committee approved stated that the new public body would have authority "subject to the approval of the Parliament of Canada, to take over all broadcasting in Canada." "SOLE MASTER OF THE AIR," the next day's Toronto *Telegram* shouted in alarm. "Now the deadly hand of bureaucracy is reaching out to strangle radio broadcasting in Canada," the *Financial Post* pronounced. But the bill set out a relatively slow takeover by the new agency, and made provision for stations not needed in the national system to continue operating on a local basis.

In an effort to ease any fears Bennett may have had about damaging the private broadcasters, adviser William Herridge sent him a memo stating, "The bill does not contemplate the automatic expropriation of existing private stations.... It is proposed rather to gradually develop government-owned stations.... Private ownership will not necessarily suffer..."

Although he had what Spry called a "conflict within his soul," Bennett was persuaded, in spite of a partly indifferent and partly hostile cabinet and caucus. "This country must be assured of complete Canadian control of broadcasting from Canadian sources, free from foreign interference or influence," Bennett said. It would be the most important legislative action of his prime ministership.

The legislation was passed in 1932 with the support of all parties. Only one Liberal, E. J. Young from Weyburn, Saskatchewan, voted against it.

"Bennett just wiped off the private broadcasters as being incapable of producing programs that would be of value to the Canadian public," says Halifax TV pioneer Finlay MacDonald, "and, looking back, he was quite right."

The bill was not as sweeping as the Aird report, which had visualized no private stations at all, nor was it as comprehensive as Spry and Plaunt had wanted. "We didn't get the BBC. We had to make a compromise," Spry later said. While public broadcasting supporters had won the fight, the prize was a system enfeebled in the crucial areas of financing and authority – flaws that would forever hobble it.

Nevertheless, private broadcasters felt the new legislation was a sharp sword poised over their heads. It was something they never forgot and some, including Walter Dales, charged that politicians saw radio as a propaganda vehicle that they wanted to control. "The Canadian government did not get into broadcasting because of any spontaneous public desire," he said later. "They interested themselves in broadcasting because of political hunger."

In the parliamentary debate, Bennett said, "No other scheme than that of public ownership can ensure to the people of this country ... equal enjoyment of the benefits and pleasures of radio broadcasting ... I cannot think that any government would be warranted in leaving the air to private exploitation and not reserving it for development for the use of the people."

In a signal to coming generations, however, he also noted, "It may be that at some future time, when science has made greater achievements . . . it may be desirable to make other or different arrangements." It was a prescient comment that private broadcasters noted and tucked away for another day.

The legislation wasn't a knockout blow, but round one in the battle had been lost by the advocates of private broadcasting. Spry and Plaunt were hailed as heroes by the cultural nationalists, and Canada was to have a public "ether highway" controlled by the new Canadian Radio Broadcasting Commission.

4

From the Frying Pan
into the Fire

Licking their wounds, the seventy private stations across Canada began searching for ways to survive under a public broadcasting umbrella. They viewed the new Canadian Radio Broadcasting Commission (CRBC) as, historian Mary Vipond says, "a tentative, experimental public broadcasting system." Their objective was to have a tame public broadcasting agency that would weaken or remove the overhanging threat of nationalization, grant them more powerful frequencies so they could make more money on advertising, and loosen regulatory constraints on such things as playing records at night and price mentions in radio ads.

The big-city stations with their aggressive commercialism led the battle, especially CFRB Toronto, CKAC Montreal, and Toronto's ever-combative Ralph Ashcroft, now the head of a new lobby group, the Dominion Broadcasters Association. It represented, he said, twenty-five stations from coast to coast, although some of them publicly rejected his representation. Largely absent from the fray was the still divided and poorly organized Canadian Association of Broadcasters. Also largely absent were Graham Spry and Alan Plaunt. Once the legislation passed, Spry, who called himself "a semi-detached Liberal," turned to politics, running and losing as a Co-operative Commonwealth Federation (CCF) candidate in a Toronto federal by-election. Plaunt went off to champion social justice, especially for young farmers, organizing the New Canada Movement and publishing a crusading weekly newspaper.

R. B. Bennett, however, was busy making some curious choices for men to run the CRBC. He appointed as chairman Hector Charlesworth, the editor of the conservative weekly *Saturday Night*, a man who knew nothing about broadcasting, thought the Aird report had little value, was suspicious of people like Spry and Plaunt, and thought radio in Canada had sunk to a very low level, especially in the West, where, he said, programs were "putrid." Looking like the bearded King Edward VII and preening with miscalculated confidence, he felt the job would be a snap. But he was neither an intellectual nor a political infighter and, although he had sought the chairmanship, it would be the most frustrating job of his life.

Reaching into Quebec, Bennett chose as the second of the three CRBC commissioners Thomas Maher, a big-name Tory, founder of a Conservative newspaper, and a descendant of an Irish soldier in General Wolfe's army. He was a director of private station CHRC in Quebec City. Maher would later resign and be replaced by another ardent Tory, broadcaster Jacques Cartier, who had played a critical role in the big Conservative party victory in Quebec in the 1930 federal election. The third commissioner was Lt.-Col. W. Arthur Steel, chief radio officer for the Canadian Corps in the First World War and an expert on the technology of broadcasting. From the start, the three commissioners were a gang that couldn't shoot straight, partly because of their own failings and partly because as soon as it had made them, the Bennett government backed away from its financial promises, making the CRBC politically vulnerable and wrapping it in a civil-service administrative cocoon.

The CRBC commissioners faced a broadcast scene that was rapidly changing and expanding. About one-third of Canadian households now had radios and the number of listeners was rising dramatically. Most stations, originally established by stores, manufacturers, newspapers, and religions to promote their products, had now turned to selling advertisements and had become fully commercial. Many of the happy-go-lucky pioneers were disappearing, replaced by hard-nosed, commercial hucksters out to make a buck. Commenting years later about the pioneers who left the radio business, Harry Sedgwick, the head of Toronto's CFRB, said, "They gave up their licences because they wouldn't spend the money needed to stay in business. They lacked courage, hope, and faith."

Pioneers who dropped out altogether included the *Toronto Star*'s CFCA, which closed down at midnight on August 31, 1933, playing "At the End of the Day." "They saw the handwriting on the wall that radio was going to be a government-run thing," says veteran broadcaster Ross McCreath. A couple of years later, CKNC Toronto went off the air. Other private stations were gobbled up by the CRBC, such as CNR Radio and the powerful Red Deer station, CKLC.

"Listeners were all our friends," William Borrett of CHNS Halifax said of the early days of radio. But now listeners were viewed primarily as potential customers for an advertiser's product more than as "friends."

Nobody, however, was yet making a fortune out of broadcasting. That was certainly true for "Big Jim" Bromley-Browne of CKOV Kelowna, who was typical of the small station owners. He had to make an on-air appeal for money to keep his station going, a forerunner of the funding campaigns half a century later run by PBS and TVO. "I am sorry," Big Jim said to his radio audience, "I tried my best, but I'm afraid it's too difficult for me to finance this venture, and unless you people can help me, I am going to have to shut it down." To his astonishment, money poured in and the station stayed on the air. It is still there almost seventy years later.

When CKOV made its appeal, the average profit of all stations was $415 a year. The bigger stations of 1,000 to 5,000 watts did better with an average profit of slightly more than $14,000 a year in 1931. Smaller stations of 250 to 500 watts lost money. The most profitable station in Canada in that year was CKAC Montreal, which netted more than $51,000. It wasn't much, but radio was rapidly moving from a pioneer into a business mode. In 1929, CFRB manager H. S. Moore had said of the station, "We never expect to make any profit on it. We did not build it to pay. The loss that we suffer is charged over to advertising." By 1931, however, that attitude no longer prevailed.

The CRBC's first move in building its national network was to buy CNR Radio, which had been sharply reduced during the Depression, for a bargain price of $50,000. This gave the CRBC the CNR stations in Moncton, Ottawa, and Vancouver, as well as equipment in numerous other cities in which CN "phantom" stations were operating. There were not many other bargains, however. Some years later, Steel said the original idea had been for the CRBC to own all stations in Canada, "but we quickly realized such a system would not work." he said. "The funds simply weren't there. So from the start, our policy was not to take over all stations . . . [it] was to work with the private stations to create a network from coast to coast."

Charlesworth set his sights on Toronto and Montreal, where he needed powerful stations. CFRB Toronto and CKAC Montreal were his targets, but they were run by swashbucklers who bet they could stare down Charlesworth and his colleagues in any impasse. They were betting a lot because, in spite of the ever-present threat of nationalization, both had invested heavily in technical equipment and studio facilities that they could lose if they lost their gamble. CFRB had about $162,000 in assets; CKAC, $207,000. They were the best-equipped stations in the country.

By 1932, with its 10,000 watts, CFRB had become the most important and powerful station in Canada, located in the heart of the country's richest and most radio-intense area. Torontonians could hear thirty different stations, including twenty-three American stations. The CRBC wanted to use the leader in that market, CFRB, for three hours every night and could, under the new legislation and with parliamentary approval, simply take over the time or even take over the station itself. Led by station manager Harry Sedgwick, CFRB took the gamble that Charlesworth and company were not as tough as the law permitted them to be. They were right.

When the CRBC offered to pay CFRB $1,000 a month to lease three hours a night of air time, Sedgwick scoffed. "It worked out at $11 a hour on time for which we ask advertisers $200 an hour," he said.

"Very unfair" and "inadequate," said station owner Ted Rogers. The CRBC warned Sedgwick and Rogers that if they rejected the offer, the public network would set up a competing station in Toronto. It didn't matter, said Sedgwick, for whom much more was at stake in this confrontation than the lease fee. If CFRB refused and got away with it, it would show that the public network was a paper tiger.

And that's exactly what happened. In the face of CFRB's intransigence, the CRBC retreated and went looking elsewhere. Next on the list was CKGW, the station run by its fiercest opponent, Ralph Ashcroft. Both the station's owner, the Gooderham & Worts distillery, and NBC in New York, to which CKGW was affiliated, were getting restive with the station. Charlesworth made a deal to pay Gooderham & Worts $12,000 a year to lease CKGW's 10,000-watt transmitter. CKGW's affiliation with NBC meant the new public network could air successful American programs from its Toronto station, such as the immensely popular *Amos 'n Andy*, singer Kate Smith, comedian Fred Allen, and cultural programs such as the Metropolitan Opera and the New York Philharmonic. Charlesworth changed the station's call letters from CKGW to CRCT. Now the CRBC had its own Toronto outlet. But it still needed a powerful station in Montreal.

The station Charlesworth wanted in Montreal was the 5,000-watt CKAC, which reached about three-quarters of Quebec's homes. Again, as with CFRB, Charlesworth could have taken over the time he wanted or the station itself, with parliamentary approval. But he backed down when CKAC told him no. Charlesworth then announced the CRBC would build its own 5,000-watt station in Montreal, for which he was roundly criticized. *La Presse*, the owner of CKAC and a long-time enemy of public broadcasting, lambasted the action, as did the *Montreal Star* and the *Financial Post*, which headlined, "BROADCAST DICTATORS PLAN NEW EXTRAVAGANCE; INVADE PRIVATE FIELD; AUTOCRATIC RADIO BOARD EXCEEDS POWERS GIVEN IT." The *Post* said building a public network station in Montreal in competition with CKAC and the other private stations was "stupid," "a flagrant crime," "an intolerable outrage." But Charlesworth went ahead anyway.

The Toronto, Montreal, and CNR stations together formed the nucleus of a national public network, to which Charlesworth added a dozen private stations that, for a fee, carried three hours nightly of national programming. The CRBC now reached about 40 per cent of the population. In the new network's first full year, the private stations were paid about a quarter of a million dollars, money welcomed especially by stations in smaller cities suffering the worst of the Depression.

The private stations not only distributed much of the new network's programming, but they also produced many of the network shows. Programs that hitherto had been heard only in local areas now got nationwide exposure. There was a pride among stations, especially those outside Toronto and Montreal, in putting programs on the network. This was "big time" for them.

Within months of getting underway, an avalanche of network programs descended on the airwaves: King George's Christmas greetings from London; *George Wade & His Cornhuskers*; *The Young Bloods of*

Beaver Bend; the Scottish music show *Cotter's Saturday Night*; *Parade of the Provinces*; and *Radio Theatre Guild*. By 1935, the CRBC network was broadcasting annually 365 variety and comedy shows, 350 dance music programs, 125 novelty shows, 45 symphonies, 29 operas, plus scores of dramas and special events. Even private broadcasters were impressed. CFRB's Ted Rogers wrote in a 1934 Toronto *Globe* article, "Radio, through [network] hook-up, gives the man or woman in the Maritimes an opportunity to think the same thoughts that are in the mind of the man in British Columbia. Radio is the greatest force ever known for unifying a nation and a people."

While they welcomed the programming, most of the private stations within the network were uneasy with the wide-sweeping rules and regulations imposed on them by the CRBC in its capacity as the regulator of all broadcasting. In its first few months, the CRBC decreed 108 different radio regulations, many of which limited the incomes of the private stations: there must be no spot advertising after 7:30 P.M., prices must not be mentioned in commercials, and advertising could not take up more than 5 per cent of total broadcast time.

Charlesworth, Maher, and Steel also ordered off the air programs that gave tips and gossip on mining and oil stocks. Charlesworth said he was cleansing the airwaves of "quackery, abuse and scurrility." The CRBC banned shows by medical quacks and fringe religious groups, such as the Remedial Movement for the Establishment of Permanent Happiness in the World. The Jehovah's Witnesses chief prophet, Judge Joseph Rutherford, was also banned from buying time on twenty-five private stations for his sermons, a rule that hit many stations in their cash registers. Charlesworth also angered some stations by confining affiliation with American networks to the handful of Canadian stations that already had it.

Charlesworth's anti-advertising stance was no secret. "The commercial rapacity of many broadcasters, their insistence on the lowest common denominator of programming and on nauseating overdoses of advertising," Charlesworth later said, "had reached the point of driving people away from their radio sets." But when R. B. Bennett failed to provide the CRBC with the funds he had promised, Charlesworth and his fellow commissioners had no choice but to seek more advertising revenue. "If we are to keep programs to our standards, we must seek revenue from advertising sources," Charlesworth explained.

Private station operators, especially CFRB's Harry Sedgwick, were alarmed by the CRBC's increased commercialism and charged that the public network, subsidized by the government as well as carrying advertising, was competing unfairly and taking business away from private stations. With its regulatory powers, he said, the public broadcaster was both a player and a judge.

The CRBC was also infuriating the private stations by raiding them for the people to run its network. Most of the CNR Radio staff had joined the CRBC when the CRBC bought the CNR stations, including, as key program director, E. Austin Weir. A few months later, Weir was fired for not getting more programs on the air and because the three commissioners felt he was "sullen," a bad manager who exceeded his authority by trying to set policy for the CRBC. "He exited from there in a great smell of sulphur and brimstone," said Vic George of CFCF Montreal.

The person the CRBC wanted to hire in Weir's place was a man who had fought against public broadcasting for the past half-dozen years, Ernie Bushnell. When first approached, Bushnell said, "I wouldn't work for that bloody outfit if it was the last thing I ever did. Frankly, we hated the guts of the CRBC." But when he was told that his station in Toronto, CKNC, was soon going out of business, Bushnell, an immensely likable, smart old rascal, swallowed his philosophical distaste for public broadcasting and accepted the CRBC job as a co-program director for the public network, responsible for programs from Ontario to British Columbia. "I couldn't lick 'em, so I joined 'em," he commented to a friend. Bushnell brought with him from CKNC most of the station's senior managers and on-air performers. They were known as "The Boys from CKNC." "Why the hell not!" Bushnell said later. "They were the only ones who knew a damn thing about radio."

For Bushnell's senior program assistant dealing closely with the western stations, the CRBC took on another enemy of public broadcasting, Horace Stovin, of CKCK Regina, who, testifying before the Aird commission and committee parliamentary hearings, had vociferously denounced the idea of a public network. "We always thought of Stovin as one of us," said Walter Dales. Stovin, a radio pioneer who opened an amateur station in 1921, was well respected by his private station colleagues and was known as "a broadcaster's broadcaster."

The third senior program director, responsible for all programs from Montreal east to the Maritimes, was yet another outspoken foe of public broadcasting, J. Arthur Dupont, who had led CKAC Montreal in its attack on the CRBC.

The three men who had been public broadcasting's bitter enemies were now in charge of all its programming. And they were brilliant programmers. The private station swashbucklers were comforted by the fact that Bushnell, Stovin, and Dupont shared their belief that radio was show business pure and simple and not an instrument for national unity, social justice, and intellectual enrichment. "We always had a friend in Horace . . . and 'Bush' and Art Dupont," said Regina broadcaster Wilf Woodill.

The three programmers were strong supporters of advertising on the air, and Bushnell urged that the CRBC "be empowered definitely and aggressively to enter the advertising field in order to supplement revenue." A few years earlier, Bushnell had set up Canada's first radio advertising agency and produced and sang broadcasting's first singing commercial, putting an ad for the Toronto Wet Wash Company to the tune of "Three Blind Mice."

While Charlesworth and his new programmers were developing the public national network and the private stations were trying to find their place in the new broadcast world, the 10.5 million people of Canada were plunged into a soul-searing Depression. Ironically, the worst of times for the people was the best of times for radio. Radio was the poor man's theatre, diverting Canadians, at least momentarily, from the factory layoffs, the repeated crop failures, and the dust-blown Prairies. Gathered around the living-room radio, families could escape the Dirty Thirties, if only for an hour or two.

"Radio was a constant companion," said Prairie broadcast pioneer Norman Botterill. "It was the most inexpensive form of entertainment and the thing they turned to . . . to take their minds off the Depression, the wind and the dirt." Radio was a lifeline to the voices and music of the rest of the world. "Happy Days Are Here Again" and "Smile, Smile, Smile" were radio's defiant, cheery musical responses to the dread of the Depression. "It saved my life," declared a woman in Barry Broadfoot's *Ten Lost Years*. "There I was," she said, "my husband cutting wood in the bush and me with three kiddies on that farm miles from nowhere. It was the world talking to me." A rich harvest of entertainment was wafting across the nation, and while CRBC and American programs brought the world to Canadian ears, there was increasing sophistication of local stations as well.

The hit-and-miss amateurism of the 1920s was long gone, especially at big-city stations such as CFRB Toronto, which broadcast big band performances, symphonies, news from the editorial room of the *Globe*, sports events, political speeches, and rallies, all handled by full-time, professional announcers. CFCF Montreal began its day with an early-morning time announcement, followed by music, programs such as *Miracles of Magnolia* and *Gloom Chasers*, a concert, stock market reports, and, as everywhere, the universally popular *Amos 'n Andy*. Prince Albert's CKBI carried *Jeff Germain and the Three Guitars*, stories by Grey Owl, and book reviews. In Regina, Bill Schultz at CKCK was on the air daily with his half-hour *Pleasant Memories* and, on Sundays for three hours, with *Golden Memories*, all designed to entertain, inspire, and comfort his Depression-weary audience.

It was a busy time, as CJRM Regina technician Leonard Cozine remembered. "We had to do an hour's live programming every night, but we only had one studio and we had four different programs. So while we were switching from one program to another, we'd put on a record and play it. And then get one group out of the studio and the other one in."

As part of the growing professionalism, performers started to be paid. Not a lot, however. At CHNC in Quebec City, actors were paid fifty cents for a half-hour program. At CFBO Saint John, Don Messer, future broadcast superstar, fiddled his heart out for $1 a program. CJRM Regina was more generous, luring Walter Budd and His Blossoms away from a rival station where they had been playing for nothing by giving the band members $2 each for a weekly half-hour program. When the station found a sponsor for the program, the band members got a raise to $2.75 per half-hour. In Winnipeg, pianist and future Happy Gang leader Bert Pearl was paid $5 for a fifteen-minute program sponsored by Maytag Washers. Actress Jane Mallett received $2 from CFRB for playing the lead in a play written by Andrew Allan, who later went to the CBC and became one of the best radio drama producers in the world. The network paid orchestra players $2 a broadcast plus two streetcar tickets. The future hit comedy duo of Woodhouse and Hawkins was initially paid $5 a show by CJCJ in Calgary.

Even station managers were paid on a hit-and-miss basis. "I got $20 a week, but my cheque often bounced," said Walter Dales. "But it was fun. We all enjoyed it." Lyman Potts worked for nothing at CHWC Regina for three years before he was paid $5 a week. When he started in radio with CFBO Saint John, future Moncton media magnate and CAB president Fred Lynds was told, "Don't expect any money, Fred. You'll get experience and you might get carfare." Later, he got $1.25 a week. "We worked hard and we worked for peanuts because we loved it," said Norman Botterill.

In the early years of radio, announcers, commentators, singers, and other on-air people were largely a happy-go-lucky bunch, forever trying to upset each other when they were on-air. "We always tried to make the other fella laugh like a jackass," said CKCK Regina announcer Wilf Collier. They would go into the studio and, while a colleague was reading the news or a commercial, do something to distract him or, rarely, her. Winnipeg actress Eve Henderson remembered her colleagues "used to do everything under the sun to make me laugh when I was doing a commercial. One Saturday, that crazy Jack Wells took his trousers off. He had put on a pair of white shorts with red hearts all over them." She got through the commercial, but with difficulty.

"The fellows were always trying to break you up when you were on-air," said Edmonton performer Kay Parkin. "They'd unzipper your dress at the back, pull your stockings down, undo your collar." The only time she broke up on-air, however, was when fellow announcer Jack Dawson "reached over and grabbed my nose. That's something you can't ignore and it really broke me up."

A typical "boys will be boys" episode occurred in Moose Jaw when, as CHAB's Sid Boyling remembered, three colleagues vied to upstage one another. Standing at a lectern, Bob McLean was reading the ten o'clock news. Fellow announcers Earl Cameron, who would go on to fame as anchor of the CBC national TV news in later years, and Jack Lawler came into the studio and took down McLean's pants. McLean kept reading the news even though his naked legs could be seen through a big window in the hall of the hotel where the station was located. "McLean, of course, had to get even," Boyling said. A week later, while Cameron was reading the news, McLean tiptoed into the studio and began undoing Cameron's pants. "Earl stopped in the middle of the news," Boyling said, "and shouted, 'McLean, get your hands off me!' McLean ran out of the studio . . . all of this went out over the air, of course."

Announcers who focused on their voice more than their mind might be able to "lift the words off the page" with a dramatic reading, but they were occasionally victimized by impish scriptwriters. Regina radio veteran Bill Speers said, "We hired an announcer named Charles Bussey. He could get the words off a page like nobody I've ever seen. [But] he didn't know what the words meant really." Writing the script one day, Speers changed slightly the sign-off line so that, with great emphasis and drama at the end of the newscast, Bussey intoned on-air, "This is Fishface Bussey announcing."

At Toronto's CFRB, newscasts came from the *Globe* editorial room, and on one occasion, the *Globe* editor reading the news stopped in mid-story, muttered a curse, and said, "Sorry, I seem to have mislaid a page. Well, it wasn't very interesting anyway."

"It didn't seem like work," reminisced one-time Hamilton announcer Ramsay Lees. "It was so much fun. Today, it's a business."

With regular network appearances, some local broadcast stars became national stars. The big band Mart Kenney and his Western Gentlemen were first broadcast by Vancouver's CJOR in 1932, which led to a CRBC network show and a high-profile career that would last nearly seventy years. His theme song, "The West, a Nest and You, Dear," was on the lips of almost every Canadian in the 1930s, 1940s, and 1950s. "You couldn't help being famous because your music and your name were constantly being heard at a time when everybody was listening to nighttime radio," Kenney said later.

Another kind of music was coming from the Maritimes, where fiddlers and country singers dominated the airwaves with such memorable songs as "When the Soup Begins to Droop Down Father's Vest." Don Messer, a chubby farmboy violinist known as "The Runt from Tweedside," and lovable rascal Charlie Chamberlain were in a group called The New Brunswick Lumberjacks, who were heard out of CFBO Saint John.

In Charlottetown on CFCY, listeners heard Ches Cooper, "the singing star of the Maritimes," offering songs such as "I'm Going to Ride to

Heaven on a Stream-Lined Train." He won first prize (a suit of clothes valued at $22) for his first radio song. "Radio in those days," he said later, "was the same as going to Hollywood. The first time I sang on the radio and came back home, I went down to Prowse's store, the local store in Murray Harbour, and all of the people said, 'I heard you on the radio today.' It was just like [being] a celebrity from Hollywood."

Thanks to his network hockey broadcasts, everyone in Canada knew the leather-lunged Foster Hewitt better than they knew the prime minister. Almost as popular was the duo Woodhouse and Hawkins, known as "The Nitwits of the Network," played by actors Art McGregor and Frank Deaville. They started in a fifteen-minute comedy program at CJCJ Calgary before moving to the CRBC network out of Winnipeg. In a routine that Max Ferguson would perfect in later years, the two comics imitated a cast of hilarious characters who became favourites across the country. Echoing many early broadcasters, Deaville said, "Radio was fun in those days. Today, it's all push-button stuff."

CFRB probably did more for women than any other station in Canada. There were a few female announcers and commentators, such as Martha Bowes in Saskatoon, Ferne Nolles in Regina, Flo Fitzgerald in Charlottetown, Anna Dexter, Abby Lane, and Helen Creighton in Halifax, and Susan Agar in Edmonton. But mostly it was male voices that dominated the airwaves. CFRB, however, was different. In the early and mid-1930s, the station starred a number of female performers and commentators, including Kate Aitken, Jane Gray, Claire Wallace, and Jane Mallett. Gray, who came to CFRB from CFPL London, pioneered in just about every kind of program from drama to cooking shows, poetry readings, horoscopes, and commentaries.

At one point while at CFRB, Gray did radio commercials and made personal appearances across the country dressed in a wig and a buckskin smock, acting as the Indian Princess Mus-Kee-Kee. She was selling the benefits of a quack medicine consisting of seneca root, pine needles, and a lot of alcohol. It was described as "real Indian medicine," a miracle cure designed to improve mental and physical health. She would go on-air, solving problems submitted by CFRB listeners and chirping about the benefits of the medicine. "I was supposed to be a real Indian princess and . . . was warned never to let anyone see me out of my Indian costume. One did anything in those days for a program." Later, she promoted a cure-all called "Kick-A-Poo" and was known as Princess Kick-A-Poo.

She was an extraordinarily effective salesperson and her fans would flock to buy whatever she advertised. "If Jane asked the women of Hamilton to jump into the bay, I think they would," said a co-worker when Gray worked at CHML Hamilton.

Actress Jane Mallett began at CKGW Toronto, performing in dramas, including a seventeen-station network program. In the early days, drama could be a hit-and-miss affair. Mallett remembered that once she "found myself talking to myself as mother, grandmother, and child. Someone had forgotten to cast the other two parts, and I was the only female in the show."

Actors often had to do sound effects as well as perform. "In one of the Canadian history plays we did," Mallett recalled, "when the Indians were attacking, I, as heroine, had to speak lines on mike while carefully rotating a sieve full of beans to simulate rain, and in the same scene at the same time, scream off mike as another character." Making sound effects became an important part of radio. To simulate the guillotine in dramas about the French Revolution, the sound of a sliding door would be followed by the smack of a heavy knife whacking into a cabbage and then the plop of another cabbage being dropped into a straw basket. Coconut shells banged together simulated hoof beats; the sound of a squeaking door was created on a violin; and the noise of walking on snow was made by squeezing cornflakes boxes. All these tricks and more were used at CFRB, where Mallett played every role from ingenue to the devil, and did serials and soap operas and even an instructional show on CFRB called *How to Be Charming*.

Kate Aitken was a dynamo who travelled the globe for CFRB (as many as twenty foreign trips a year), interviewing Italian dictator Benito Mussolini and other world leaders. Whether for programs or interviews, she was always running late, usually arriving at studio out of breath and shouting, "I'm here! I'm here!" Over the years she was named Woman of the Year, Best-Known Female Voice in Canada, and Top Woman Commentator. In her singsong voice, Aitken did sixteen shows a week, in addition to writing for the *Montreal Standard* and being director of women's activities for the Canadian National

Exhibition. A fair drinker, she occasionally launched into temperance lectures on her programs. Given her timetable, it's no wonder she was all business and little chit-chat with studio guests.

If Kate Aitken had a rival, it was Claire Wallace, who started at CFRB in 1935, a year after Aitken arrived. Wallace wrote a column for the *Toronto Star*, entitled "Over the Teacups," but her fame came from radio and her five-nights-a-week program *Teatime Topics*, even though the sight of a microphone made her quake. "She was so nervous, you could see her legs quivering under the table," said fellow CFRBer Gordon Sinclair. "Somehow, it improved her delivery."

Wallace became one of the country's highest-paid radio commentators. She had a nose for a story and was able to elicit improbable confessions, such as the head of the Salvation Army saying she swam daily in long black tights, or Dale Carnegie saying he could not make friends with or influence his ex-wife, no matter how hard he tried. As well as interviewing celebrities such as Dwight Eisenhower, Eleanor Roosevelt, Madame Chiang Kai-shek, and Emily Post, Wallace also "interviewed" a talking dog, a snake, and Gene Autry's horse.

Toronto's CFRB boasted the most extensive programming of any private station in Canada on the insistence of its founder, Ted Rogers. Rogers the inventor had become Rogers the businessman, who felt Toronto needed higher class programming than was being offered by the city's five stations in 1927. On the new 1,000-watt station's opening night, CFRB began with Jack Arthur conducting a symphony orchestra in a three-hour inaugural program. Rogers himself wasn't there, preferring to stay at home and listen to how it sounded on the radio.

For its first couple of years, operating out of the second floor of a downtown art gallery, CFRB shared a frequency with other stations and offered just an hour's programming in the morning, an hour in the afternoon, and up to two hours in the evening. By 1930, CFRB had its own wavelength and was broadcasting regular newscasts, sports commentary, popular and symphonic music, lectures, interviews, children's and women's programming, drama, special events, and, more important than all, Saturday-night NHL hockey, sponsored by General Motors and delivered by the biggest, most popular radio voice in Canada, Foster Hewitt. CFRB was the key, originating station on ad hoc networks that broadcast hockey and other events across the nation. "Until 1936, CFRB did most of the big shows in Canada," said Bill Baker, who was with the station from its first broadcast. It also aired many of the popular prime-time American programs through its affiliation with CBS.

CFRB gained audience and kudos for its extensive news coverage of the birth of the Dionne quintuplets in 1934, broadcasting three shows weekly with the quints' doctor, Allan Roy Dafoe. When the Moose River mine in Nova Scotia caved in, in 1936, CFRB was there with its own correspondent, Jim Hunter, who at one point was on the air every 20 minutes for 120 consecutive hours, his gravelly voice providing tense immediacy to the story. His broadcast rival in covering the story from the mine site was CRBC's J. Frank Willis. "Millions of people in a state of unparalleled emotion . . . never left their radios," said the U.S. entertainment industry paper *Variety*. It was one of the first "you are there" broadcasts, and Willis was picked up not only by Canadian stations, but by 650 stations in the United States as well.

Willis went on to radio stardom, as did the hard-drinking, hard-working Hunter, who became one of Canada's most popular newscasters. The colourfully dressed, opinionated Hunter was not loved by all, however. Once, he got into a vigorous argument with a colleague in the Toronto *Telegram* newsroom where he did his newscasts. When Hunter went on-air inside the news radio booth, his colleague heaved a spittoon through the studio window. With glass flying all around him, Hunter continued the newscast without missing a beat.

CFRB announcers seldom threw things but occasionally succumbed to practical jokes around the microphone. Once, when the Imperial Oil Symphony, under well-known conductor Reginald Stewart, ran over the allotted time on a thirty-station network program, announcer Charles Jennings (father of ABC News anchor Peter Jennings) slipped into a small broadcast booth and while the music of Tchaikovsky's *Fifth Symphony* was faded by the engineer, he closed the program.

However, Stewart and his orchestra, thinking they were still on the air, carried on for several minutes before concluding. At that point, Jennings decided to teach Stewart a lesson about getting off the air on time. As related by writer Donald Jack, when the music ended, Jennings said into a dead microphone, "Ladies and gentlemen, you have just heard what is probably the worst performance of Tchaikovsky's *Fifth Symphony* since a group of Italian futurists experimented with an orchestra of retarded orangutans. We should like to apologize for the missing second movement. The orchestra was too busy shooting craps. As for the conductor, Dr. Reginald Stewart, my aunt Chloë could have done better and she's not only tone deaf, she's been dead for years.

"This is CFRB Toronto. Good night."

Stewart and the symphony were dumbfounded. Finally Jennings laughed, told them it was a joke and that he hadn't been on-air. They never forgave him.

Ted Rogers, the Broadcast Hall of Famer and founder of CFRB, died at age thirty-eight in 1939. His legacy included Harry Sedgwick, who deserves much of the credit for the creative and financial success of CFRB. When he began running the station in 1933, Sedgwick was determined to have a happy, talented, and well-paid staff that he believed, correctly as it turned out, would produce good programs and big profits. Announcers were paid only $25 to $30 a week in salary, but earned much more from announcing advertisements for about $2.50 each. "Take away as much money as you can out of here," he told them. "That's fine with me." Sedgwick applied the same principle to himself, earning a salary of only $3,000 a year, but also taking 10 per cent of CFRB's profits, which earned him as much as $150,000 a year.

In the few years before Sedgwick arrived, CFRB was not a money-maker, but Sedgwick turned the station's fortunes around by enthusing and enriching his staff, by his driving style and love of raucous parties with the staff and with advertisers. "He was a pretty rough-and-tumble guy with a heart of gold," says fellow broadcaster Murray Brown, who knew Sedgwick in his later years. "He wielded a very big stick. There is no doubt about that."

Sedgwick led CFRB for twenty-six years, spearheaded the CAB's attacks on the CRBC and the CBC, and laid the groundwork for the ultimate victory of private broadcasters over the public system. With his bulky physique clad in English tailoring, his rich baritone voice tinged with his native Yorkshire accent, and a broad smile creasing his war-scarred face, Sedgwick was at home in the salons of the élite, the boardrooms of business, and the corridors of government. Associates described him as "looking like a bulldog with the heart of a St. Bernard."

As CAB president, Sedgwick travelled repeatedly across Canada, smoothing out irritants among member stations and winning the moniker "Mr. Private Broadcasting." His message was simple, as he explained to a 1934 parliamentary committee on broadcasting: "[We] are all before the bar of the listening audience, and subservient to its interest. . . . There will be a much happier listening audience if it is left largely to take care of itself and express its disapproval by refusing to listen rather than have a commission arbitrarily enact regulations as to what the public itself wants."

If CFRB and Harry Sedgwick were the sophisticates of private broadcasting, the quintessential small-town hustler was pudgy cherub Roy Thomson. For him, there was no sense of romance, no technological fascination, no excitement about the miracle of broadcasting. He was in it, pure and simply, for the money. It was, he thought, a way to riches, and he was determined to make a success of his radio station in North Bay, Ontario.

Like most private broadcasters of the time, Thomson came up the hard way: a high-school dropout at thirteen, a clerk in a coal yard at fourteen, an entrepreneur who flirted with bankruptcy a couple of times, he was always brimming with optimism and convinced that fame and fortune were just around the corner.

For him, they were. Thanks to his start in radio, he eventually became a billionaire radio and newspaper tycoon, hobnobbing with royalty, presidents, and prime ministers and becoming a lord of the realm in Britain. But such a glittering future for the baggy-clothed, enthusiastic travelling salesman would have been hard to predict when he decided in 1931 that the way to sell more radios in his appliance warehouse in North Bay was to start a radio station in the city. The problem was, he had no money and no transmitter, but such minor inconveniences didn't deter him.

With his brother-in-law, he drove to Toronto to call on Ernie Bushnell, then the manager of CKNC, because he had heard that the station had an old 50-watt transmitter it wasn't using. Its tubes were missing, its wiring was dodgy, and it was covered in dust having lain around unused for years. But Thomson was determined.

"How much do you want for it," he asked Bushnell.

"$500."

"I'll take it!"

As Bushnell remembered the conversation, Thomson then said, "Mr. Bushnell, before we make a deal, I think it's only fair to tell you I haven't any money. I'll have to give you a promissory note."

Bushnell talked to his boss, who laughed and said, "Why not? It's no good to us."

Thomson and his brother-in-law picked up the transmitter, about the size of a small chest, carried it down two flights of stairs, stuffed it into the trunk of his car, and drove off to North Bay.

Two days later Bushnell got a call from North Bay and Thomson told him he needed tubes for the transmitter. "What the hell did you expect for $500?" Bushnell said. But Thomson quickly added, "Mr. Bushnell, I'm in trouble . . . I'm going to ask you to lend me $160. Add it to my note and ship the tubes to me."

"So I did," said Bushnell, "and that's how Mr. Thomson started in the broadcasting business. Roy had more courage and foresight than most of us."

Thomson not only borrowed money from CKNC to get started, he borrowed CKNC's engineer – Jack Barnaby – to set up the North Bay station. Then he sweet-talked Barnaby into quitting his job with CKNC, where he was being paid $45 a week, to run the North Bay station – CFCH – at a salary of $25 a week plus a promise of a glorious future.

As Thomson himself admitted, he was stingy, as is illustrated in his hiring of future broadcast executive Tom Darling. Darling was first given a job in Thomson's appliance business for $35 a week. "The second week, I got $30," said Darling. "By the third week, my cheque was only $25. My salary kept going down at the rate of $5 a week until I was getting nothing." At that point, Thomson gave him a job at the radio station for $15 a week, the same wage he paid announcer Stan Burnett, whose first paycheque had bounced. Thereafter, employees were told not to cash their cheques for three or four days while Thomson chased up enough commercials to cover them.

Waving their rubber cheques, Thomson's employees found a friend in Phil the Greek (some say he was Chinese), the owner of a small café who would cash their cheques when the bank wouldn't. "This man Thomson will make good one day," Phil would tell the CFCH employees,

Ted Rogers, Sr., the father of today's head of Rogers Communications, at work in 1922 in the wireless workshop of his Toronto home. At age twenty-five, he revolutionized broadcasting by inventing the batteryless radio, and in 1927 started CFRB in Toronto. (*Courtesy Rogers Communications Inc.*)

The Rogers Batteryless Radio sold for as much as $370, a lot of money in the late 1920s and early 1930s. Rogers' motto was: "Just plug in, then tune in." (*Courtesy Rogers Communications Inc.*)

"Radio Wheels": The *Toronto Star* station CFCA became a special attraction in city parks and beaches in 1922 with its Radio Station No. 1 truck. The radio reporter with the truck was Foster Hewitt. (*Courtesy Rogers Communications Inc.*)

A piano and guitar recital in a 1920s radio studio. (*Courtesy CAB*)

Listening to the radio aboard a CNR transcontinental train in 1927. (*Courtesy CAB*)

Movie stars Douglas Fairbanks and Mary Pickford at the CKAC Montreal studio in 1922. The microphone is in the lampshade. (*National Archives of Canada PA-139111*)

(*Courtesy Rogers Communications Inc.*)

T. J. "Jim" Allard, the pit bull of private broadcasters who, as chief lobbyist, led the CAB to triumph in its broadcasting war with the CBC. His tough-talking, quarter-century reign at the CAB ended when he was deposed in 1973. (*Courtesy CAB*)

Glen Bannerman was the CAB's first full-time senior executive, appointed as president in 1940. He was ousted in a "palace coup" five years later. (*Courtesy CAB*)

Once described by a cabinet minister as "the most dangerous lobbyist in Ottawa," Michael Hind-Smith was a powerful force for the cable industry for fifteen years starting in 1975 after a high-level career at the CBC and CTV. (*Courtesy CAB*)

Prime Minister William Lyon Mackenzie King at the end of his VE Day broadcast to the nation in 1945. He was an enemy of private broadcasting and a stout protector of the CBC. (*National Archives of Canada C-23277*)

Prime Minister John Diefenbaker, the patron saint of private broadcasting, paved the way for private station domination of the airwaves when he defeated the Liberals in 1957. He "defanged" the CBC and encouraged the establishment of the CTV network and more private stations. (*Courtesy CAB*)

In the mid to late 1960s, Prime Minister Lester Pearson wanted to return the CBC to its dominant position in broadcasting after the Diefenbaker years, but political realities prevented him. (*Courtesy CAB*)

G. R. A. Rice, who began CJCA
Edmonton in 1922 and later
established CFRN Edmonton.
(*Courtesy CAB*)

Colonel Keith Rogers, a First
World War Signal Corps veteran,
brought radio to Prince Edward
Island when he founded CFCY
Charlottetown in the early 1920s.
(*Courtesy CAB*)

Kenneth Soble graduated from
amateur hour hosting to running CHML, a radio station in
Hamilton, Ont. Later he ran the
Hamilton TV station CHCH, the
first affiliate to break away from
the CBC network to become an
independent station in 1961.
(*Courtesy CAB*)

Ernie Bushnell, a private broadcaster in the 1920s and a public broadcasting senior executive in the 1930s, 1940s, and much of the 1950s, returned to his private broadcasting roots in Ottawa in 1959 with a successful application for a TV licence. (*Courtesy CAB*)

Roy Thomson, the founder of Northern Ontario radio stations in the early 1930s, later became so frustrated with Ottawa's regulations he moved to the United Kingdom, where he became a billionaire media owner and a member of the House of Lords. (*National Archives of Canada PA-203080*)

At a thirtieth birthday party for Canada's richest radio station, CFRB, in 1957, Harry Sedgwick, president of CFRB and a key player in Canadian broadcast history, slices the cake while Jane Gray, "the sweetheart of Canadian radio," watches. (*Courtesy CAB*)

as he confidently stuck their cheques on a hook by the cash register. The cheques eventually were honoured by the bank.

When he couldn't get cash for commercials, Thomson would take goods instead, especially from Italian grocery stores. "They'd pay him off in Parmesan cheese, Romano cheese, olive oil, olives, and tomato paste," said veteran broadcaster and Thomson's friend Johnny Lombardi. "He told me, 'My cellar is just full of Italian food.'"

In the station's first year, Thomson made a profit of $5,400. Thirty years later, Thomson was one of the richest men in the world, saying that broadcasting had been "just like a licence to print your own money."

Within a year or so, the thirty-nine-year-old Thomson began expanding on a hope, a prayer, and a lot of nerve, opening stations in Kirkland Lake and Timmins and elsewhere, and then going into the newspaper business. Living up to his reputation for parsimony, he left behind him a trail of memorable comments. "For enough money, I'd work in hell," he once said. When someone pointed out that you can't take it with you, he replied, "Well then, I'm not going." The most beautiful music, he said, "is a spot commercial at ten dollars a whack." Thomson's attitude was, "It don't mean a thing, if it don't go *cha-ching.*" It was an attitude to broadcasting sharply at variance with the ideas of Graham Spry and Alan Plaunt.

While Thomson and Sedgwick were marching to similar radio success with distinctly dissimilar methods, their public sector rival, CRBC, was lurching from one pothole to another. A torrent of complaints poured in to the CRBC about too many French programs being aired in the West, about the quality of programming, and about the regulations that the private stations felt prevented them from earning more money. Private broadcasters were alarmed that Canada might follow France, which in 1934 had banned radio advertising altogether. In support of the private stations, CBS vice-president Lawrence Lowman complained from New York that the limits imposed by the CRBC on advertising were "impossible," "arbitrary," and "radical." Ralph Ashcroft, president of the short-lived Dominion Broadcasters Association, denounced the provision in the Broadcasting Act, which gave authority to the CRBC to expropriate stations. "The sword of Damocles hangs over stations . . ." Ashcroft said. "And they do not know when it will fall." Indeed, Ashcroft's own station, CKGW Toronto, had been taken over by the CRBC, although willingly when the station owners sold out to the public broadcaster.

In the first half of 1935, while R. B. Bennett was out of the country, the private station campaign to undermine the public broadcaster came to a head. CFRB Toronto, CKAC Montreal, and CKLW Windsor, all CBS affiliates, had a plan ("a plot," Charlesworth called it) to get government approval to raise their stations' power to 50,000 watts each, enough to drown out the CRBC's signal in those cities. "It would practically hand over the entire radio business to the two big networks of the United States," Charlesworth said. This campaign against the CRBC was strengthened when two strong Conservative party supporters, Arthur Ford, editor of the *London Free Press*, which ran CFPL in London, and M. G. Campbell, president of CKLW Windsor, lobbied the government for better frequencies and criticized the CRBC in a discussion with Sir George Perley, who was acting as prime minister in Bennett's absence. Perley was persuaded by their arguments and, with cabinet's approval, renewed the CRBC's mandate for only two more months.

Unfortunately for the private broadcasters, when Bennett returned to Ottawa he was furious with both his colleagues and the private stations, cancelling the power increases for CFRB, CKAC, and CKLW, and extending the CRBC for a full year. Bennett lashed out at the private stations, telling the House of Commons that "a very persistent and determined effort is being made to destroy this Commission. . . . Always insidiously is the attack made against the publicly-owned facility . . . I should not yield this facility to any private enterprise."

For their pains, Charlesworth and Bennett found little comfort among supporters of public broadcasting, who felt betrayed by them for failing to produce the kind of public broadcaster they wanted. Charlesworth was described privately by *Winnipeg Free Press* Ottawa correspondent Grant Dexter as "sinister," "desperate," and "a double dyed scoundrel." Graham Spry was appalled at the CRBC, saying the public broadcaster was "a failure . . . a total disaster," and adding that "the Commission has become an instrument for subsidizing private enterprise." Alan Plaunt said Bennett was a "betrayer" and Charlesworth an "ignoramus."

Canadian newspapers thought they could run broadcasting better than the CRBC, and in 1935 at a meeting of Canadian Press directors, a resolution was approved stating, "Control of broadcasting should be in the hands of the publishers and their news-gathering association, the Canadian Press." No further action was taken on the resolution, however.

In truth, the clumsy, underfunded, overmandated, politically vulnerable, and quite unworkable public broadcaster never had a chance, and the beleaguered CRBC staggered on to its inevitable oblivion. Ralph Ashcroft offered his reasons for the CRBC failure: "Through inexperience, ignorance, and arrogance, they have antagonized almost everybody."

The coup de grâce came through a political soap opera called *Mr. Sage*, a series developed for the Conservatives in the 1935 election campaign by a private broadcast supporter, the J. J. Gibbons Ltd. advertising agency in Toronto, and aired by the CRBC. Some CRBC staff also performed in the fifteen-minute dramas that ridiculed Mackenzie King. "Scurrilous and libellous" said an outraged King, who swore to get revenge if elected.

When the Liberals swept back into power in late 1935, Charlesworth and the CRBC were swept right out. Doing most of the sweeping, and working in the shadows with Liberal philosopher king and financial angel Vincent Massey, was Alan Plaunt, who had revived the Canadian Radio League and put all his eggs in a Liberal basket. During the campaign, he provided the Liberals with ammunition about the failures of Bennett, Charlesworth, and the CRBC.

With Mackenzie King back in power and the implacable, relentless Plaunt spearheading the cause of public broadcasting, the worst nightmares of private broadcasters seemed about to overwhelm them. "He [Plaunt] had Mr. King in his pocket," Jim Allard later noted. "He was the only man who could see Mackenzie King at any hour of the day without an appointment. In fact, he had Mr. King, Pickersgill, Paul Martin and Brooke Claxton all in his pocket. . . . His political connections were awesome. He was probably closer to Mackenzie King than anybody, save the Prime Minister's mother."

King, in fact, had offered Plaunt the job of being the prime minister's principal secretary, but Plaunt turned it down because he wanted to concentrate on getting into law his vision of public broadcasting.

Unlike in 1932, this time Plaunt was on his own. Graham Spry's work with the new CCF meant that he was now out of favour with the Liberal establishment, particularly with C. D. Howe, who was a fast-rising powerhouse in the new King government. "I was in very bad odour at the time," Spry later admitted. Howe, as minister of Marine, was responsible for broadcasting, and one of the first documents to land on his desk after the election was a twenty-four-page memorandum from Plaunt outlining a public broadcasting blueprint that proposed, in contrast to the CRBC, the Canadian Broadcasting Corporation (CBC), a more powerful, better organized, better funded public broadcaster, responsible to Parliament, not the government. It would also emasculate private broadcasting.

Plaunt's proposal reiterated most of the earlier Aird report recommendations. King and other powerful Liberals backed it and, most importantly as it turned out, his ideas were enthusiastically endorsed by Edward Pickering, Mackenzie King's young assistant private secretary and a close friend and admirer of Plaunt. So close that Pickering named his son after Plaunt.

This clearly signalled serious trouble for the private broadcasters. They feared tough regulations about advertising and programs and eventual expropriation by an all-powerful public broadcaster. They didn't seem to have a chance against such a formidable adversary as Plaunt, who had extraordinary influence for a young man of just thirty-two years.

But this time, the private broadcasters were better organized than they had been in 1932. Now they were led by the sophisticated, tough, and smooth-talking Toronto CFRB manager, Harry Sedgwick, who had fought and won a battle with the CRBC over the public broadcaster's plan to take over CFRB's evening programming. Sedgwick, the newly elected president of a reorganized, revitalized, and better funded Canadian Association of Broadcasters, had a few tricks up his sleeve. For one, there was C. P. Edwards, C. D. Howe's principal adviser on radio and a man who had worked with Marconi Wireless in 1910. He was now director of radio in Howe's Marine Department, and was not only leery of public broadcasting, but was also a friend of CFRB owner Ted Rogers. This gave Sedgwick invaluable access to Howe's office. This time, too, the private broadcasters had more newspaper support, more business support, and a more focused message. This time, they had their act together.

Their first objective was to torpedo Plaunt's proposals, particularly his idea of giving the public broadcaster – the CBC – both an operational function, with a network and high-powered stations, and a policy function to regulate and police all broadcasters. This dual role would be more comprehensive than that granted four years earlier to the CRBC, and it infuriated Sedgwick and his CAB colleagues, who began a counterattack through Edwards.

Plaunt and his Radio League associate Brooke Claxton – soon to be a Liberal cabinet minister – had given Howe and Edwards draft legislation to put before Parliament, but Edwards, listening to Sedgwick and Rogers, was not prepared to rubber-stamp Plaunt and Claxton's bill. He wanted a separate regulatory agency.

"All private stations," he wrote to Plaunt, "should be placed under the control of the Minister and not the control of the Corporation. . . . The main complaint of the private stations . . . [is] that they were regulated by and at the same time, competed with, the Radio Commission."

Howe, always an empire builder, agreed with Edwards and instructed him to ignore Plaunt's bill and draw up one favouring private broadcasters, which he would then endorse. Plaunt and Claxton were furious, knowing that Howe's bill would nullify their and Aird's idea that the CBC should ultimately take over all broadcasting in Canada.

Howe had his bill instead of the Plaunt-Claxton bill sent to a special parliamentary committee that, after debate, was expected to forward it to the House for approval. During committee hearings, Howe argued forcefully against the CBC having both regulatory and operational responsibilities.

Sedgwick and his CAB colleagues rejoiced at Howe's approach and offered modifications to shrivel further Plaunt and Claxton's ideas for the CBC. In a joint proposal, the CAB, the Association of Canadian Advertisers, and the Canadian Association of Advertising Agencies suggested a government body to provide relatively light broadcast regulation as in the United States, government subsidies for private stations to ensure high-quality programs, and establishment of a public agency that would have no stations of its own but would provide private stations with programs. The Association of Canadian Advertisers dismissed the Plaunt-Claxton proposals for public broadcasting, telling the parliamentary committee, "This objective is entirely unsuitable for Canada. . . . It will never function efficiently. . . . We urge that it should be abandoned."

Public radio, or "government radio" as the private stations called it, was holding back the development of broadcasting in Canada, the committee was told by Glen Bannerman, head of the Association of Canadian Advertisers, a man who, five years later, would become head of the CAB. Zeroing in on the possibility of expropriation of private stations by the public broadcaster, Bannerman said, "We cannot expect stations to undertake costly major developments while there continues to be a prospect that they will eventually lose their licences." This uncertainty, he said, hurt Canadian performers and producers, lowered the quality of Canadian programs, and encouraged Canadians to tune in to higher quality American programs.

Bannerman and Sedgwick both argued that radio should provide primarily popular entertainment, not educational and socially uplifting programming. Show business is what Canadian listeners want, they said. Liberal MP Paul Martin, a public broadcast supporter, was not entirely persuaded this was the case, saying, "Radio is the most powerful instrument in the moulding of national character."

When Sedgwick appeared before the committee, to demonstrate private broadcasters' good intentions, he said that his station, CFRB, broadcast numerous charity appeals and hundreds of public service programs ranging from church services to advice to farmers and housewives, classical music, and educational programs. In the past twelve months, he told the committee, CFRB had broadcast the launching of the *Queen Mary* oceanliner, the Oxford-Cambridge boat race, Toscanini from Paris, Hitler from Berlin, and Rudyard Kipling from London.

Sedgwick urged that private stations be allowed higher power to extend their reach, noting that American stations often overwhelmed Canadian stations because they, in total, had 2.5 million watts compared to a total of 64,000 watts for Canadian private stations. He also pleaded that private broadcasters be allowed to sell more commercials.

Support for Howe and Edwards' ideas and those of the private stations even came from within the CRBC. Ernie Bushnell, a CRBC program director, handwrote a fourteen-page note to use when he appeared before the committee in which he endorsed the idea that regulation and supervision should be the responsibility of C. D. Howe's department. Even Hector Charlesworth, a couple of years earlier, had floated the idea of removing regulatory authority from the CRBC, but nothing had been done about it.

Bushnell also denounced "idealists and pure theorists" who wanted public broadcasting to focus on issues of national unity, information, and education. What the public wants, he said, was simply "good, wholesome entertainment."

In the first draft of its report, the committee favoured Howe's approach. When he read it, Plaunt became a tornado in pants, launching a ferocious counterattack on two fronts: public and private. In letters, phone calls, and visits, he roused editorial support for public broadcasting, especially within newspapers that had backed the Liberals; he persuaded churches, universities, unions, and farm and other organizations to issue statements of endorsement; he got prominent individuals to make representations to the committee; and he wrote articles attacking Howe's approach, saying it would be the death of public broadcasting. Plaunt also was constantly lobbying supportive committee members, such as newly elected Liberal MP Paul Martin.

In short, Plaunt used every card in his awesome Rolodex of power-brokers to gain support. Most important of all his contacts was the prime minister. If Harry Sedgwick and the private stations had C. D. Howe as a champion, Plaunt had Mackenzie King. "Mr. King's intervention at several stages was to prove crucial," Pickering said later.

Thanks in part to Pickering, Plaunt saw King at least half a dozen times during this period, making sure that the prime minister read Plaunt's testimony to the committee and warning him that Howe's approach would destroy public broadcasting. "Mackenzie King thought the legislation was going to develop along the lines of the Aird report," Pickering remembered. "Instead of bringing in the Aird report, the minister [Howe] was influencing it toward a commercial, privately owned orientation. His whole background was private enterprise." King told Pickering that the committee had "got off the rails" and commissioned him to get it to change its mind, to reject Howe's bill, and to adopt Plaunt's proposals. "He instructed me to work with Mr. A. L. Beaubien, the Chairman of the Committee, and get things back on the track along the lines of the Aird Report, without disclosing his intervention," Pickering later wrote in a private note.

Caught between Howe and King, Beaubien said, "I'm only chairman of this committee and I am in the hands of its members." Once Pickering told him of the prime minister's strong, private feelings, however, Beaubien knew he really was in King's unseen hands. With Pickering's surreptitious help, he got the committee back on track. "We were very much aware of the political intrigue that was taking place," said Walter Dales. "Surely any corporation to spring from this hotbed of political manoeuvring would be forever tainted with partisanship."

The committee soon approved Plaunt's approach for the CBC and rejected its earlier support of the ideas of Howe, Sedgwick, and the private broadcasters. "I don't think Mr. Howe ever really grasped what the concept of public broadcasting was," Pickering said. Even worse for the private stations, the committee reaffirmed "the principle of complete nationalization of radio broadcasting in Canada." Private broadcasters were horrified by the committee's recommendation that "in determining the compensation to be paid for the taking over of any private stations, no allowance shall be made for the value of the licence terminated by the taking over of such stations." Walter Dales' reaction was typical: "This could be all taken away from us." Softening this threat of immediate expropriation, the committee added, "Pending the accomplishment of this, radio listeners will continue to be dependent on private stations for much of their entertainment."

The House of Commons passed the new bill in 1936. As soon as the CBC was established, a sour Hector Charlesworth, his ego in shreds and his reputation in tatters, was fired as Canada's broadcasting czar. He blamed the CRBC's demise on Plaunt and the public broadcasting supporters. "It was this group with the collusion of some hostile officials who foisted on Mr. Howe the new set-up and lobbied it through the Commons," he said. The CBC, Charlesworth warned, would be "a Frankenstein."

Plaunt was exultant in his triumph over Charlesworth, Howe, and the private broadcasters. He'd won a far more ringing endorsement of public broadcasting than Bennett's 1932 legislation. Writing to the BBC's Gladstone Murray, who had his heart set on becoming the CBC's general manager, Plaunt said his campaign had been "an extraordinary experience of intrigue, bamboozling, publicizing, and worse. But it has succeeded and very much worth the effort. The whole sordid business . . . is certainly a tale to tell."

But the private broadcasters were far from surrender and they tried to write a different ending than the one Plaunt envisioned. If there had to be a CBC, they wanted *their* man to run it, not some BBC official like Gladstone Murray. Once again, the adversaries lined up: Plaunt, Mackenzie King, Claxton, Vincent Massey, and their supporters on one side, the private broadcasters led by Harry Sedgwick, C. D. Howe, and his aide, C. P. Edwards, on the other. At first, the private broadcasters lobbied for Harry Sedgwick to be named to run the CBC, an extraordinary suggestion since Sedgwick had been so vehemently outspoken against its establishment. It would have been in line, however, with the earlier CRBC appointments of Ernie Bushnell, Arthur Dupont, and

Horace Stovin, who had similarly spoken out harshly against public broadcasting before joining the CRBC in senior executive positions. Believing that Edwards was leading the campaign for Sedgwick, Plaunt told friends, "He is playing the double game of his friends the Rogers at CFRB . . . to get their man Sedgwick in as general manager, if possible."

Mackenzie King distrusted Sedgwick, however, and quickly dropped him as a candidate. The private broadcasters, Howe, and Edwards then zeroed in on Reginald Brophy, a senior NBC executive in New York and a former manager of CFCF Montreal. Howe was deadly opposed to Gladstone Murray and fought hard in cabinet on behalf of Brophy, while Edwards, whom Plaunt labelled "a son of a bitch," spread the word that Murray was a drunk and unreliable. But once again, Plaunt's torrential lobbying, his persuasive powers, and his interlocking friendships among the high and mighty of Ottawa won the day.

Although Mackenzie King was concerned by the rumours of Murray's excessive drinking, which turned out to be true, he was more worried about Brophy's American connections and cast his vote for Murray. The cabinet gave its approval. This meant a clean sweep for Plaunt and public broadcasting. In spite of their increased professionalism and improved lobbying techniques, the private radio stations were simply no match for Alan Plaunt.

Meanwhile, at the urging of his friend and adviser, *Winnipeg Free Press* editor John Dafoe, King named a highly talented and strongly Liberal board of governors for the CBC, including Plaunt and feminist Nellie McClung. As chairman, King appointed Leonard Brockington, a forty-eight-year-old immigrant from Wales who was reputed to be one of the toughest lawyers in Canada and the country's best-known after-dinner speaker. He would soon symbolize for the private station operators everything they hated about public broadcasting, their dislike of the man almost but not quite eclipsing their hatred for Alan Plaunt. While private broadcasters viewed radio as, essentially, vaudeville, the new CBC board's view of broadcasting was summed up succinctly by Nellie McClung when she declared, "Radio is the greatest university in the world."

5

The Worst of Times

Private broadcasters were at their nadir. In the public policy battle for the airwaves, the private broadcasters had been routed in their efforts to shrink, if not kill, public broadcasting. They also lost the fight over who the CBC general manager would be when Gladstone Murray was given the job instead of Harry Sedgwick or Reginald Brophy. In a showdown with C. D. Howe over the building of high-powered CBC stations across the country, the CBC also won and went on to build 50,000-watt stations in Ontario and Quebec and other high-power stations in Saskatchewan and the Maritimes, thus fulfilling the dreams of the Aird commission. At one point, there was talk that instead of spending money to build the powerful new stations, the CBC might simply take over key existing private stations. Fighting back, the private broadcasters (including CFRB, which had Howe's support) lobbied for higher power, but a CBC committee chaired by Plaunt turned them down flat. The private broadcasters had made their point, however, and the CBC abandoned its plan to appropriate key stations and instead built its own, using smaller stations across the country as affiliates in areas not served by CBC-owned outlets.

Howe had tried to diminish the CBC's role by demanding that it concentrate on producing programs and put on a back burner any thought of high-power stations for itself. In an angry outburst, he said the government couldn't afford the CBC's plans and urged the board to "face realities" and be "practical." Leonard Brockington fired back a seven-page letter sizzling with indignation – "Your conclusion is incorrect and your observation unfair" – and threatening that the whole board would resign unless their plans were approved.

Nobody talked to C. D. Howe that way, but, with Plaunt's behind-the-scenes persuasion, Mackenzie King let Howe know that he sided with the CBC. Howe grumpily caved in, and in a speech in Moncton he announced, "In future, private stations will not be allowed to expand beyond 1,000 watts, while existing larger [private] stations will not be permitted to increase their present power."

It was the most astonishing policy defeat in the entire political career of the all-powerful C. D. Howe, who soon would be known as "The Minister of Everything" in King's government. To add insult to injury, Plaunt, as chairman of the committee considering radio licence applications, rejected an "urgent" recommendation from Howe for a licence to be given to a friend of his.

Even critics of public broadcasting, such as the Toronto *Telegram* and the *Financial Post*, at least momentarily stilled their attacks on the CBC, as did most of the private broadcasters themselves, who seemed stunned by the Plaunt-Brockington-CBC onslaught. Lurking in the background as always, providing soft-voiced but overpowering support for the CBC, was Prime Minister Mackenzie King, whose hands were everywhere, although his fingerprints were never to be seen.

Worried about the public influence of newspapers supporting the Conservatives, which he thought might in time lead to fascism, King confided to his diary, "There remains radio as a corrective to this tendency, so long as radio is kept under government control. This becomes more necessary with private control of great newspapers."

Unlike the CRBC, which paid private stations to supply programs to the network between 1932 and 1936, the CBC concentrated on producing its own programming. This meant that many performers moved away from local private stations to the all-powerful CBC. Among them were orchestra leaders Mart Kenney and Don Messer, pianist Bert Pearl, comedian Alan Young, Kathleen Stokes of Pearl's Happy Gang, Foster Hewitt, musician Bob Farnum, clarinetist Bert Niosi, actors Tommy

Tweed and John Drainie, and hosts Bernie Braden and Elwood Glover. CKAC Montreal alone lost two-thirds of its local performers to the CBC. In another blow, the CBC in 1938 halved the amount it paid the private stations to carry its programs, and eventually eliminated any payment. The money was replaced, however, when the CBC began sharing with its private station affiliates the advertising revenue from sponsored network programs.

The rout of private stations in their fight for the airwaves is dramatically seen in the figures on their frequency power. At the end of 1936, the total power of private stations was 64,000 watts, while the CBC had 14,000 watts. Two and a half years later, private stations had a total of 74,000 watts and the CBC had 212,000 watts.

Surfing along on the crest of power and influence, and with a dollop of arrogance mixed in with its missionary enthusiasm, the CBC seemed invincible. Its programming was well received by the public, especially programs on the 1937 coronation of King George VI and, a couple of years later, the 10,000-mile tour of Canada by the King and Queen, the most technologically complicated radio programming ever undertaken up to that time.

"The CBC has apparently won an easy victory over the private stations," said *Variety*, "providing more abundant, more diversified and more complete radio entertainment than [is] possible for private interests." It was also a victory for Canadian programming, according to Leonard Brockington. "If tomorrow the CBC ceased to exist," he said, "every private station in Canada . . . would be delighted to be the member of an American chain."

When the CBC announced it was doubling the amount of advertising it carried to $500,000 a year, private broadcasters feared that ad money would move from them to the CBC, particularly with the CBC seeking local advertising. Even more alarmed by the increasing commercialization of the CBC were the newspapers. Most of them had been strong, original supporters of public broadcasting, in part because they felt a public broadcaster would be much less of a rival for advertising than a private system.

Brockington, Plaunt, and Gladstone Murray tried to ease the newspaper fears, telling editors and publishers that most ads on the CBC were national, not local. In the long run, they said, advertising on the CBC would be minimal. "We look upon the elimination of commercial advertising from the CBC certainly as part of our ultimate policy," Brockington said.

The government decided on a licence fee increase to $2.50, which mollified the newspapers to some extent. The increase, however, antagonized listeners, who complained about the licence fee itself and about a change in the rules requiring a licence for every radio, instead of one per household.

The CBC stirred up opposition among Conservatives when it aired commentaries from two University of Toronto professors, who said Canada had the right to be neutral in the looming Second World War. Ontario Conservative Leader George Drew charged that the CBC was being run by "parlour pinks" and that the CBC commentaries represented "an attack on the very basis of our democracy." Former Conservative prime minister Arthur Meighen, one of the original strong supporters of public broadcasting, denounced the CBC for using "some pink professor" to tell Canadians "that Britain was a traitor to democracy." The CBC, he said, was exercising "Gestapo methods."

Another assault on the CBC came from the young, aggressive publisher of the new *Globe and Mail*, George McCullagh, who earlier had been turned down by the CBC for a station licence. The CBC now denied his request to broadcast a series of political commentaries that he would pay for on his vision of Canada's political future. McCullagh said this was outrageous, compared Brockington to Hitler, and said it was "dictatorship on our doorstep." After the CBC turned him down, McCullagh bought time on nineteen individual stations, sending out his commentaries on a transcription for simultaneous release on all the stations.

Accusations were made that the CBC was, as the Toronto *Telegram* reported, "the servile creature of the King Government." The *Globe and Mail* stated the CBC was "an instrument of politics and privilege . . . it has been the privilege of a small group of socialists to use our national radio network for the dissemination of their propaganda under the pretense of presenting 'the other side.'"

The CBC largely ignored these criticisms; it was too occupied by an internal battle royal between Alan Plaunt and his erstwhile protégé,

Gladstone Murray, over Murray's drinking problem and his expense accounts. Bob Bowman, a CBC executive and son of one-time *Ottawa Citizen* editor Charles Bowman, said, "He had a weakness for drinking. If he started drinking, it was just too bad." Bowman said he'd been told that private broadcasters had deliberately tried to get Murray drunk in public places as "a conspiracy on the part of privately owned radio stations to destroy Gladstone Murray." Ernie Bushnell said he knew of one incident when officials of CFCN Calgary put a case of whisky into Murray's train compartment, most of which Murray consumed going back to Ottawa. On his tour of western stations, Bushnell said, Murray had been repeatedly entertained "in some rather raucous parties."

Plaunt now turned against his former friend, as did Graham Spry, who said later, "He was a terrible mistake. He was a drunkard and turned into a right-winger of the most awful vintage." Eventually Murray was forced out, and in going, he charged that there was "a left-wing enemy" plotting to take over all private stations. "A conspiracy existed," Murray later said, "to abolish private radio and give the CBC monopoly control throughout Canada." While not conspiratorial, the principle of nationalization was in both the 1932 and 1936 broadcasting legislation. The 1942 Parliamentary Committee on Radio also reaffirmed the principle of nationalization. The fact that it never happened, Murray credited to C. D. Howe, writing in a letter to Arthur Meighen, "Fortunately C. D. Howe turned out to be an ally and with his help, the private radio stations were saved. . . . It might have been better if public radio had never been undertaken in any form."

Murray also disagreed with Plaunt's view of CBC programming, saying, "We are in the show business, primarily." Years later, after he had gone back to private broadcasting, Ernie Bushnell commented on Murray's firing: "I had nothing but the greatest admiration for Gladstone Murray. . . . There wasn't a soul at the top after [him] who knew broadcasting from a bale of hay. . . . Alan Plaunt's . . . a son of a bitch so far as I'm concerned."

By the time of Murray's departure in 1942, it was not the same CBC that had begun with such exuberance half a dozen years earlier. Alan Plaunt succumbed to cancer in 1941, dying at age thirty-seven. His legacy was praised by Leonard Brockington, who said, "When the history of national broadcasting is written, Alan Plaunt's name will be honoured above all others." Brockington himself had resigned a couple of years earlier. With Plaunt and Brockington gone, the CBC board was less aggressive. To private broadcasters, the CBC leadership no longer seemed invincible.

By the start of the Second World War, three-quarters of Canadian homes had radios, and through programs on its own stations and carried on affiliated private stations, the CBC tried to "inspire the nation" during the war years with patriotic dramas, comedies, music, and vivid, almost hero-worshipping front-line reportage and commentaries. Private station newscasters also got substantial audiences, especially Elmore Philpott of CKWX Vancouver, John Collingwood Reade of CFRB Toronto, and Robertson Davies of CHEX Peterborough. As the 1943 Parliamentary Committee on Radio stated, "Radio in the present war . . . is the most vital morale builder at a nation's command." Even so, most Canadians still preferred American shows. A 1942 Elliott Haynes rating survey showed the five most popular shows in Canada were all from the United States: *Edgar Bergen and Charlie McCarthy*, *The Jack Benny Show*, *Fibber McGee and Molly*, *Lux Radio Theatre* and *The Aldrich Family*.

While most critical voices were stilled amid the wide praise for CBC wartime programming, there were mutterings among those who objected to the CBC's "Ready, Aye, Ready," response to the government. The CBC, they complained, had become a propaganda voice for the government's wartime policies.

Shortly before he died, even Alan Plaunt had bemoaned the CBC's subservience to the government, noting in a private memorandum, "The Corporation has, since the outbreak of war, been rapidly becoming merely a tool of the party in power." What upset Plaunt and outraged Conservatives was that while Liberal cabinet ministers were on the CBC constantly, Conservatives were hardly ever heard. Plaunt lamented, "Nobody except Cabinet Ministers and other government yes men are invited to speak. . . . The Corporation has lost all vestiges of independence of thought or action."

The Conservatives couldn't have agreed more. They were especially angry when the CBC refused to give outgoing party leader Arthur Meighen air time for his farewell address to the 1942 Conservative Party

Convention in Winnipeg on the grounds that it was too political. The CBC's decision turned the Conservative party as a whole into a powerful supporter of private broadcasters.

"Fascism is here!" thundered Meighen to the applause of Conservatives from coast to coast. "Radio of Canada," he said, "has been for years, is today, and Mr. King intends it will continue to be the effective monopoly, tool, and instrument of a partisan government headed by himself." There was some truth in Meighen's remarks. The CBC had made a ruling that there could be no partisan political broadcasting outside of election campaigns. This gave the Liberals a distinct advantage since they could claim their broadcasts were government business, not partisan politics. As a result, in 1942 Liberal MPs made statements on CBC stations seventy-five times while Opposition MPs were on the air five times. Mackenzie King spoke fourteen times over the CBC and the Conservative leader of the Opposition spoke just once.

A year later, the CBC rejected a speech by Meighen's successor, John Bracken, because, the CBC said, Bracken was too partisan in his comments. When he became premier of Ontario shortly after this incident, George Drew claimed that the CBC was denying him enough time on-air to report to the people of Ontario.

As quickly as it made enemies of the Conservatives, the CBC began to lose friends among the Liberals. Brooke Claxton, who had co-drafted the legislation that created the CBC, bitterly complained that the corporation was giving too much air time to the CCF; Leo LaFlèche, the minister responsible for the CBC, tried to stop the CBC from reporting news that he felt damaged the government; and Justice Minister Louis St. Laurent, another original public broadcasting supporter, was angry at the CBC for reporting on prison disturbances because he felt it encouraged trouble in other prisons. The CBC agreed to stop such reporting. Even Mackenzie King himself expressed concern at one point over some CBC commentaries that he felt gave a wrong impression of government policy.

There was also criticism of the CBC's fast-rising advertising income. CBC gross ad billings were more than $3.5 million in the last year of the war, a far cry from the maximum of $500,000 the CBC had declared as its objective in 1937. It was money the newspapers and big-city private stations felt should be going to them. The Periodical Press Association complained to Parliament about the CBC's accelerating commercial revenue. "It is not fair," it said, "that the press of Canada has to compete with a commercial competitor which does not pay taxes and which has $3 million in subsidies in the form of licence fees."

Taking advantage of rising anti-CBC sentiment at the end of the 1930s, Harry Sedgwick and the CAB had begun a tenacious campaign against what they saw as a CBC stranglehold stifling free enterprise, curtailing freedom of speech, and threatening expropriation of private stations. Despite their complaints, the private stations were growing richer, especially the big-city broadcasters, and they put more money into their lobbying organization, the CAB. Until 1941, the CAB had only one employee, but in that year, the stations hired Glen Bannerman, a high-powered old ally from the Association of Canadian Advertisers, as president and general manager.

One of Bannerman's first actions was to help found the *Canadian Broadcaster*, which became almost a house organ for the CAB with its constant, uncompromising, and often vitriolic attacks on the CBC. In 1944, when the CBC established the Dominion network (consisting of one CBC station, CJBC Toronto, and thirty-four affiliated private stations) to air nighttime entertainment shows, the *Broadcaster* thundered, "[This] means that the bells may shortly be tolling the death knell, not just of private radio, but of the whole democratic structure of our system of competitive business."

The Dominion network would last until 1962, when it was merged with the Trans-Canada network and by which time the CAB's campaign for a private radio network had died with the arrival of television.

From its beginning, the *Canadian Broadcaster* under its editor, Richard Lewis, was the voice of the hard-line privateers of broadcasting, associating public broadcasting with government dictatorship. Originally, Lewis had wanted the CAB to sponsor his magazine, but while the CAB did not do this, it told him, "Run it yourself and we'll get you all the advertising we can." Lewis, who thought of private broadcasters as family, provided a platform for the CAB. "By God, you've been worthwhile," Bannerman once told Lewis.

When Bannerman was named CAB president in 1940, Harry Sedgwick became chairman, and his brother Joe, a backroom power in the Conservative party, became its legal adviser. With the forceful, influential voices of Plaunt and Brockington gone from the CBC, the Sedgwicks and Bannerman became more vigorous in proselytizing the private broadcasting holy writ. One of their first moves was to demand an easing of the

CBC's restrictions on the money-making opportunities for private stations. They wanted approval of beer and wine advertising; more time for advertising; permission to quote prices of products being advertised; the right to air advertising in newscasts; and the authority to set up private regional and national networks at any time; permission to play records and transcriptions at any time of the day or night; and the freedom to affiliate with American networks.

They also wanted the CBC to stop airing advertisements, at least local commercials, and a bigger share of network advertising for private CBC-affiliated stations. They also wanted to reduce the number of CBC "mandate" programs that the private affiliates were obliged to carry. "Make the listener the final judge," they said, "not professors and bureaucrats." And as more kilowatt power led to more advertising revenue, they also demanded the removal of the CBC limit on power increases for private stations.

The CBC grudgingly made a few concessions to these demands: prices up to a dollar could be mentioned in ads; transcriptions could be used for an hour or two at night by those stations using what the CBC considered to be a desirable number of local performers on-air; ads could be aired at the beginning of newscasts and the sponsor mentioned at the end. By 1947, beer and wine companies were allowed to sponsor programs with some restrictions, and temporary network hookups among private stations were allowed for up to thirteen weeks, provided the stations involved followed CBC program policies. No national network independent of the CBC would be allowed, however.

This was all well and good, but what the private broadcasters most wanted was to have the threat of nationalization overhanging private stations removed and regulatory authority taken away from the CBC. The CAB wanted the CBC to have no broadcast outlets at all, but simply to make programs that the private stations could accept or reject. We must, the CAB said, "return to the basic principles of liberal western democracy."

The CAB's position was endorsed by the Conservatives, the Social Credit party, and even by a few Liberals. The private broadcaster demands, the CBC countered, were more rooted in commercial greed than philosophical concerns, suggesting, perhaps tongue-in-cheek, that Parliament should consider a law to limit private station profits.

Through the early war years, the CAB slowly gained supporters. Again and again, Joe Sedgwick complained, "Here is a corporation that is competing with us seriously in many cities and yet at the same time makes regulations which govern us."

The CBC and the Liberal government had consistently denied there was any real competition between the public and private sectors of broadcasting, but a chink in that defence opened up when the minister responsible for the CBC rejected the public disclosure of CBC internal affairs by saying, "Why put our corporation in the disadvantageous position vis-à-vis its competitor?" That reference to "competitor" was just what the CAB had been waiting for. It proved its contention that the CBC was indeed a competitor, said the CAB's Glen Bannerman, who added, "The Corporation [is] in the position of making the rules and regulating its competitor."

The CAB made the same arguments again before the parliamentary committee in 1943, but with more intensity as Joe Sedgwick compared nationalized broadcasting to Nazi radio or that of Mussolini or Vichy, France, leaving the impression that this was the direction public radio in Canada was going. He reiterated the accusation that the CBC was private radio's competitor as well as its judge. In response, the CBC's interim general manager, J. S. Thomson, denied there was competition. "The real distinction between the CBC and the private stations is that the CBC is a national institution providing programs for the whole of the Canadian people on a national basis. The private stations are local stations providing . . . a local service. There is no competition between these two services."

If the private stations were angered that their "competitor" was also their "judge," their nerves were positively shattered by the ever-present fear that expropriation by the CBC was just around the corner. "After twenty-one years of pioneering, do we lose the homestead?" asked Gordon Love of CFCN Calgary. "Will private enterprise survive or will public ownership engulf radio [and] limit facilities to sympathizers and stooges, and free speech become but a cherished memory?" The private stations, Joe Sedgwick said, "lived like a man on the edge of a volcano." How, he asked, can the private stations fulfill their programming responsibilities when they are continually threatened with extinction? "Operating under the threatening shadow of expropriation, it was remarkable that so much energy and resources were devoted to the broadcasting of good programs and the development of better technical facilities," Walter Dales said. The private stations, said veteran broadcaster Lyman Potts, "were fighting tooth and nail for their lives."

The parliamentary committees of the early 1940s, dominated by Liberals, listened to but ultimately rejected the CAB's complaints, sticking to the system of broadcasting envisaged in the 1936 law. The MPs also criticized multiple station ownership, urging a policy of one station per owner and saying that only in the most unusual circumstances should one person own more than one station. This was enough to discourage Roy Thomson from expanding his radio business and propel him into building a multibillion-dollar newspaper empire.

A serious blow for the CBC came in 1944 with the death of J. W. Dafoe, a key adviser to Mackenzie King and the editor of the *Winnipeg Free Press*. He had made the paper a staunch supporter of the CBC, but he had lost power at the newspaper. A month before his death, an editorial, written by *Free Press* owner Victor Sifton, whose family had heavy investments in private radio, urged that the CBC be stripped of its regulatory functions. So, too, did the Liberal *Vancouver Sun*, which stated, "The private station is in the position of a store keeper whose big competitor next door is also the lawmaker, the regulator, the policeman. Finally, the private station can be put out of business . . . by the CBC by the cancellation of its license."

In the House of Commons, John Diefenbaker took up the CAB's cause. The CBC, he said, should be cut back to being a producer of programs and nothing more. "An independent body should be set up," he said, "similar to the radio commission in the United States. . . . The broadcasting corporation [CBC] is in the position of being both litigant and judge and jury. It is in the position of being, as someone has said, a cop and a competitor." His comment was a warning of things to come for the CBC.

Diefenbaker came back to this point in the 1944 parliamentary committee hearings, at which he was a political champion for private broadcasters, advocating a dual system with an independent regulatory agency and two equal broadcasting systems, one private, one public. His position was echoed by Glen Bannerman, who told the annual CAB meeting that year that the current system of CBC domination of broadcasting was "becoming too centralized, too monopolistic, and too cumbersome." He said that the CBC represented a "distinct danger to freedom of the air, to freedom of speech, and to the exchange of ideas."

One indication of the growing influence of the private broadcasters was the presence at the 1944 CAB annual meeting of Gen. Leo R. LaFlèche, the minister responsible for broadcasting. That was the first ever formal face-to-face meeting between the CAB and the minister, and the CAB took the opportunity to lay out its demands. LaFlèche was impressed and considered the possibility of setting up a joint CAB-CBC consultative committee to discuss in advance of announcement any regulations the CBC might propose. It was never established, but the minister's attitude gave hope to the private broadcasters that the government was at least listening to them. But one important member of the government was still not listening, Prime Minister Mackenzie King, who in a warning to LaFlèche and his cabinet colleagues said, as he wrote in his diary, "Our policy is government ownership and control and members of the party must not begin to favour private interests in competition, but hold to the policy laid down by the Aird Commission."

At the 1944 committee hearings, CBC chairman Réné Morin rejected the CAB's concept of broadcasting, saying that Parliament had always insisted on CBC control of all broadcasting and he saw no reason to change. The *Canadian Broadcaster* promptly denounced him: "Who is this man Morin, this self-appointed oracle who has the effrontery to declare that Canadians shall have no say in the programming of Canada's own broadcasting system?"

CCF Leader M. J. Coldwell, a strong proponent of public broadcasting since 1932, leapt to the CBC's defence. "That law," he said, referring to the 1936 legislation establishing the CBC, "specifically states there shall be one dominant radio corporation in Canada and the privately owned stations . . . are given the privilege of operating subject to the regulations laid down by the regulatory body which is set up by Parliament and which is the CBC."

Nonsense! said the private broadcasters. Future CAB head Jim Allard endorsed the fear expressed in the *Canadian Broadcaster* that ". . . our whole system of living is tottering [and may] crash down into the chasm of socialism."

Joe Sedgwick formally requested that Parliament consider a dual system of equal private and public partners with an independent regulatory agency. In addition, he again made a strong plea that the CBC allow private stations to increase their power beyond the CBC-imposed limit of 1,000 watts. Four months later, the CBC agreed to raise the limit to 5,000 watts. The handful of stations that already had high power, such as CFRB Toronto, CKAC Montreal, CFCN Calgary, and CKY Winnipeg, were not allowed an increase.

The 1944 radio committee listened more carefully to the CAB arguments than any previous committee, but in the end it ruled that the CBC had been fair in dealing with private broadcasters. "Ever since 1928," it added, "every Parliament, every political party, every Parliamentary Committee enquiring into the question has been in favour of a system similar to the one we now have."

For the first time, however, the Conservatives on the committee refused to sign its report. They had been convinced by the CAB's arguments and now joined its relentless campaign to overturn the 1936 law.

The private broadcasters' campaign was also significantly helped by an initiative from Ken Soble of CHML Hamilton. He had run the station since 1936 after being master of ceremonies for a group known as Ken Soble and His Amateur Hour. At the 1944 CAB meeting, Soble, who had been working in radio since he was sixteen, proposed and the CAB endorsed setting up an Ottawa radio bureau to produce a program called *Report from Parliament Hill*. It would feature MPs reporting to their constituents on their Ottawa activities and current issues and would be aired by private stations across Canada at no cost to the MPs. Soble had test run the idea for CHML and found it valuable both for Hamilton MPs and for his own access to them. It would become even more politically valuable for private broadcasters across the country when set up for national distribution.

The CAB chose Jim Allard to establish the Radio Bureau in Ottawa and to run *Report from Parliament Hill*. Allard, an executive of CJCA Edmonton, had been working on the program for Soble and for Taylor, Pearson, Carson, the operators of a number of western stations. Once in Ottawa, Allard made sure parliamentary friends of the CAB got air time, and it was through the program that Allard became a good friend of John Diefenbaker. Writing to "My dear Jim," the Saskatchewan MP thanked Allard for letting him be on the broadcast and urged him to be sure the program was heard in his Prince Albert riding. The *Report from Parliament Hill*, Diefenbaker told Allard, "deserves the highest praise."

Later Allard expanded the service so that when the House of Commons was not sitting and the MPs were away from Ottawa, private stations airing the *Report* would carry reports on political events produced by Allard and by members of the Parliamentary Press Gallery. In time, about one hundred stations carried *Report from Parliament Hill*. Allard described it as "the most effective public relations device in a political sense that broadcasting ever had." Allard also provided to private stations a daily five-minute report from Ottawa distributed on script to stations by the news service British United Press. It, too, was much appreciated by politicians.

As the war ended, the private stations were still the underdog in Canadian broadcasting, but they were rapidly gaining political allies and developing more sophisticated public relations techniques. The private broadcasters were now clearly on the rebound from their nadir of 1936.

6

The March Back

While the well-connected, pragmatic Sedgwicks and Glen Bannerman were centre stage in the campaign to eviscerate public broadcasting and elevate private broadcasting, a bitter, deeply ideological battle was begun by two western broadcasters, Jim Allard and Walter Dales. Allard worked in the public spotlight, while Dales toiled behind the scenes. Both had been at CJCA Edmonton in the mid-1930s, where they found they were philosophical soulmates and swore to annihilate the CBC.

The seeds of Canadian public broadcasting had germinated in the fall of 1930 over a bottle of fine wine sitting on a starched white table-cloth in an elegant Hull restaurant – Café Henry Burger – a healthy stone's throw across the Ottawa River from Canada's Parliament Buildings. While sipping the wine and patting their lips with white linen napkins, Graham Spry and Alan Plaunt bemoaned the Americanization of Canadian radio. They felt radio's majestic educational potential was being destroyed by the tawdry reality of hucksters selling soap, tooth-paste, and laxatives. Private broadcasters, they believed, were debasing the public mind with vapid programs and barbaric commercialism. "The money-grubbers," Spry called them.

Radio, Spry and Plaunt felt, should not be just a billboard for adver-tisers and a platform for Americanism; it should offer the riches of the theatre, concert hall, and university. Their model was the BBC, not NBC.

Over their wine, Spry and Plaunt decided to establish the Canadian Radio League, which they would use as their pulpit. After the dinner, the two evangelists of public radio set off on their crusade. The future of the nation, they believed, was at stake.

What dumbfounded their private broadcasting adversaries was the speed with which Spry and Plaunt worked, their sophisticated, persuasive techniques, and their acquaintance with everybody who was anybody in the higher reaches of the Canadian political, economic, and social worlds. They were the ultimate networkers among the élite of Canada.

They persuaded the powers-that-be, including the "High Tory" Prime Minister R. B. Bennett and Mackenzie King, of the necessity for a public broadcasting-dominated system.

In contrast to the chic Hull restaurant where Spry and Plaunt had met, Allard and Dales met seven years later to plan their counterattack in a noisy, downtown Edmonton beer parlour, amid clattering glasses and glances from local ladies of the evening. "We went to the Cecil Hotel beer parlour . . . and there, we made our pledge to do battle with Spry and Plaunt's Radio League," Dales recalled years later in an unpublished book manuscript.

"When I realized that there was pressure from a group of idealists to gain control of radio broadcasting in order to 'educate and enrich' us all," Dales said, "I made up my mind that I'd far rather trust it to outfits who were after my nickels for their chewing gum or soap, or patent medicine or pills than I would trust it to a bunch of Victorian idealists after my mind. They seemed to me to be far less honest and direct in their approach than the broadcasters and advertisers out to make an honest buck."

Allard agreed. Although he had been what a friend described as "a left-wing radical" in his early days, now he worried about plots by socialists or worse among supporters of public broadcasting. He thought that Spry and Plaunt flatly detested private enterprise and hated anything American. They and their supporters, he believed, were "wide-eyed, woolly idealists who really didn't know what was going on at any time." They were, he told Dales, collectivist-minded intellectual busybodies, snobs who were out of touch with the people and part of a left-wing international conspiracy to nationalize broadcasting around the world. "These people," he later wrote in a letter to an Ohio professor, "see no value at all in the comfort and convenience made possible by automobiles, refrigerators, vacuum cleaners and would prefer to see those things destroyed and the simple, non-Ph.D. peasants living in quaint thatched huts and dancing around the maypole on the village grass at suitable intervals. I assure you that this is intended neither as humour nor exaggeration, but is an accurate reflection of their fundamental thinking."

"Graham Spry," Dales said, "seemed to us to be more concerned with promoting socialism than he was with broadcasting." As for Plaunt, Allard described him as "a dilettante millionaire of Ottawa and obviously a very strange man."

Allard held a simple view of what Canadians wanted from their radio and television sets. When they turn on a TV or a radio, he said, people turn off their minds.

Although Allard himself was well read and a quiet but substantial supporter of the arts, he denounced what he called "the power élite" for trying to foist off on "ordinary" Canadians operas, ballet, symphonies, and lectures instead of popular entertainment programs. "They remain convinced, moreover," he said, "that if the rest of us can only be sufficiently instructed, properly regulated, and frequently exposed to their concept of entertainment, we will all see the light." In a letter to a friend, bemoaning "this curious desire to do good by changing other people's lives," Allard said, "It is probably true that we would have an ideal society, or something close to it, if every human being could be conditioned to mind his own business."

He also didn't much like professors, most of whom criticized private broadcasters, and in a memo to the CAB board following a meeting with a number of educators, Allard said, "Some of the university professors I have met recently strike me as textbook cases of paranoia. . . . Many of these people have nothing to do. . . . All of them strike me as people who have never really been loved . . . and are probably totally incapable of giving or receiving affection. There's a great yawning void in their lives. . . . [They have a] passive, listless attitude. . . . Their eyes . . . dull, flat, lifeless."

Allard and Dales waged their war for decades. It was the battle of their lives. Both seethed with a sense of injustice about the CBC: Allard was thin, red-headed, defiant of authority, and scornful of "do-gooders," and Dales, who rode freight trains during the Depression before becoming a broadcaster, saw Canadian public broadcasting surrounded by dark conspiracies. "They were two peas in the same pod, and very far to the right," says an old colleague, Lyman Potts.

The Scottish-descended Allard won a 1927 Diamond Jubilee history essay contest at the age of thirteen, became a truck driver and coal-mine worker. He had begun his radio career in 1934, when he worked for four months without pay at CJCA Edmonton as a sweeper and coffee gofer before finally getting a paying job at the station as a switchboard operator for $50 a month. He soon became a writer and editor and moved to Ottawa a decade later. He had an unusual sense of humour and would occasionally startle his CJCA colleagues with a loud screech, which he claimed was "the mating call of an insane, sex-starved aardvark." Dales was a writer and public relations executive for CJCA, where he worked with Allard, and later managed a station in Trail, B.C., before he, too, went east.

As they drank their beer at Edmonton's Cecil Hotel, Dales told Allard how he was going to reach the grassroots of Canada with a pro-private broadcasting message by befriending the editors of weekly papers. He'd already begun visiting them in northern and central Alberta to promote CJCA, talking about the value of private radio and writing a weekly column for their papers. The first column had been carried by fifteen papers, leading Dales to remark, "I was astonished that newspaper editors could be conned out of so much free space." Soon, Dales was also writing editorials for the weeklies, pushing his views on radio. "Allard and I," he said, "considered the views of the country weeklies to be the best barometer of public sentiments. These editors were pointing to the CBC's failure as a unifying influence and to its invidious position as judge over its competitors."

While writing his columns and editorials, Dales also wrote and hosted a weekly half-hour radio program on CJCA, praising the virtues of the weekly papers and urging listeners to subscribe to them. In turn, the weekly editors "showed me propaganda for so-called 'public service broadcasting' that kept coming across their desks," he said.

"Fortunately for private broadcasters, the country weekly editors took note of this excessive regulation and began to editorialize strongly for a separate, independent body to regulate broadcasting. The politicians knew that when the hometown paper came out against the CBC regulations, this would be the mood of its readers, too."

For the rest of his life, Dales wrote columns for weekly papers in Alberta and later in other parts of the country in which he extolled private radio, excoriated the CBC, and won important support for private broadcasters. The Canadian Weekly Newspaper Association became a CAB ally in demanding an end to the CBC's regulatory role and the establishment of a separate, independent regulatory agency. Many weeklies also denounced CBC "thought control," referring to the public broadcaster's choice of speakers for its current affairs programs. "Country editors saw the danger and their editorials on the subject became regular and powerful," Dales said.

Allard and Dales were as dedicated and as alarmed about the future of Canadian broadcasting as Plaunt and Spry had been seven years earlier when they had begun their drive for public broadcasting. For them, the devil was in the broadcasting laws of 1932 and 1936, and the enemy was Plaunt and Spry's Radio League. "While our material was winning the approval of country editors and the general public," Dales later wrote, "the more facile arguments of the League were being accepted holus-bolus by the so-called intelligentsia – college professors, commentators and community thought leaders. Worst of all, we were losing the politicians."

Dales and Allard were determined to change this. "It occurred to me," Allard memoed Harold Carson, his boss at CJCA, "that private broadcasters ought to have effective and powerful representatives in Ottawa." In response, Carson wrote, "Dear Jim: I like your idea. Be in Ottawa April 12."

They and their private broadcasting associates would never accept a supplementary role, "strangulated" by regulations, as Dales put it. They also resented the way Spry, Plaunt, and their supporters characterized private broadcasters. "Private exploiters!" said Dales. "That's what they called us." Allard was equally wounded by such attacks. Both men were disdainful of the CBC's supporters. "Some were eager to sell socialism; some wanted jobs with the Corporation; some were concerned about the radio threat to newspaper advertising," Dales charged.

Dales and Allard met frequently in Ottawa, to discuss policies and to plan strategy and tactics for their campaign. "Jim Allard used his influence to get stations to use my material, and Harry Sedgwick was kind enough to recommend my work wherever he could," Dales recalled. "He and his brother Joseph Sedgwick, an outstanding lawyer, often included me in strategy sessions having to do with the future of private broadcasting."

The Sedgwicks, Allard, Dales, and their colleagues first sought only equality with the CBC: a "dual system comprised of a nationally-owned organization operating in conjunction with the independent stations," as the CAB said. Once that was achieved, they intended to aim for private domination of broadcasting and, in time, the marginalizing of the CBC. These were still pipe dreams in the 1940s, but nevertheless the real goals of the true believers. "I was more convinced than ever that the less government had to do with broadcasting, the better for democracy," Dales said later.

The two men began an assault on what they said were the "long-haired," "pointy headed," "stuffed shirts" and "snobs" who were part of an international plot to impose dictatorial government broadcasting. The roots of the conspiracy, they felt, lay in communist Russia and Nazi Germany and the fruit, they believed, was the CBC. "There was something rotten in Europe, and a big fat glob of it had come to settle over Canadian broadcasting," Dales wrote in a comment on the birth of public broadcasting.

"Certainly there were sinister forces at work in the background. The entire economy of the western world was shaky and many Canadians looked with great admiration at Germany and Italy. . . . The socialist gospel, too, had won many converts among Canadian intellectuals at the time. A surprisingly large number of them either leaned toward communism or joined the movement secretly. . . . Naturally they favoured nationalization of broadcasting and did everything they could to sway the Aird Commission in that direction.

". . . We knew what the people wanted. They wanted fun and reassurance and inspiration and they certainly didn't want their radio fare dictated by the very government they felt had brought the Dirty Thirties upon them."

Allard couldn't have agreed more with Dales' view of broadcasting. He told Carleton University student Hugh Saunderson, who was writing a thesis on Canadian broadcasting, ". . . a man returns [home] from work, turns his set on and turns his mind off. He does not want to think of troubling matters like unemployment, pollution or other social and political issues. He wants to be insulated from worldly problems and transplanted into a world of fantasy where everything is worked out by program's end."

Echoing Dales' accusations of conspiracy, Allard charged that the Canadian Radio League was "a curious organization" with "mysterious financing" and that Spry and Plaunt hated private enterprise and anything American. They had, he said in a letter to a colleague, a "disdain for Coca-Cola and bathtubs. . . . Their ideal society would contain no businessmen at all." He accused them of "incredible contradictions and inaccuracies" and "unsupported allegations."

"It seems to me," Allard said in a letter to an American professor, "that Canada, in terms of policy and aspirations, is run by a tightly knit establishment. It also seems to me that this establishment is further removed from reality and from the viewpoint and aspirations of the population than is generally the case in other countries." Canada was run, he felt, by a "curious mixture" of politicians, big business, and intellectuals.

To a degree, there was a measure of truth, as well as a lot of paranoia, in Allard and Dales' conspiratorial apprehensions. Graham Spry was indeed a bleeding-heart liberal who went left to the CCF, and Alan Plaunt saw the CBC as an instrument for public good and social change. "I look upon the CBC," he said, "as a hopeful experiment in a new type of public organization combining the principles of independent flexible management, together with ultimate Parliamentary responsibility. I believe it to be a model for other experiments in the public conduct of business."

Plaunt came from a rich, conservative family and his cousin, W. B. Plaunt, once commented, "Alan was always considered just a little on the pink side, a little too radical in his approach to things."

But Allard grudgingly admired Plaunt and Spry's tactical successes. "It cannot be denied that they played with admirable skill," Allard said. "Without doubt, they were extremely clever publicists and strategists. . . . The League's activities offer a model for the serious student of political influence, public relations and manipulation of parliamentary opinion."

He believed that Spry, Plaunt, and their supporters were part of the international conspiracy to nationalize radio everywhere in the world. A good example of what worried them was the CBC's 1946 takeover of the frequencies of CFRB Toronto and CFCN Calgary. The CBC had long coveted these frequencies to improve the reach of its own stations and had for years warned CFRB and CFCN, as well as CKY Winnipeg, that at a future date it would move them to a different spot on the dial.

CKY Winnipeg offered no resistance since it was, in any event, in the process of being sold to the CBC. CFCN's H. Gordon Love, however, denounced the CBC, saying, "We do not concur in or submit to [these] conditions." Harry Sedgwick of CFRB and his brother Joe at the CAB declared that they would fight with "all possible pressure" to stop the CBC from taking over the CFRB's frequency for use by the CBC's Dominion network key station in Toronto, CJBC. The Sedgwicks said the CBC's objective was to get more advertising through the new frequency, and what was worse, it was selling ads by discounting the price by up to 20 per cent. Harry Sedgwick also accused the CBC of trying to get CBS to switch its affiliation from CFRB to the CBC. The CBC denied the accusations and rejected Sedgwick's request for 50,000 watts for CFRB, saying that at 10,000 watts, CFRB had twice as much power as almost any other private station.

In a forceful and emotional statement to the 1946 Parliamentary Committee on Radio, Harry Sedgwick denounced those who criticized the profits made by CFRB and other private broadcasters. "When we started in this business," he said, "many people thought us fools to invest time and money in so visionary an enterprise, and it is easy now for those who never lifted a finger or invested a dollar to help create this modern miracle, to indulge in cheap sniping at those who did the work and risk, and who made it succeed." Sedgwick said CFRB used much of its revenue to provide staff with paid annual holidays, Christmas bonuses, and establish a pension plan for employees. As he had done before, Sedgwick also offered a long list of public service programs aired by CFRB. Thus, he said, to force CFRB to change its channel now was unfair treatment of a good corporate citizen.

Equally articulate and forceful before the committee was CFCN's Gordon Love, who said his station devoted a great deal of time to public service programs and even offered to sell the station to a cooperative of Alberta citizens if the CBC would let CFCN keep its frequency and be boosted from 10,000 to 50,000 watts. CFRB and CFCN said that of 194 newspaper editorials on the issue, 189 had supported their position.

In the House of Commons, the Conservatives and the Social Credit party did their best to prevent the CBC from getting the $2 million necessary to finance its expansion plans. They denounced the plan as "socialism," "communism," and "totalitarianism." But in the end, the committee supported the CBC and rejected CFRB and CFCN's protests about the frequency changes.

J. A. McDougald of the Argus Corporation, new owners of CFRB, was determined to get some concession from the government to help offset the revenue loss he foresaw with the changed frequency. He went to Ottawa to see External Affairs Minister Louis St. Laurent. As compensation for the frequency change, McDougald wanted the power increase that the radio committee had rejected. It was the least the government could do, McDougald said, because it would cost CFRB $600,000 to change its frequency. St. Laurent agreed to the trade-off, making CFRB as powerful as the 50,000-watt CBC key stations and giving it more listeners than it had ever had before.

When CFRB's frequency change officially took place, the CBC also gave permission to CKLW Windsor to raise its power to 50,000 watts and to CKAC Montreal to raise its power to 10,000 watts. (CFCN Calgary was not given permission to go to 50,000 watts until 1960.) With the power increases, the private broadcasters took on a much larger role on the Canadian airwaves.

CAB president Glen Bannerman was an old hand in Ottawa who knew how to work the corridors of government power. He was, however, uncomfortable with some of the more strident comments made by the private broadcasting hard-liners, including Allard and Dales. Although he was no slouch with his own public criticism of the CBC, he preferred to have a diplomatic cover over his iron fist. "Shouting doesn't get you anywhere in Ottawa," he said. "You just have to be patient and reason your way to objectives."

Patience and diplomacy, however, were in short supply among some of the CAB members and supporters, particularly *Canadian Broadcaster* editor Richard Lewis, who demanded a blunt, hard-hitting style for the association. "[The] attitude of sweet reasonableness resulted in nothing much for the private broadcaster," Walter Dales later commented. There was a need for a "more aggressive posture" by the CAB, he said, "a need to fight." Behind his back, some started calling Bannerman "the bland Mr. Bannerman."

At the same time, there was another group of private station operators – mostly in the smaller communities – who were uneasy with the CAB's central demand, repeatedly voiced by Bannerman, for removal of regulatory responsibility from the CBC and establishment of an independent agency to administer the rules and regulations of broadcasting.

The combination of forces against him soon became too much for Bannerman. As Jim Allard later said, a "vicious palace revolution" occurred at a late 1945 CAB board meeting when, without Bannerman there, the board abolished his role as president and general manager. Harry Sedgwick telephoned him to say the CAB would henceforth have an elected president and an appointed general manager, neither of whom would be Bannerman. Shortly after, Bannerman became a senior public servant in Ottawa, where he spent the rest of his career.

As a result of this internal bickering, the CAB was in organizational disarray for a couple of years and the CBC was suddenly strengthening, thanks to Mackenzie King's appointment of a genial, well-connected "boy wonder" to run the CBC. A. Davidson Dunton, a thirty-three-year-old Montreal newspaper editor, seemed to be destiny's darling. Quickly reversing low morale among the CBC creative staff, his effervescent, articulate style also appealed to many private broadcasters, even though his self-described politics were "left Liberal to right CCF." "Dunton won a pretty fair following among the private broadcasters," said Walter Dales. "They liked him. Many felt safe under the umbrella of the CBC as directed by Dunton."

At the time, one of the private broadcasters' complaints was the CBC's ban on mentioning prices in commercials. Lyman Potts remembers Dunton's reaction to the ban: "He came to the station and at a meeting with about a dozen of us asked, 'What problems have you guys got?' 'Well,' I said timidly, 'it seems kind of stupid, but we can't tell prices on the air.' 'That's dumb!' said Dunton [who had already been thinking about eliminating the long-time restriction]. 'Write me a letter and I'll change it.' Everyone around the table practically fell on the floor. I got in touch with Jim Allard at the CAB and he wrote a letter, requesting the change and promising not to have more than three price mentions per commercial. 'I don't care how many price mentions,' Dunton said. 'We're taking the regulation out.' And bless him, they did."

Dunton had an immensely likable manner, with all the qualifications of an intellectual, but, as Dales said, he was as earthy as any independent broadcaster. "The general feeling among broadcasters, particularly in the smaller cites, was that Davie Dunton's a good fellow and t'will all be well," said Dales. But Dales thought differently. "Dunton always seemed to me to be the real danger to the future of private broadcasting. I suspect that if the private broadcasters had fought less resolutely, he would eventually have put them all out of business entirely."

Jim Allard was a key player in the CAB's response to Dunton and the CBC. Allard was now the association's public relations director and, together with Clifford Sifton of Winnipeg, he prepared the most comprehensive presentation to the 1946 radio committee the CAB had ever made. The CAB's statement was given by a delegation of private broadcasting leaders, including some of radio's pioneers: F. H. "Tiny" Elphicke of CKWX Vancouver; Col. Keith Rogers of CFCY Charlottetown; Dick Rice of CFRN Edmonton; and Phil Lalonde of CKAC Montreal.

Once again, they demanded the MPs strip the CBC of its regulatory authority and establish an independent Radio Board of Appeal as a final arbiter. "We submit," the CAB stated, "that no government with any claim to being democratic combines in one body the legislative, executive, judicial and police powers." Besides, Dick Rice said, "They [the CBC] are not close enough to the public. Private broadcasters are better than anybody to respond to public attitudes about programming."

But the private broadcasters backed off from their long-time dream of an independent national radio network. "We more or less gave up that idea," said Harry Sedgwick. However, they did argue for permission to set up regional networks. With the CBC's Dominion and Trans-Canada networks and with the coming of television, the broadcasters reckoned that there was not enough advertising revenue to support a private radio national network.

The private broadcasters, however, did not cite any CBC injustice in its regulatory role. "Officials of the CBC have usually endeavoured to be fair and just, even generous, in using their powers," the CAB stated.

Throughout their battles with the CBC, private broadcasters carefully drew a line between the people they dealt with at the CBC on programs, advertising, and day-to-day operating matters and the CBC board members responsible for overall policy. "We got along fine with the people at the CBC," said Lyman Potts. "They were really a bunch of nice guys at the operating level. They were very benign. You always figured they wouldn't be too hard on you. I had a good many friends at

the CBC, but still everybody had their elbows up and we were very resist-
ant to these regulations."

Even hard-liner Walter Dales felt CBC management tried to be fair.
"They did not, to my knowledge, abuse their power." But, he added, "it
hovered over the head of [private] station management everywhere and
could affect their judgment in countless insidious ways. The room for
abuse was there, and some station managers were all too eager to please
the government of the day so that they would be in good odour at
Ottawa when begging concessions."

The CBC responded to the CAB demands with its by now customary
riposte that Canadian broadcasting was a single, not a dual, system.
"Network broadcasting and nationwide coverage . . . are the functions of
the national system," it told Parliament. "Service to the community
areas is the function of the private system."

The private stations had been making their arguments about a dual
system for years, but this time there was a glimmer of hope. In its final
report, the parliamentary committee congratulated the private stations
for their "quite strong and sincere arguments." While the MPs did not
think that any change in regulatory authority was desirable, "On the
other hand, your Committee is not yet prepared to say that the idea
ought to be dismissed at once. Your Committee . . . recommends that
further study of it should be made."

A door to the CAB's long-time dream of an independent regulatory
agency had been pushed slightly ajar. But if this gave hope to the private
broadcasters, they were decidedly unhappy with the committee's
comment that if private stations had too many commercially sponsored
programs, they might not be properly discharging their public service
duties, and this should be considered in renewing the station licences.

Soon after the committee issued its report, the CBC indicated it was
going to measure promises against performance in considering licence
renewals. The private broadcasters were outraged and launched a
nationwide campaign denouncing the CBC, led by the CAB and orchestrated by Jim Allard, who was gaining greater influence in the association.
The CAB placed advertisements covering a third of a page in seventy
newspapers across the country damning the CBC. Over two weeks, the
association ran a series of five ads with headlines such as, "OUR RADIO
LAWS SPELL MONOPOLY," "CANADIAN RADIO LAWS ARE STILL IN THE
OX-CART DAYS," "CANADIAN RADIO NEEDS FREEDOM TO GROW UP."

It flooded the Canadian airwaves with commercials attacking the CBC-controlled broadcast system. In addition, hundreds of newspaper articles and radio programs joined in the condemnation of the system. The *Canadian Broadcaster* called the CBC "a power drunk tribunal" and labelled Davidson Dunton "a dictator."

The CAB, now representing eighty-nine stations, obtained letters of support from leading citizens and local and regional organizations and passed them to the committee. Ten thousand copies of a thirty-seven-page booklet called *Control of Radio: An Urgent Canadian Problem* were distributed to high schools, universities, libraries, doctors' and dentists' offices, beauty parlours, barbershops, and key individuals. Editorials and columns were printed and reprinted across Canada in daily and weekly papers, much of the newspaper material produced by Walter Dales. His columns, under the pseudonym Ambrose Hills, were appearing in more than one hundred weekly papers and a number of dailies.

The Canadian Daily Newspaper Association endorsed the CAB's demand for a separate regulatory body, as did the Association of Canadian Advertisers. The Canadian Chamber of Commerce said private broadcasters should have more security of tenure and that it favoured a separate regulatory agency. In early 1947, the annual meeting of the Progressive Conservative Association of Canada passed a resolution denouncing the CBC and demanding an independent regulatory board. "The CBC, as presently administered," the Conservatives said, "is a menace to freedom of speech and freedom of enterprise. . . . The control of radio should be removed from political domination and vested in an independent board."

The Tories' resolution was endorsed by George Drew, who soon would become the national leader of the Progressive Conservative party. Thanks to Jim Allard's efforts, it was also endorsed by numerous churches and civic organizations across the country, such as the Vancouver Board of Trade. The CAB organized a Community Station Week designed to show how private stations were serving their communities. It announced it was setting up a committee to develop "a basic philosophy for the broadcasting industry of Canada." Allard also organized private station executives to speak at service clubs, sending them reams of backup material to use.

The CBC was under seige. "This campaign seems to be making an impression," CBC executive Ron Fraser memoed to his boss, Davidson

Dunton, and CBC officials became concerned about the support the private stations were generating. "Probably never before," Dunton said later, "has the country seen such a concentration of radio time, newspaper space, and other pressures marshalled in an attempt to influence legislation."

The CBC's supporters joined the fray. The editor of *Saturday Night*, B. K. Sandwell, characterized the CAB's campaign as "flagrantly misleading propaganda." Normally not philosophical bedfellows, CCF Leader M. J. Coldwell took up Sandwell's line of attack. "The CAB has built itself up, until today it is a powerful propaganda agency, operating as I believe, against the best interests of the country and . . . likely to destroy the independence of this country and place it more and more under the cultural and economic control of the United States," Coldwell said in the House of Commons. "I regard that as treasonable and subversive activity – just as treasonable and subversive as the activities of those who sell our country to a communist power or to Russia. I can see no difference between the two."

Private broadcasters were outraged. Jim Allard called it an "obviously absurd charge" and issued a list of 359 Second World War veterans with 130 war medals who worked for private radio.

An almost equally strong attack on the CAB came from the minister responsible for broadcasting, Dr. J. J. McCann. "An unscrupulous campaign has been carried on in an attempt to discredit the Canadian Broadcasting Corporation and at the same time to expand commercialism," he told the House of Commons. "Certain private radio interests have been campaigning for a change in radio laws which they think would give them more freedom to make profit and to exploit the public. . . . We believe in a nationally owned, nationally controlled and nationally operated system for all the people of the country. It will be nationally operated by the Canadian Broadcasting Corporation and nationally controlled by them. . . ." This was McCann's voice, but Mackenzie King speaking. His support, backed by the Liberals and CCF MPs on the radio committee, guaranteed a pro-CBC report by the committee. Allard was outraged by McCann's attitude, saying he had "a totally paranoid hatred of private broadcasters."

While they did not win the war, Allard and the CAB did win some battles this time. In its report, the committee recommended that stations be licensed for three years rather than one, and urged consideration be given to raising the power ceiling for all private stations, all of which the CBC subsequently did. More significantly, several Liberal MPs privately indicated that in spite of the prime minister's support of the CBC, they were willing to consider the CAB's central demand to take regulatory powers away from the CBC and give them to a separate agency. Even the chairman of the committee, Ralph Maybank, felt that way, saying, "I personally would have no objection to a regulatory board. I am not strongly for it, but I would have no objections to it."

In its final report, however, the radio committee reaffirmed the CBC-dominated radio system, including its role as regulator. Once again Conservatives on the committee refused to sign it, and one Liberal broke ranks and opposed the committee support of the CBC.

Another threat to the CBC's dominance was the increasing number of stations being licensed. Altogether, there were now about 110 private stations in Canada, most of them not part of the CBC network. Inevitably this had led to audience fragmentation and a shrinking audience share for the CBC, as had the granting of high power to CFRB, CKLW, and CKAC. Permitting other private stations to go higher than the 5,000-watt ceiling would compound the problem for the CBC. This clearly violated the past policy of only CBC stations having high power, and had significant long-term consequences on the shape of Canadian broadcasting. "All you have to do is grant enough licences and you destroy the public character of Canadian broadcasting," R. B. Bennett had said presciently in 1936. If too many licences were issued, he said, "then the Corporation is destined to be supplanted in its public operations by private enterprises."

In spite of Davidson Dunton's best efforts, the private broadcasters were now generating more public and political support than ever before, thanks mostly to the effective campaign organized by Jim Allard. When the man who had succeeded Glen Bannerman as head of the CAB resigned in 1948, Allard was named general manager. He was named CAB executive vice-president in 1953, remaining in that post for twenty years. Allard brought more discipline and strategic planning to the CAB, making it more quickly and effectively responsive to broadcasting issues, and cementing relations with the Conservatives.

That same year also saw a leadership change in the newly renamed Progressive Conservative party that was enormously beneficial to private broadcasters. John Bracken, a long-time supporter of public broadcasting, retired as party leader. He had known and admired Graham Spry and had never endorsed the criticism of the CBC as articulated by his fellow Conservatives George Drew, John Diefenbaker, and Donald Fleming. Now he was replaced by Drew, who charged the CBC was a tool of the Liberal party and possibly harboured communists.

The third significant change that year, and by far the most critical one for broadcasting, was Mackenzie King's retirement. No one had been more important in the development of public broadcasting than King. He was the CBC's guardian angel. Time and time again he had stepped in when C. D. Howe and other lukewarm government supporters of the CBC had threatened action that would diminish the authority of the public broadcaster. He had been the biggest enemy the private broadcasters had.

King's replacement, Louis St. Laurent, was a man who, like King, seemed as though he didn't entirely approve of the twentieth century, but he was an original and continuing supporter of public broadcasting. However, he did not carry the powers of persuasion nor the Machiavellian skills that King had so forcefully wielded. St. Laurent's inability to keep the Liberals squarely behind the CBC was of great advantage to the private broadcasters.

By 1949, private broadcasters had four thousand employees. Radio was rapidly becoming a significant sector of the economy. Its growing influence was helped by the number of Liberals who had gone into the business of broadcasting and were now beginning to put forward the CAB's positions in Liberal policy debates.

The developing strength of station owners was matched by the power of their stations. When the CBC came into existence, private stations had five times the power of the public network. By 1939, the CBC had dramatically reversed that figure. It had a total 216,000 watts to 74,000 watts for the privates. By 1949, however, the privates had climbed back to be almost even with the CBC: 342,000 watts compared to the CBC's 397,000 watts. Two years later, there were 133 private stations with a total of 370,000 watts. At this rate, it wouldn't be long before the private stations surpassed the CBC in power. They already were well past the CBC in total assets, owning nearly $30 million, three times the CBC.

What was remarkable about the long march back from its near death in 1936 was private broadcasting's ability to maintain a united front in the face of many different and potentially destructive tensions among the station operators themselves.

Some wanted an all-out war with the CBC. Some wanted a live-and-let-live approach. Big-city and small-town stations differed sharply in their needs. Eastern, central, and western stations often had conflicting objectives. The regional tensions within the CAB were illustrated by the formation of the Maritimes Association of Broadcasters, the Western Association of Broadcasters, the British Columbia Association of Broadcasters, and the Central Canada Association of Broadcasters, all pushing their regional concerns, but all operating more or less under the CAB umbrella. Some stations wanted to focus their efforts on local communities, while others wanted the bigger audiences and greater commercial revenues of regional and national networks.

Sometimes the arguments among private broadcasters almost came to blows. At the 1949 annual CAB meeting in St. Andrews, New Brunswick, "It was only the personal intervention of cooler heads that prevented physical violence," Allard later said.

Walter Blackburn of CFPL London, William Borrett of CHNS Halifax, Harold Carson of the Taylor, Pearson, Carson stations in the West, and many among the smaller stations felt they were better off with the CBC as regulator rather than having to deal with some new body. "At least the CBC fellows knew what the hell it was all about," Borrett said. "I never had any trouble with them, [but] a lot of the private operators were quite restless under so-called government regulations and supervision. Just the same, I think most of them would admit it was necessary in many instances. The CBC, I always found, was very cooperative and very helpful." Blackburn felt much the same way, warning that a separate regulatory board might be more restrictive than the CBC. "I argued hard and fought but with no success," he later said.

Finlay MacDonald of CJCH Halifax remembers talking to Harold Carson about the CAB's effort to split off regulatory functions from the CBC. "I spent an evening in Harold Carson's house, and he said, 'This is just horseshit! We're getting along great. They're giving us stations and now we're going to destroy all of this. These goddamn fools are rushing around to get a separate regulatory body and we'll end up with 14,000 bureaucrats for Christ's sake and more regulation.' He saw through it," said MacDonald, "but he did nothing about it."

"The CBC was sort of like a benevolent father," said veteran radio executive Andy McDermott. "The people who hollered loudest for a separate regulatory board eventually realized that they probably had bought a pig in a poke." Veteran broadcaster Bill Speers said, "It was the worst possible thing we could have done."

But even with all the differing and often competing preoccupations, the CAB, dominated by the tough-talking big-city stations and led by Allard, managed to present an appearance of unity to the public and the politicians. Credit for that goes not only to Allard, but also to Harry and Joe Sedgwick, Harold Carson, and a handful of others.

The Taylor, Pearson, Carson stations were unique in the Canadian broadcasting landscape because most were owned by someone else, but managed by a company formed in the early 1930s by three broadcast pioneers who, like so many of the early broadcasters, almost accidentally fell into the business.

In 1928, Harold Carson was an automotive supply dealer in Lethbridge, Alberta, who, so the story goes, won ownership of a Lethbridge station, CJOC, in a poker game. He kept the station because he thought he could use it to promote the radios and radio batteries he had in stock. At the same time, in Edmonton, Hugh Pearson and James Taylor were also in the auto parts business and also sold radios and batteries. They had run a small Edmonton station to promote radio sales in the mid-1920s, but after four years had sold it to avoid bankruptcy. In 1933, they went back into radio broadcasting, establishing another Edmonton station.

Taylor, Pearson, and Carson met for the first time at a Chicago car dealers' convention, and all were fascinated by the potential financial rewards of owning radio stations. The three formed a company in 1934 and tried to buy CFAC, the station owned by the *Calgary Herald*. The *Herald* wouldn't sell but did agree to make a deal with them under which they would manage the station, splitting the profits 50-50 with the paper. They then made a similar management deal with the Edmonton *Journal*'s station, CJCA. In time, Taylor, Pearson, and Carson's management business was responsible for about a dozen radio and TV stations across the country, including stations owned by the Siftons and

Southams. Eventually, their company would become a major broadcasting force through its successor, Selkirk Holdings Ltd., and its subsidiary, All-Canada Radio and Television Ltd., which represented more than seventy stations.

Jim Allard described the three broadcasting pioneers as "Harold Carson, the entrepreneur; Jim Taylor, the gambler; and Hugh Pearson, the bookkeeper." They had a decentralized management style, paid their executives well, and were among the early providers of staff benefits such as life insurance, health and accident insurance, pension plans, and other fringe benefits. They also gave free rein to station managers to run the stations as they wanted. "They were smart," said M. V. Chesnut, who managed several stations for Taylor, Pearson, Carson. "They didn't interfere in the day-to-day operation of a station. I've never known one of the partners in any way to say you should be broadcasting this or that. They were perfectly content to hire a manager on his record and let him do what he wanted to do. All they wanted was a pretty picture at the right-hand bottom corner of the financial statement."

Taylor was the public relations expert and hard-driving salesman and, according to Allard, "abused alcohol pretty badly, was completely ruthless, was extremely bad tempered, but he was an absolutely superb salesman, a man of imagination and of considerable vision." Pearson was a superior administrator and prudent with a dollar. Carson, Allard said, later also had problems with alcohol, smoked big cigars, and was "a very sensitive man." "He was a veritable giant," said Norman Botterill, one of his managers. "He inspired his managers, inspired loyalty."

Carson was the entrepreneur of the trio who, in the mid-1930s, set up a company in Toronto to solicit national advertising for their stations. When the CBC's Trans-Canada network was established in 1938, Carson tried to become the CBC's commercial representative but was turned down.

Carson also wanted to set up his own across-Canada radio network and pushed hard through the CAB for the right to have such a national private system. When his request was rejected by the CBC, he turned his attention to the transcription business and bought Canadian rights to such popular American programs as *The Lone Ranger*, *The Green Hornet*, *Tarzan*, and a few Canadian-made shows. This move attracted many more advertisers to the Taylor, Pearson, Carson stations.

As far as the private broadcasting hard-liners were concerned, the trio's one fault was their unwillingness to go into full battle with the CBC. "Our only complaint against them was that they might be too submissive to the wishes of the politicians in order to be allowed freedom to operate," said Walter Dales. But, he added, "Carson was a big man – big in every way – in size, in outlook, in his personal weaknesses, and in his fight to overcome them. Every man who ever worked with him loved him."

The same could not be said for another Canadian radio entrepreneur who began his chase for radio's pot of gold in the 1930s and found it in the 1940s: Jack Kent Cooke.

Cooke, who started out working with Roy Thomson, was a peerless huckster, stingy, not to say a cheapskate, a ruthless workaholic who revolutionized Canadian radio. A salesman's son, the teenaged Cooke sold encyclopedias and Bibles door-to-door in Toronto's east end, was a stock-exchange runner, a racehorse walker, and the leader of a band – first called Jack Cooke and His Band but later known as Oley Kent and His Bourgeois Canadians. Playing for dancing teenagers at Toronto's Balmy Beach Canoe Club, the band got $60 a night, $2.50 for each of the other eleven band members, and $22.50 for Cooke. Described by schoolmates as a hard-eyed little guy who could be verbally intimidating, Cooke fell in love with radio listening at night to music from a Chicago station. He practised announcing in his bedroom and in 1934 at the age of twenty-two applied for a CFRB announcer's job. He was turned down. Two years later, as a Northern Ontario salesman for Colgate-Palmolive, he approached Roy Thomson in Timmins for a job. "I like you. I'm going to hire you," said Thomson after listening to Cooke's persuasive, confident voice talking excitedly about a business of which he knew nothing. But he did know how to sell, and that salesman's magic is what Thomson heard.

At the age of twenty-four, when he'd been married for two years, Cooke gave up a job paying $70 a week, big money during the Depression, to grab Thomson's offer of $23.85 a week to run Thomson's money-losing station in Stratford, CJCS. In a few months, under Cooke's sales drive, CJCS was making a profit, and Thomson sold the station and moved Cooke to Toronto to sell national advertising for his other stations. Then he brought Cooke back to Northern Ontario to manage his stations in Timmins, Kirkland Lake, and North Bay for $100 a week.

They formed a partnership, bought a station in Rouyn, Quebec, for $21,000 ($2,000 down), and then sold it a year later for $105,000. They also bought stations in Amos and Val-d'Or, Quebec, ran stations in Kingston and Peterborough as well as Northern Ontario, and visions of a broadcast empire began to dance in their heads. But the CBC, which frowned on multiple ownership, restricted their plans to expand further. Even so, Cooke was a millionaire by the time he was thirty-one. The Thomson-Cooke partnership foundered when Cooke took on a high-paying consulting role with an Ottawa station and refused to share his fee with Thomson.

Cooke moved into big-time Canadian broadcasting in 1944, buying on his own for $500,000 the Toronto station CKCL, which he renamed CKEY. He brought flash and excitement to the Toronto radio scene, upsetting tradition, piling on commercials, introducing new program styles, making new radio stars, and rivalling the mighty CFRB. "Make no mistake, Jack revolutionized radio in Canada," said CKEY on-air personality Bill Brady. Announcer and actor Lorne Greene left the CBC, where he'd been known as "The Voice of Doom" because of his wartime newscasts, to do four sponsored newscasts a day for CKEY. Early in his career Greene had worked for $5 a week for an ad agency where, among other tasks, he sang jingles. He had been told after one early audition, "Don't become an announcer, Lorne. You haven't the voice for it."

Cooke broke the traditional fifteen-minute program block of most Canadian radio, allowing programs to run an hour or two hours. One of the first programs to benefit was the immensely popular *Make Believe Ballroom* music show with disc jockey Keith Sandy. One of Cooke's innovations went too far, however, when the CBC, as regulator, charged Cooke with radio piracy in broadcasting a play-by-play reconstruction of NHL hockey games aired by a rival station, Foster Hewitt's CKFH, which had exclusive broadcast rights to some of the games. Many stations reconstructed games from news agency reports, but Cooke was taking the play-by-play from CKFH broadcasts and airing CKEY commentary moments later by popular sportscasters Joe Crysdale and Hal Kelly. They were caught when Hewitt, suspecting what Cooke was doing, announced three fake penalties. Seconds later, CKEY reported the same fake penalties. Cooke denied the radio-piracy charge, but the CBC board found him guilty and ordered him to stop.

Cooke demanded that there be no dead air on CKEY, filling every second between programs with musical bridges, jingles, and stings, and he brought in twenty-four-hour-a-day programming. He was accused of running far more ads than the CBC regulations allowed. He was a cyclone of action, a smiling cobra who was a friend one moment and a frightening adversary the next. And the money was rolling in, enabling the flashily dressed Cooke to drive about in a blue Cadillac convertible, travel in style to New York City, stay at the Waldorf Astoria, sail in his yacht about Lake Ontario, and carry on with beautiful women such as popular American singer Kay Starr. "I'm the goddamndest romantic you'll ever meet," he told a magazine writer years later. "I like women at all times of day and evening. I just plain like women."

He was rich beyond even his wildest early dreams, expanding his business interests from radio to ownership of magazines, a baseball team, a publishing house. He kept a sharp eye on spending at all times, and paid his staff as little as possible, making an exception only for Lorne Greene, who earned $25,000 a year. He often gave out new titles instead of pay raises. "He'll promise you the sun and the moon. He'll give you anything but money," one colleague commented.

His legendary stinginess is illustrated in a story told by writer Alex Barris, who saw Cooke for the first time in the office of *Liberty* magazine, which Cooke owned. Cooke came into the editor's office to borrow a coat hanger because he'd locked his keys inside his car. When the editor looked out the window, he saw the car was parked in front of a locksmith. "He'll get you out in a minute," said the editor. "My God, that'll cost five dollars!" shouted Cooke, grabbing the coat hanger and rushing out the door.

In 1960, seeking bigger fields to conquer, Cooke left Canada for the United States. There, he became a billionaire sports mogul in basketball, hockey, and football, reaped a fortune from cable TV, owned Manhattan skyscrapers worth hundreds of millions, bought a 500-acre Kentucky thoroughbred ranch worth $43 million, and acquired the *Los Angeles Daily News* for $176 million.

Altogether, not bad for a high-school dropout and one-time $23.85-a-week station manager in Stratford. Even Roy Thomson, no slouch himself as a salesman, was impressed with his erstwhile radio protégé. Using Canadian broadcasting as their springboard, both Thomson and

Cooke catapulted themselves into the billionaire class. Another thing they had in common was a lack of patience for both the CBC's policies and the private broadcasters' battles against them. Their focus was on selling, not policy-making. Instead of fighting, they left, Cooke for the United States and Thomson for the United Kingdom, where their future fortunes lay.

But for Harry and Joe Sedgwick, Harold Carson, Jim Allard, Walters Dales, and their colleagues, the CBC was the enemy and Ottawa the battleground. With Mackenzie King's resignation, a major confrontation now loomed between private and public broadcasting advocates. Also looming large again was an old and dangerous adversary of the private broadcasters, Vincent Massey.

7

Playing Politics

"**V**incent Massey was the type that lived in days when His Majesty went by, you tipped your forelock." That was Walter Dales' acerbic comment on the long-time supporter of the CBC, who in 1949 was named chairman of a royal commission on arts and culture, especially broadcasting. A few years later, Massey became Governor General.

With characteristic sharp-edged diplomacy, CAB legal adviser Joe Sedgwick wrote that Massey, then the chancellor of the University of Toronto, was "the fine flower of Toronto and Oxford, scholar, diplomat, man of affairs and culture – everything, indeed, but a man of business." Most private broadcasters felt that Massey was an upper-class snob, whose aristocratic style and élitist sense of superiority may have been appropriate when he was Canadian High Commissioner to Britain but were decidedly the wrong qualities for someone sitting in judgment of Canadian broadcasting. Worse still, Massey had been a close ally of Alan Plaunt in the early battles for public broadcasting and was an influential figure in Liberal party circles. Dales, Allard, and their supporters thought that if ever there was a high-society egghead who had never met a payroll, Massey was it. Worse, none of the royal commissioners was a businessman: four of them were high-ranking academics and the fifth was a professional engineer.

To add to the dismay of private broadcasters, just as the commissioners were beginning their work in mid-1949, a federal election was held in which their strong political supporter George Drew led his Progressive Conservatives into a humiliating defeat at the hands of Louis St. Laurent and the Liberals. The private broadcasters saw their hope of a quick-and-easy triumph over the CBC go down the drain.

For two years, the CAB had been lobbying for a national inquiry into broadcasting in hopes that it might be sympathetic to many of its demands. Current rules governing broadcasting belonged to the "horse and buggy days" and badly needed revision, the association said. Now about nine out of ten homes had a radio, and television was just around the corner, but the royal commission, to the CAB's mind, was "stacked" 4-1 with academics predisposed to favour public broadcasting.

While the idea of the royal commission was first put forward by the private broadcasters, the government had become increasingly attracted to it as a way of deflecting some of the criticism aimed at the CBC and at itself. Among the critics was Conservative Leader George Drew, who repeatedly lambasted the CBC's "indecent broadcasts," its "blasphemy in the air," and "the mental poison being carried over the air waves of Canada." John Diefenbaker chimed in with protests about CBC "pornography," and others accused the CBC of promoting "godless communism" and giving air time to anarchists and atheists. Social Credit Leader Solon Low said the corporation was being manipulated by "diabolically clever subversive agencies in ideological warfare." It was providing a soapbox, he said, for "international gangsters who are scheming world revolution." Quebec Conservative MP Louis-Joseph Pigeon urged the House of Commons to "throw out these people with warped ideas, leftist ideas ... Pierre Elliott Trudeau, Gérard Pelletier and Jean Louis Gagnon who should be permanently kept away from the national network." There were similar, privately voiced sentiments even within the Liberal cabinet. Alphonse Ouimet, in an oral history recording, told of one unidentified cabinet minister telling him, "You are having a bunch of communists on the air ... Marchand, Trudeau, Pelletier, Gagnon, Laurendeau. ... Get rid of them all!"

The most popular announcer in Canada at the time, the CBC's Joel Aldred (a former RCAF squadron leader and war hero – and a man with a golden voice), denounced his employer for "wasting money on high brow programming" that was "too artsy." The CBC was, he said, "a wonderful example of socialistic monopoly at work." His criticism was heartily endorsed by Drew and Diefenbaker, who protested noisily when the CBC later fired Aldred. A parliamentary committee, however, rejected Aldred's criticism as "dangerously sketchy" and "inaccurate," saying, "Mr. Aldred's evidence, where it was not hearsay, was merely opinionative. . . . The committee was not impressed."

Nevertheless, the controversy was fanned by the private broadcasters, most of whom felt any criticism of the CBC would move them closer to their goal of less regulation. So, as Canadian governments so often do when faced with criticism and unpalatable problems, the Liberals announced a royal commission. It was one of Louis St. Laurent's first moves after he succeeded Mackenzie King as prime minister.

Massey and his fellow commissioners studied broadcasting, culture, and the arts for two and a half years. They heard from more than 1,200 witnesses, read 462 briefs, and met with representatives of about 350 different organizations. The CAB and the CBC each made two presentations, one at the beginning and one near the end of the hearings.

As soon as the Massey commission was announced, Walter Dales and Jim Allard got together to work out a strategy for the private broadcasters. Dales moved quickly to get the Canadian Weekly Newspaper Association to turn up the volume on its criticism of the CBC. "The country weekly editors . . . began to editorialize strongly for a separate, independent body to regulate broadcasting," he said.

J. H. Cranston of the weekly papers association told a parliamentary committee in a vitriolic attack on the CBC that there was a "potentiality for evil" in the CBC-dominated broadcasting system and that there were great "dangers" for freedom. "It is a battle," Allard wrote in the *Canadian Broadcaster*, ". . . that we should and must continue to wage until it is won or until the belief in freedom perishes in the hearts of men." George Chandler of CJOR Vancouver, an ally of Allard, warned that "the forces of socialism" were curtailing broadcasting freedom.

Dales and Allard wanted a tough-talking, no-nonsense approach in the CAB's presentation to the Massey commission but ran into opposition from the CAB's board, which was divided between hawks and doves. "Because the private broadcasters were not united enough to fight hard, the strategy Allard and I had favoured did not win acceptance," Dales later said with some bitterness. "Honey rather than vinegar was the choice of the CAB. [They] hoped that by a cooperative and behind-the-scenes negotiation, the broadcasters could win more approval."

Leading the internal battle for a softer approach was the CAB's new president, William Guild, Harry Sedgwick having retired because of ill health. Guild managed the Taylor, Pearson, Carson station in Lethbridge, Alberta, and was strongly influenced by his boss, the moderate Harold Carson. Even without the fiery rhetoric Dales and Allard wanted, the private broadcasters still made a vigorous case to the commissioners. As well as the CAB, thirty-five stations made individual presentations, although seven of them differed with the CAB and supported the current broadcasting system.

In his initial statement, Guild put forward the CAB's position that broadcasting was, in reality, a dual system, not the single one mandated in the 1936 Broadcasting Act. He argued that the single system idea had been destroyed by the CBC itself through the licensing of so many private stations. "The privately operated stations in Canada are in fact providing the primary radio service and . . . the national system should function as an outgrowth of their service," Guild said. He claimed that competition was "stifled," and it was "undemocratic and dangerous" to have control in the hands of the CBC, which, he said, is "at one and the same time . . . competitor, regulator, prosecutor, jury and judge."

"Radio broadcasting in Canada today," Guild said, "is a business – a business in which private enterprise is engaged in competition with a publicly owned and largely publicly financed company."

There is no such competition, Davidson Dunton responded. "Our field is in national network broadcasting, whereas their field is local community broadcasting," he said.

Guild pleaded for less regulation, saying stations should be able to put on the air whatever programs they judge the public wants, and not have them subject to the dictates of bureaucrats. He also requested a lessening of restrictions on commercials (at the time, the CBC still banned ads for brassieres, girdles, and laxatives) and the removal of the CBC ban on commercials at the end of newscasts. "This removal will enhance the value of newscasts," Jim Allard said.

CKEY Toronto owner Jack Kent Cooke took a tougher line at the Massey commission, when he said the CBC should not own or operate any stations at all, only produce programs from which the private stations could pick and choose. Harry Sedgwick said the CBC should provide only Canadian programming. He urged elimination of the licence fee for listeners and proposed that the CBC be given an annual grant from Parliament of $9 million as compensation and to allow it to forgo advertising.

But you've got it all wrong, the Massey commission told the private broadcasters. Broadcasting should enrich the mind and refine taste, it said, adding that broadcasting was "a social influence too potent and too perilous to be ignored by the state."

Private broadcasters knew they were in for a public spanking when they first looked at the commission's five-hundred-page report and saw it began with a quotation from St. Augustine. The report rapidly became a Bible for Canada's cultural élite. It rejected the arguments of the private stations. Massey himself said most of the CAB's claims were "ridiculous" and "absolute and unqualified nonsense."

The report stated, "The principal grievance of the private broadcasters is based, it seems to us, on a false premise that broadcasting in Canada is an industry. Broadcasting in Canada, in our view, is a public service directed and controlled in the public interest by a body responsible to Parliament. . . . The only status of private broadcasters is as part of the national broadcasting system. . . . The statement that the Board of Governors of the Canadian Broadcasting Corporation is at once their judge and their business rival implies a view of the national system which has no foundation in law and which has never been accepted by Parliamentary committees or by the general public."

In other words, said the commission, private broadcasting is a privilege, not a right. Private broadcasters are subordinate, not equal, to the CBC. "The most important function of private stations . . . is that they serve as a regular or occasional outlet for national programs, thus giving the national system a coverage which could not otherwise be achieved except at great public expense." Massey also dismissed the argument that the CBC was stifling freedom of speech, and said the private stations gave the impression that "financial considerations are more important than the theory of freedom."

At the same time, the report admonished the CBC for not exercising tighter control over the private broadcasters and urged considerably more and better Canadian content on the private stations. "We cannot believe that there is any justification for their undistinguished programs," the report said. "While the programs of some were satisfactory and of a very few praiseworthy, those of far too many . . . could only be described as regrettable . . . inexpressive and unimaginative."

The private broadcasters had not expected much from the Massey commission, but this was worse than they had feared. As Walter Dales later said, "They got an acid scalding for their programming; the CBC was told to regulate them more sternly." "Biased and misleading," "unwise," "absolute and unqualified ivory-tower nonsense" were some of the private broadcaster reactions on the commission's findings. To friends, Allard called the Massey report, "the last gasp of the WASP élite."

In response to the Massey recommendation that more Canadian talent be used by private stations, the CAB said, "Broadcasting should not be forced to subsidize those who desire to become artists but have neither the talent nor the ability." It was reminiscent of the arguments against Canadian content articulated by private broadcaster spokesman R. W. Ashcroft two decades earlier.

The CAB denied the Massey criticism that there were too many commercials on the air, saying that advertising "is greatly in the public interest." That idea was ridiculed by CCF Leader M. J. Coldwell, who said commercials were "an insult to the intelligence of the Canadian people. . . . Those who sponsored these singing commercials must regard the public of Canada as a nation of morons." The CAB also rejected the Massey fear that without public broadcasting, Canadian airwaves might have been taken over by American networks. "Never at any time was there any danger of absorption of Canadian stations into the American orbit," the CAB said.

The principal CAB demand for a separate regulatory agency was dismissed by a majority report of the commissioners as a misreading of the purpose of the single national system, and it warned that such a separate body "would either divide or destroy, or merely duplicate the present system. . . . A completely separate body treating public and private radio broadcasting with judicial impartiality could not fail to destroy the present system upon which we depend for national coverage with national programs."

But one member of the Massey commission disagreed. Civil engineer Dr. Arthur Surveyor, in expressing reservations about some of the commission's report, recommended just such a separate regulatory agency, saying it was a matter of fairness. He noted that 90 per cent of Canadian radio stations were privately owned, and proposed a Canadian Broadcasting and Telecasting Control Board to have authority and jurisdiction over both the CBC and private broadcasters. While this was only Surveyor's position and not accepted by the commission as a whole, it was nevertheless a significant milestone for private broadcasters in their long battle to whittle down the CBC's powers, and it provided a road map for the Conservatives when they came into power.

Apart from this, gains for the private broadcasters were few and far between in the Massey report: a recommendation to extend station licence renewals to five years; a suggestion that the CBC review its regulations to see if any were no longer necessary; a recommendation that the CBC get out of all local advertising, except in communities where there was no private station. The private broadcasters also won a recommendation for a modified right of appeal from CBC rulings.

When a bill incorporating most of the Massey recommendations was passed by Parliament, Conservatives spoke out sharply against them and reiterated their demand for a separate radio regulator. George Drew called the Massey report "out and out nonsense," and John Diefenbaker said that the public interest could be safeguarded only by an independent regulatory agency. The government, however, once again rejected these proposals.

"The Massey findings," Allard said, "failed dismally to lower the temperature of the debate boiling around broadcasting policy. Instead, the heat was intensified, frequently approaching hysteria." And nowhere was that more evident than in the arguments over public versus private television, a new medium now looming on the horizon.

John Aird himself had seen experimental television in the London laboratory of British scientist John Baird in 1928, when Aird was on his fact-finding mission. The concept of television had been developed in the 1880s, when it was called "seeing by telegraph." Although history remembers them for developing radio, by the early 1900s, Marconi and Canadian scientist Reginald Fessenden saw TV in the future as well. Serious experimenting with the new medium, which began in the early years of the century, was interrupted by the First World War. After the war, Baird began intensive testing in his London laboratory and produced the first television pictures in 1925. By the late 1920s, experiments were widespread in Europe, the United States, and Canada. "Radio pictures will be commonplace within five years," *Canadian Magazine* forecast in 1929. Television "will one day revolutionize culture," said *Saturday Night.* "Television is just around the corner," *Radio Week* predicted.

Professor Jean Charles Bernier of L'École Polytechnique in Montreal was among the early Canadian experimenters, as was Len Spencer, chief engineer for CKAC Montreal and one of the station's original four employees. "RADIO EYE ADDED TO EAR," headlined the *Montreal Gazette* in a story on Spencer's experiments. Another key player in the development of TV in Canada was J. Alphonse Ouimet, a McGill graduate who, as a child, had built his own crystal set and as a McGill engineering student in the late 1920s had built a small TV set. Spencer and Ouimet worked together to put on Canada's first television program for CKAC in October 1931. A year later, CKAC, much as CFCF had done in Montreal in the early radio days, was experimenting with one hour a day of television, showing the talents of local fiddlers, violists, singers, and bands.

In 1932, in Toronto, Ted Rogers of CFRB was also experimenting with TV, putting Gordon Sinclair and Foster Hewitt and a group of musicians before a camera and using the windows of a downtown Toronto department store as a studio. Pictures of the men appeared on a set four feet away. It was the first public demonstration of TV in Toronto. By the end of the year, there were seven experimental TV stations in Canada, all developed by private entrepreneurs; three in Montreal, one in Toronto, one in Vancouver, one in Saskatoon, and one in Mont-Joli, Quebec. CFCF in Montreal and Ted Rogers in Toronto applied for TV licences in 1938 but were denied.

War interrupted the development of television, not only in Canada but in Britain, Europe, and the United States. But as soon as hostilities ended, the television explosion began. Within months, stations were on the air in the United States, Britain, France, and Russia. By the end of 1950, there were 150 stations around the world offering "photographed radio."

In Canada, private radio swashbucklers lined up with applications to the CBC for TV licences. They could see the riches just waiting for them in this new invention. "One of the quickest roads to a fortune in Canada," said Graham Spry. By 1944, thirty-four applications had been made to the CBC, and in 1946, CFRB was back again with a new application, along with seventeen other would-be TV stations. In 1949, there were more applications, including detailed plans from broadcasters Jack Kent Cooke and feisty Hamilton broadcaster Ken Soble. The CBC turned some down and ignored the rest, making it an easy target for attack by the CAB. Conservative politicians, led by George Drew and John Diefenbaker, used the CBC's rejection of private TV applications as a weapon against the ruling Liberals and, in their view, its lapdog, the CBC.

"Television has been held back . . . in this country by the policy of the CBC," said Diefenbaker. "There are private operators who are ready to risk their money to carry on through the experimental stages," said Drew. Manufacturers also started pressuring for a quick start, calculating the fortune to be made selling sets to viewers and equipment to stations. "The CBC cannot block the aspirations of private entrepreneurs indefinitely," *Saturday Night* editorialized, "without earning for itself a reputation of capriciousness and tyranny."

But the Liberal government was alarmed at the potential cost of a national television service, and no one more so than C. D. Howe. "If private operators think it worthwhile to risk that much money, let them go ahead. . . . For the government [to do so] would be a dead loss," he said. Prime Minister St. Laurent was not so sure, and J. J. McCann, still the minister responsible for broadcasting, told the House of Commons it was not "prudent" to spend CBC money on TV or to encourage private companies to do so. So the government and even the CBC dithered in a "wait and see" attitude. "It would be a mistake to encourage the introduction in Canada of television without sufficient financial support," said CBC general manager Dr. Augustin Frigon. Frigon also had doubts about Canadians wanting TV. "Do you seriously think people will keep sitting in front of a little screen?" he asked Alphonse Ouimet.

By early 1949, CBC chairman Davidson Dunton had decided it was time for television to come to Canada. Saying that it would be "a great social force," he suggested a sharing of resources between private and public interests. The CAB promptly proposed that a separate television company be run jointly by the CBC and private broadcasters. Dunton rejected that idea and proposed to the government that the CBC should establish television before any private licences were granted. He warned that private TV by itself would be "swamped" with American programs. The Massey commission agreed, saying, "The pressure on uncontrolled private television operators to become mere channels for American commercial materials will be almost irresistible."

Howe and several other cabinet members urged that TV be left to the private sector with the CBC functioning only as a regulator and adjudicator of the private stations. McCann and Prime Minister St. Laurent, however, were uneasy with that approach. St. Laurent told the House of Commons, "I do not think these [TV] frequencies should be lightly turned over to private ownership and exploitation." The government did say, however, that "it is not the intention . . . to exclude private operations from the field of television." But it added, "The general direction of television broadcasting in Canada will . . . be entrusted to the Board of Governors of the Canadian Broadcasting Corporation."

Finally, in March 1949, the federal government approved CBC television stations for Toronto and Montreal. The rapidly increasing Canadian viewing of American TV shows emanating from U.S. border cities forced the government's hand. It was the same fear of an American invasion of Canadian airwaves that had led R. B. Bennett to authorize Canada's first national public radio system in 1932.

The CBC and the government set a target date of 1951 for the start of TV in Toronto and Montreal, but the date was postponed until September 1952 because of a shortage of steel and equipment caused by the Korean War. By the time television arrived in Canada, there were 146,000 sets already in use across the country, bringing in American programs. Within fifteen months, there were 1.2 million sets, and 2 million by 1956.

Initially, the St. Laurent government had said private TV stations could be licensed in any Canadian city, one station per city, but by 1951, influenced by the Massey report, government policy had changed. Now private TV would be allowed only in cities where there was no CBC-TV outlet and only after the CBC had established a distribution system for the national programs the private stations would carry. When that would be, no one was sure. McCann told the House of Commons that the Conservatives and Social Credit parties "appear to be in a great hurry to see some private operators get television licences . . . from which they might hope to make a good deal of money." They will have to wait, he said.

With the public clamouring for television, there were lots of entrepreneurs willing to take their chances and bring television right away to Canadians. "We . . . had our applications ready and waiting to go," said Walter Blackburn of CFPL London. "We knew from what the Hon. C. D. Howe was saying . . . [that] he wasn't prepared to give the CBC everything."

But Howe's cabinet colleague J. J. McCann had long been uneasy about private broadcasters. Soon after McCann became the minister responsible for broadcasting, he had told Jim Allard, "As long as I'm the responsible minister, there will be no private television in the country, and if by some unhappy mischance it does come about, the people you represent will never be considered for licences." Two weeks after that meeting, Allard saw Howe, who, Allard said, took the opposite position. "His view, strongly held," Allard remembered, "was if television came to Canada, private enterprise should be responsible for it and the CBC totally uninvolved because of the expense."

Once Canadian TV began on the CBC in September 1952, Conservatives and private TV applicants raged that television was available only to the CBC. "CBC-loving highbrows" were frustrating free enterprise and denying TV to Canadians other than those in Toronto and Montreal, the *Vancouver Sun* wrote. George Drew argued in the House of Commons, "Why should public money in Canada be allocated for the purpose of giving telecast programs to the areas of Toronto and Montreal? . . . No sound reason has been put before the House for allocating one cent. . . ." He told the CAB, "It seems to be the most fantastic nonsense." C. D. Howe privately agreed with Drew. "If I were living in my own town of Port Arthur, I'd kick like a steer at paying taxes to bring television to Montreal and Toronto," he told friends.

CAB head Jim Allard began a spurt of intense lobbying. Private broadcasters already had the highly vocal support of two political parties, the Progressive Conservatives and the Social Credit. Toronto CCF MP Joe Noseworthy said the two parties, "through the years have supported CAB just as intently as if they had been directly sent here to do that. . . . Any recommendations which have been put forward by CAB as opposed to CBC have had the support of the two groups."

The CAB also had the support of the Canadian Chamber of Commerce, the Southam, Sifton, and Thomson newspaper chains, and influential individual papers such as the Toronto *Globe and Mail*. But Allard knew he had to do more. He now had to chip away at Liberal support for the CBC; it was the only way he could alter government policy. He was helped in this by the fact that some Liberals were getting into the business of private broadcasting. They were his targets, especially highly influential Liberals such as Don Jamieson of Newfoundland.

Jamieson was a close ally of Jack Pickersgill, a backroom Liberal who had easy access to the prime minister. Jamieson was the best-known radio personality in Newfoundland and co-founder of a radio empire that wanted a TV licence. Prominent Ontario Liberal John Wintermeyer, who represented a Kitchener TV licence applicant, was another of Allard's targets.

The most immediately useful senior Liberal, however, was Duncan MacTavish, who was a business associate of Jack Kent Cooke and whose company owned a private radio station in Ottawa. He also had represented private broadcasters before the CBC board. He was president of the National Liberal Federation, and one of his vice-presidents was Irving Keith of Winnipeg, a lawyer for private radio stations. In October 1952, one month after CBC-TV began in Toronto and Montreal, the advisory council of the National Liberal Federation held its annual meeting in Ottawa, and Allard saw an opportunity to score an important lobbying victory.

Allard wrote "Extremely Confidential" letters to supporters outlining the CAB's intensive lobbying campaign aimed at the nearly three hundred Liberals attending the advisory council meeting, and he urged CAB stations to add their own pressures on delegates. CKEY's Jack Kent Cooke had prepared a detailed document entitled *The Case for Private Television Broadcasting*, and it was the basis for a resolution introduced by Keith, urging immediate approval of private television in Canada and abolition of the listeners' licence fee. (The licence fee was eliminated a few months later.) J. J. McCann strongly opposed the resolution, but despite his pleas, 85 per cent of the delegates approved the resolution, the first major victory for the CAB among the Liberals. A few days later, the Association of Canadian Advertisers announced its support of the Liberal advisory council resolution.

A delighted Allard noted that the Liberals at the meeting had "openly revolted against the government's entire broadcasting policy. It was an extremely stormy meeting."

A month later, for the first time, a dozen CAB directors met with the prime minister to make their case for private broadcasting. Finlay MacDonald of CJCH Halifax was among the group and remembers Allard saying, in reference to broadcasting legislation, "I realize, Prime Minister, that you've been very, very busy and haven't had an opportunity to bring a number of things up to date." "He went on and on," MacDonald says, "and in a very patronizing way. At which particular moment, the meeting came to an abrupt halt. St. Laurent blew his stack! He said, 'Mr. Allard, I have been told of my unfortunate tendency to not bring things up to date. . . . I appreciate you coming here.' There was nothing left to do but get up and say, 'Thank you, Prime Minister, for a very useful, profitable conversation.' That was it, and we got up and left."

The CAB told reporters that its brief to the prime minister had been "sympathetically received."

Within a few weeks, the government announced that CBC-TV stations would be established in Halifax, Winnipeg, and Vancouver as well as Ottawa, which had been previously announced. The CBC had asked for stations also in Edmonton, Regina, Saint John, St. John's, and several in southwestern Ontario. But, listening to arguments from Howe about the cost of CBC-TV, the cabinet, including St. Laurent, hesitated, and the decision on those stations was put off.

The government said it was ready for private station hearings in cities where there was no CBC-TV station. No private TV network was possible, however, without the approval of the CBC board of governors, and that was not forthcoming. Explaining the new government policy, McCann told the House of Commons, "Under this plan, the private stations licensed will carry national program service, besides having time for programming of their own."

"Our view," said Transport Minister Lionel Chevrier, "is that the private station . . . [is] not a competitor of the CBC, but [is] a complement to the CBC . . . I'm sorry to say that the Tories have abandoned the enlightened and patriotic policy which Mr. Bennett adopted twenty years ago. They have gone back to the traditional Tory policy of handing over the exploitation of the public domain to their wealthy political friends." Chevrier also attacked the idea that private TV stations could produce programming "by Canadians, about Canada." "It is perfect nonsense," he told the House of Commons, "for anyone to suggest that private enterprise in Canada, left to its own devices, will provide Canadian programs."

The St. Laurent government's decision, while finally launching private TV, was greeted coolly by the private broadcasters. "A faltering, fumbling step," said Jack Kent Cooke. CAB lawyer Joe Sedgwick added, "Why can't we have privately operated TV stations ... in every centre in Canada where entrepreneurs can be found willing to risk capital?" John Diefenbaker thundered that the government's decision was "a denial of every right of private broadcasters."

Jim Allard said the new government policy "places staggering power in the hands of the Canadian Broadcasting Corporation, permitting it not only to maintain its present regulatory powers, but to decide for itself in what area it will have a complete television monopoly. This policy will set back for years the provision of television programs that Canadians will look at and the general development of the television industry." He argued that the Liberal government's decision to limit private TV licences was an infringement on freedom of speech and democracy.

Allard later softened his criticism when private stations began getting licences and when the government indicated it would not give the CBC as many television stations as it had asked for. George Chandler, the tough-talking Vancouver broadcaster, remained unmollified. "Government policy remains monopolistic, has caused long delays, refuses Canadians a choice of programs, and in many areas has driven Canadians to rely on American TV service," he charged. More forcefully, Clifford Sifton noted in a letter to Allard, "The CBC is made to appear to be an independent dictator, but is in fact under the absolute power of the Cabinet."

By June 1953, the CBC board had approved seven private stations and first on the air in October of that year was CKSO in Sudbury; a month later, CFPL London was the second private TV station. Within about a year, fourteen private TV stations had been approved. In 1952, the Montreal and Toronto CBC-TV stations had reached 20 per cent of the Canadian population. With the arrival of private TV and the launch of the three additional CBC stations, by 1954, TV was reaching 75 per cent. A patchwork network was developed by the CBC, which shipped recorded programs to stations pending completion of a microwave relay system. The private stations were carrying about twenty-five hours a week of CBC programs. By 1957, they were carrying thirty-eight hours a week of CBC programs. There was no coast-to-coast CBC network until 1958.

While cries echoed across the country for Canadian TV, warnings were also heard about the new medium fostering a nation of couch-potato idiots, just as there had been critics of radio in the 1920s who warned of "radio-itis" or "spectator-itis." *Maclean's* magazine was alarmed about "tele-vidiots." *Globe and Mail* columnist J. B. McGeachy said TV "may destroy conversation and could even make thinking obsolete." (Plato once said more or less the same thing about the invention of writing.) Movie director Alfred Hitchcock said the TV screen was "a rectangle charged with emotion." When playwright George Bernard Shaw was asked for his reaction to television, he said, "I'm afraid to look!"

Meanwhile, to the horror of private broadcasters, the CBC board had picked up the worries expressed by the Massey commission over insufficient Canadian programming on private radio stations. In late 1952, the CBC suggested regulations that would set a range of Canadian content minimums from just under 50 per cent between 8:00 A.M. and 11:00 P.M. for radio stations in big cities affiliated with the CBC Trans-Canada network, to 40 per cent for unaffiliated stations and between 30 per cent and 38 per cent for stations in small communities. As a sweetener, the CBC also proposed allowing private stations to have slightly more time for commercials.

More ad time was fine, but the Canadian content proposals set off a firestorm of protest. Astutely, Jim Allard, rather than protesting only about the cost of using more Canadian talent, declared that the proposed Canadian content rule "is the complete negation of freedom of speech." It was dictatorship versus freedom, he said, adding, "and we're for freedom." He issued a seventy-six-page pamphlet entitled *The Case for Freedom of Speech*. In a highly aggressive tone, it charged that the proposed Canadian content regulations were undemocratic, imposed thought control, and reeked with "narrow and bigoted nationalism . . . [and] cultural inbreeding." Allard's accusations were bitterly denounced by Dr. Eugene Forsey of the Canadian Congress of Labour, who said, "This notion that freedom is being cramped and restricted by the CBC is nonsensical and fatheaded!"

But Allard countered that the regulations could lead to a ban even on the Bible and non-Canadian writers and musicians such as Shakespeare, Beethoven, Gershwin, Chopin. Predictably, the *Canadian Broadcaster* echoed Allard's line. "CANADIAN IF IT KILLS US," was its headline over a story stating, "This regulation . . . would practically destroy what vestige of freedom of speech remains on the air." It said the CBC was an enemy in the struggle for freedom, "the tombstone of private enterprise," "undemocratic," "greedy" for power, and "overloading stations with culture." Setting a percentage of Canadian content, it said, was like the government ordering Canadians to travel 65 per cent of the time on the CNR or Trans-Canada Airlines.

CKEY's Jack Kent Cooke denounced Canadian content regulations as "narrow, nationalistic nonsense" and called for "cultural democracy." He said that Canadians wanted American programs, "undoubtedly the fastest rising culture in the world today." Don Jamieson of CJON St. John's said, "Public preference for United States programs of virtually every type is obvious and growing." To prove that point, Jim Allard said that three-quarters of Toronto television viewers were watching the Buffalo, N.Y., stations, not the CBC Toronto station. (By 1954, the audience for the Toronto CBC station had risen to 35 per cent.) Allard told Clifford Sifton, "The simple truth is that the entire world wants American entertainment."

Joe Sedgwick claimed that the private stations couldn't afford to hire much local talent. "You can't do the impossible and you can't do it without money," he said. "We can't afford to produce live shows with fees for actors and orchestras." But Sedgwick's real complaint wasn't the cost of Canadian content, he opposed the very idea of Canadian arts and culture in a mass medium like television. "Such Canadians as have a choice prefer U.S. television, commercialism and all, to Canadian culture . . . by a margin of four to one. . . . Culture is running a poor last. If, as all surveys show, the mass of the people prefer commercial radio and TV, then in my view, that is what they are entitled to."

"These proposals tighten the straitjacket around Canadian broadcasting and fit in with the ideas of the long-haired, arty groups who believe that we the public are too dumb to know what is good for us," said George Chandler of CJOR Vancouver.

Six months after the Canadian content regulations were proposed, they were dropped by the CBC, the battle lost, at least for the time being.

The additional commercial time that had been proposed along with the content regulations was approved, however, and put into effect.

The private broadcasters were on the comeback trail. At the Ontario Young Liberals annual meeting in 1953, the rising Liberal star Keith Davey, a Toronto broadcast advertising salesman, strongly advocated stripping the CBC of its regulatory authority. British Columbia Young Liberals also called for a separate regulatory agency, and later the National Conference of Young Liberals, in open defiance of the prime minister's wishes, endorsed the idea of removing the CBC's regulatory function. Under provincial Liberal pressure, the Manitoba legislature passed a resolution with a large majority urging more private stations in the province and approving a separate regulatory board.

Allard's tough approach was working. Finlay MacDonald, who was CAB president in 1954–55, says Allard's success stemmed from his determination, his encyclopedic knowledge of the corridors of Ottawa, and his aggressive style, too aggressive for MacDonald's taste. "He was a take-charge guy, a hard worker, intelligent, who knew more than anybody else about copyright and fought for private broadcasters, saving them a lot of money on copyright. You had to admire that. He may have felt that the majority of the CAB just didn't give a shit about anything except advertising and he could do whatever he liked. But some of us saw through him . . . saw through his bullshit."

But not everyone did.

"With a high pressure campaign," stated the *Canadian Forum*, "the private broadcasters have succeeded in convincing a goodly portion of the Canadian public and the Liberal Party that they were suffering a serious injustice because of the government's decision to establish a national television service before granting licenses for private TV stations. . . . The campaign consisted chiefly of vilification of the CBC as a monopoly that was threatening freedom of information in Canada." At one point in a heated meeting with Allard, the CBC's circumspect Davidson Dunton burst out, "Oh, for Christ's sake, Jim!"

Nevertheless, Allard and the tougher idealogues among his CAB colleagues knew they were gaining support for private broadcasting. When MacDonald stepped down as the CAB's president, his replacement was inclined to give Allard more room to operate. CAB hard-liners had been disappointed in the re-election of the St. Laurent Liberals in 1953, even though there were more Conservative and Social Credit MPs and twenty fewer Liberals, which led to more political support for private broadcasters.

Private broadcasting won another victory with the granting of a TV licence for St. John's in 1955. The CBC board of governors had recommended a CBC station be established in Canada's easternmost city. Its second choice was a licence for CJON St. John's, run by Don Jamieson and his partner, Geoff Stirling. It was up to the cabinet to make the final decision and, the CBC thought, give its blessing to the public broadcaster. But Jamieson's close friendship with Jack Pickersgill, who was now in the cabinet as secretary of state, and with the Liberal premier of Newfoundland, Joey Smallwood, paid off. "Jamieson and Stirling were quite a power team," says Murray Brown.

The two Newfoundlanders flew to Ottawa to lobby senior Liberals. They met with Pickersgill, among others, and, on their behalf, Pickersgill argued in cabinet that a CBC outlet in St. John's would be a waste of taxpayers' money when Jamieson and Stirling were prepared to invest their own money in setting up a TV station. McCann fought strongly for a CBC station, but Pickersgill persuaded the cabinet, and Jamieson and Stirling were given the licence. "There were at least a dozen better ways to spend a million dollars of public money for the benefit of Newfoundland," Pickersgill said. "I knew that Geoffrey Stirling and Don Jamieson ... were prepared to finance a private television station ... McCann, as Minister for the CBC, pressed [the CBC's] case vigorously, but the Cabinet decided the issue in my favour."

It was the first time the cabinet had overruled a licence recommendation by the CBC board. Allard said the CBC board had been dumb to offer the cabinet a second choice for St. John's.

One result of this award was the introduction to the world of Canadian broadcasting of a singular man who would forever defy convention. Geoff Stirling, a one-time St. John's newspaper publisher, built a broadcasting empire in St. John's, Montreal, Windsor, and elsewhere with his audacity, street smarts, and quixotic management style. "He was absolutely astonishing," says comedian Roger Abbott of the Royal Canadian Air Farce, who once worked as an executive at Stirling's Montreal radio station. "He was rarely in town, and he'd arrive for two or three days and then disappear and we might not see him again for months. But if he didn't like something he'd heard on the air, he'd call up the station and fire the announcer.

"Around 1969 or 1970, he became convinced that the price of gold was going to skyrocket. So he gave us all a gold coin and urged us to go out and buy many more," Abbott recalls. Flamboyant Toronto media magnate John Bassett received similar advice. "When gold was $35 an ounce, Stirling urged my dad to buy gold. 'Mortgage your house! Borrow anywhere, but buy gold,'" Bassett's son Douglas recalls Stirling telling his father. "Gold went to a high of about $715, but my dad never did buy gold."

"Stirling had a terrible time with names," Abbott says. "Twice at a meeting he called me 'Francine.' Another time we were having a cocktail party and he tried to introduce his wife but couldn't seem to remember her name. Eventually he called her 'Mrs. Stirling.'"

In those days, Abbott says, Stirling usually wore a T-shirt, jeans, and alligator boots, and his curly black hair hung over the collar of his leather jacket. Some years later Stirling changed his dress style. One-time All-Canada Radio and Television president Ross McCreath remembers Stirling attending CRTC meetings wearing a robe, beads, and sandals. "He'd go to India from time to time to be with his guru there," McCreath says. "For him, nothing was impossible with his great enthusiasm. He would get up before the CRTC and say things nobody else would dare, calling them names and then the next minute he'd have them in the palm of his hands. He could charm the socks off anybody."

Stirling once visited his radio station in Windsor and called the staff out into the parking lot. "He made a couple of announcements and then he fired them all," says McCreath. "An unbelievable, fascinating man." In his later years, Stirling moved to a mountaintop in Arizona.

The award of the TV licence in St. John's to Liberal supporters Stirling and Jamieson was certainly not the first time politics had played a part in granting broadcast licences. Jim Allard remembered that when the owner of the *St. Catharines Standard* wanted a licence in his home-town, he and Allard visited C. D. Howe, who gave his support but warned, "If you ever on that broadcasting station run an editorial in opposition to the Liberal party, I'll cancel the licence at once."

Allard also recalled when Liberal Fisheries Minister Jimmy Sinclair wanted a radio licence in Vancouver to go to a strong Liberal supporter. In an Ottawa hotel room, he met with Allard and three Vancouver radio operators who might normally oppose a new station in town: George Chandler of CJOR, Bill Rea of CKNW, and "Tiny" Elphicke of CKWX. Sinclair demanded that they support the application. According to

162 • THE SWASHBUCKLERS

Allard, Sinclair said, "It is essential that [the applicant] get it in order that we have a voice of Liberalism on the Lower Mainland. I want your support. I want you to write a letter of support." All three did, and Sinclair's Liberal friend got the licence.

In the mid-1940s, when the CCF government in Saskatchewan wanted to take over CHAB in Moose Jaw, the Liberal government in Ottawa killed the idea because it didn't want the CCF to have a station it could use to broadcast the activities of the Tommy Douglas government.

Adding to the CBC's problems in the mid-1950s, an increasing number of senior Liberals were becoming disenchanted with some CBC programs, which reflected a broad spectrum of opinion on current issues, including opposition to some government initiatives. Private broadcasters, whose program emphasis was more on entertainment than current affairs, came in for no such criticism. They also were gaining favour with politicians through the CAB's *Report from Parliament Hill*, which generally skirted around controversy and gave MPs an opportunity to broadcast whatever they liked to their constituents. Private broadcasters also won support for sponsoring the Dominion Drama Festival and broadcasting several of the dramas.

A festering sore point for Allard, Dales, and the CAB hard-liners, however, was the attitude of the Ottawa Parliamentary Press Gallery, which, they charged, was strongly pro-CBC because of payments to reporters for their commentaries and participation on panels. In Dales' mind, this was a form of bribery. "Being human, large numbers of them reached for this plum," Dales later wrote, "and in reaching, some of them may have praised the CBC where criticism would have been more in order. Others may have moderated their views regarding nationaliza-tion. . . . It seemed to us even staunchly right-wing commentators became very mild when an opportunity to be a name broadcaster for the CBC was in prospect."

In his regular column, which ran in weekly papers, Dales charged, "The Press Gallery now contains a large number of newsmen eager to please CBC . . . and, consequently, their broadcasts and their news dis-patches ought to be looked at with care." Dales also accused *Maclean's* of being "an unofficial house organ of the CBC." He said Allard "kept me well supplied with figures and facts on press gallery activity," and "plenty of reporters in Ottawa were making about as much money from the CBC as they were getting from their publishers."

Dales believed that many politicians were also being seduced by their appearances on the CBC. "Many backbench politicians, too, noticed that those favoured by the CBC with regular appearances gained tremendous advantage on the hustings . . . many of the top politicians feared the CBC more than they feared the electorate."

"Personally," said Dales, "my own fear was that the CBC was getting far too politically powerful."

Another attack on the CBC came in accusations that the CBC was undercutting the private stations in its advertising rates. The CBC was "giving big advertisers a cheap ride," said Dales. "I couldn't prove it," says Finlay MacDonald, "but I know damn well they did." Don Jamieson made the same assertion. "It is a fact" that the CBC undercut ad rates, he said. *Canadian Broadcaster* editor Richard Lewis charged that the CBC had reduced its television advertising rates by about 50 per cent in order to get more commercials.

A few Liberals joined the Conservatives in denouncing the CBC for encouraging sex. New Brunswick Liberal MP Henry Murphy complained in the House of Commons about a CBC-TV program on ballet that, he said, showed "long-haired nut boys cavorting around in tight, long underwear."

There was also concern expressed by some politicians about the CBC's commentaries on the rise of social democratic political parties in Europe and on McCarthyism in the United States. Ontario Premier Leslie Frost accused the CBC of being "a propaganda machine for the party in office in Ottawa . . . the Liberal party. . . . Everything is being loaded against the opposition parties."

Some politicians thought the CBC was a propaganda machine not for the Liberals, but for communism. "There is a liaison between communist headquarters and the CBC," said Newfoundland Liberal MP Chesley Carter. Expanding on his accusation, Carter later said, "I am a little frightened by the amount of brainwashing and subversive propaganda which goes out over the CBC day after day at taxpayers' expense. I am appalled at the extent to which the CBC provides a national platform for subversives and points of view which originated in the Kremlin."

C. D. Howe attacked the CBC for echoing Tory policy in a program on unemployment. Other cabinet ministers, including Brooke Claxton, were outraged at a planned discussion on a controversial book critical of Mackenzie King. The CBC bowed to their pressure and abandoned the program. St. Laurent also complained about a talk given on the CBC by a University of Manitoba professor that criticized Canadian foreign policy. Even McCann apologized in the House of Commons for a CBC Radio play honouring labour martyr Joe Hill. The Liberal dyspepsia with the CBC was also reflected in softening enthusiasm for the CBC in the reports of the parliamentary broadcasting committee hearings.

All this heartened the private broadcasters, who felt the tide was moving their way. M. J. Coldwell in 1953 had written to a friend, "Step by step, over the years, they [the CAB] have encroached on the area Parliament designated as exclusively the responsibility of the CBC. The Conservatives have for years been their mouthpiece in Parliament. . . . The propaganda in the press through the CAB itself is, of course, intense. [And] there is a strong element within the Liberal party directly interested – some of them personally interested – in private radio and television and I feel there is indeed grave danger of temporary success for CAB."

To the CAB's alarm, however, supporters of public broadcasting, disorganized since the 1936 hearings that gave birth to the CBC, had begun to stir. At St. Laurent's private urging, noted historian and ardent public broadcasting advocate Professor Arthur Lower of Queen's University put together a small band of like-minded thinkers, hoping to form a new version of Graham Spry and Alan Plaunt's Radio League. "The League looks more dangerous every day," CKWX's Sam Ross wrote in alarm to Allard from Vancouver. Allard told one of his legal representatives, W. J. "Bud" Estey, later a Supreme Court Justice, that he intended to plant "spies" in the new Radio League. More openly, the CAB tried to become a member of the league and influence its policies from within. The effort, however, was rebuffed. Estey said, "The Canadian Radio League had everything – doctrinaire socialists, misguided but well-intentioned people, many minority groups, but it lacked the guy in the street."

Lower and his key league colleagues Pierre Berton, Professor Frank Underhill, and educator E. A. Corbett not only felt that private programming was too American and too commercial, but they also had harsh words for the CBC for being too easy on the private stations. "I'm beginning to despair of the CBC authorities," Lower wrote to Spry. "They seem to have no reply at all to the aggressiveness of the private broadcasters."

As CAB president, Finlay MacDonald of CJOH Halifax was far more sympathetic to the CBC than most of his colleagues. "We have an obligation to protect the CBC from unjustified attacks," he told the 1954 CAB annual meeting. "As a national program institution, we can be proud of the CBC. Give or take an issue or conflict of personalities, I fail to see anything sinister in their attitude." That was certainly not Allard's viewpoint, and MacDonald's comment signalled future trouble between the two men.

After Army service in the Second World War, MacDonald had begun his broadcast career announcing the news on CJFX Antigonish while he was still a student and later at CJOH Halifax while getting his law degree. As manager of CJOH, he endorsed the CBC as the broadcast regulator and said that the CBC should be paramount in Canadian broadcasting. Private stations, he said, were not equal to the CBC, but were "links in the national system."

In contrast to MacDonald, Don Jamieson was at times virulent about the public broadcaster, once referring to its staunch supporters as "misguided eggheads or bribed stooges . . . who advocate state control." But Jamieson also criticized many of his fellow private broadcasters, saying, "Within this industry we have too many operators who have grown fat and complacent." He called them "cockroach broadcasters." "They have abdicated control of station programming to advertisers and agencies," Jamieson said. "We are not mere salesmen or manufacturers. We are broadcasters and . . . we have a serious responsibility in what has been called, with considerable truth, the struggle for men's minds." Denouncing dissension within the CAB, he called for a stronger, more united association to battle public broadcasting.

Despite their differences, Jamieson and MacDonald were kindred spirits in their distaste for many of the tactics of the CAB's Jim Allard and the hard-line anti-CBC private broadcasters. Late one night during Jamieson's term as CAB president, he and Allard got into a loud, alcohol-fuelled argument. It was after a CAB meeting in Jamieson's Ottawa hotel suite, and Allard upbraided Jamieson for "doing everything the wrong way," saying that if Jamieson only would listen to Allard, "I could make you prime minister." "He just tore strips off me," Jamieson told Murray Brown of CFPL London and Allan Waters of CHUM Toronto, whom he'd called at 3 A.M. to describe his encounter with Allard. They had traipsed up to his suite in their pyjamas and found a fuming Jamieson saying, "I just had the worst fight of my life with Jim Allard . . . a terrible battle."

"Jim had had a lot to drink and just screamed and went into a rage," Brown says. "Don was really upset and I've never forgotten that night."

In 1955, in response to concerns about the rapidly rising costs of CBC television, the CAB's campaign to remove the CBC from its regulatory role, and increasing political distemper and divisions within his cabinet, St. Laurent decided to set up another royal commission to examine the roles of public and private broadcasting. The chairman was a Liberal insider with impeccable business credentials, Robert Fowler, whose name had been suggested by Brooke Claxton. Private broadcasters looked for support from the commission, particularly since Fowler and his two colleagues – a banker and a former editor-turned-diplomat – were likely to be more sympathetic to them than the academics of the Massey commission.

The militants at the CAB immediately set to work to make their case against the CBC. "It was suggested to me by the Sedgwick brothers, Joe and Harry, and by Jim Allard," said Dales, "that I get to Hamilton and spend a few days with Mr. Ken Soble of the CAB board, so that we might offer some thoughts on what kind of brief the Association might present to the Fowler Commission. . . . Some felt the 'honey' approach had failed in the past and that we must go after what we wanted forcefully, phrasing our requests in colourful language." This they did, expressing their deep bitterness at the CBC for thwarting their efforts on behalf of private broadcasters. This led Fowler to complain about the CAB's "devious propaganda wrapped in colourful verbiage." Even the Toronto *Telegram*, normally a strong supporter of the private broadcasters, said in an article that the broadcasters' brief "was so loaded with irrelevancies and unsubstantiated charges against the CBC that the legitimate case of private broadcasters was lost."

Allard and the CAB again trotted out their complaints about the CBC being "cop and competitor," but, even under intense questioning by Fowler, they could not cite any examples of significant unfairness by the CBC in its regulatory role. It was in the principle, they said, that the potential for unfairness existed. They also felt that the CBC board tended to assume an air of superiority in dealing with them. Allard later explained, "You were making a presentation in the middle of hostile, sarcastic remarks with one-half of the board reading newspapers and the other half asleep 90 per cent of the time. We were up against a star chamber kind of thing." Broadcasters were deferential to the CBC board, he said, because they feared reprisals if they criticized the CBC. In a letter to Vancouver radio executive George Chandler, Allard wrote, "Broadcasters appearing before the Board have acted like guilty schoolchildren trying to explain to the principal why the window was broken."

Geoff Stirling of CJON St. John's said that CBC stations should be sold or rented to private broadcasters and that the CBC should give the private affiliated stations a bigger share of national advertising on the network programs they carried. Malcolm Neill of CFNB Fredericton said the CBC should prepare a daily package of non-commercial programs that it would pay private stations to air. He said the fear of American culture dominating Canada was a "red herring." The CBC treats private stations as "second class citizens," Neill charged.

CAB lawyer Bud Estey told the commission that Canadian broadcasting was being held back by the CBC's refusal to license a large number of private TV stations. His comments were supported by the Canadian Chamber of Commerce and the Canadian Federation of Mayors and Municipalities, among other bodies.

The CAB also complained about too many constraining regulations, saying, in a play on Mackenzie King's comment about conscription, "Regulation if necessary, but not necessarily regulation."

CBC supporters disagreed. Donald MacDonald, secretary-treasurer of the Canadian Congress of Labour, told a parliamentary committee, "The apparently harmless plea for an independent regulating body is, in fact, a demand that the CBC should be done to death; slowly perhaps, but nonetheless surely."

"Time after time," *Maclean's* editorialized, "[Fowler] demanded and failed to get examples of the tyranny and persecution by the CBC that elicited such heart-rending screams from the private stations. Some of the examples were palpably false. Others were nearly twenty years old."

Fowler himself complained that the CAB "has issued much one-sided or misleading information . . . and this propaganda has largely gone unanswered by the CBC. The outcome has been to give shape in the public mind to analogies based on incomplete knowledge or insufficient reflection, to enroll the Canadian instinct for freedom behind hidden mercenary motives and to foment misunderstanding and confusion among the well-meaning." Allard explained the CAB's harsh comments in a letter to Don Jamieson: "In order to get something changed, there has to be at least some element of attack in one's presentation which is bound to lead to controversy."

The case made by Allard and his colleagues was blunted somewhat by the desertion from the CAB brief by a number of key broadcasters, including Finlay MacDonald of CJCH Halifax, Murray Brown of CFPL London, and Corey Thomson and Jack Tietolman of CKVR Verdun, all of whom felt Allard was too abrasive in style and substance.

The CBC, MacDonald said, was a "nerve centre and backbone around which the national character has grown and will continue to grow." He urged that the CBC keep its regulatory authority, saying it had been fair in its judgments and regulations. MacDonald said later that Allard and the CAB hard-liners "were always going around screaming that they were competing with the judge and the prosecutor, that they were getting a raw deal. They just couldn't see beyond their noses, and they were insisting upon a separate regulatory body. They didn't realize that the regulatory authority of the CBC was frankly applied with great gentleness. They never had it so good."

Allan Waters, then relatively new to broadcasting in Toronto at CHUM, wrote to MacDonald, "Congratulations. You have the guts to get up and say what I suspect a lot of the others are thinking. . . ." Disagreeing with the CAB's central demand, Waters said, "If we get an Independent Regulatory Body, we will find that we have got 'a lion by the tail.'"

"I wish to congratulate you," said another broadcaster uncomfortable with Allard's leadership, C. H. Witney of CFAR Flin Flon. The CAB, he told MacDonald, seemed like "a master followed by many sheep." He worried about "the tendency to follow blindly" the course charted by Allard and his supporters.

The CBC's Alphonse Ouimet wrote to Fowler complaining about Allard's tactics, saying there was "a day and night difference between the attitude of our [private] affiliates and that of the body that speaks for them. The attitude of our affiliates has appeared to us to be an understanding one, a friendly one. . . . On the other hand, the CAB attitude has appeared to be belligerent and nasty. . . . The CAB seems to be systematically, ruthlessly and also without civility, seizing every opportunity to discredit our operations."

On March 28, 1957, the 172-page Fowler report was submitted to Parliament. It praised most CBC programs, urged a much more aggressive commercial emphasis at the CBC, criticized the CBC board for being too easy on private broadcasters in its regulatory role, and denounced private broadcasters for failing to develop Canadian programs and talent. Private stations had "hidden mercenary motives" in their appeal against CBC regulations, the report stated. It also stated a private TV network in Canada was not economically viable at the present time. But it gave the private stations explicit assurances on the permanence of private broadcasting. "The mixed Canadian system of public and private ownership is here to stay. . . ." the commission declared. "Private operators should stop worrying about the bogey of nationalization that has filled them with suspicion and fear in the past." Fowler added, "We have made it clear that private broadcasters are an integral part of a single system."

But the big news in the report was a recommendation for a new regulatory authority, one that would oversee both private broadcasters and the CBC. At first glance, it would seem to be what the CAB had been asking for. Closer reading, however, indicated it would not be much different from the present approach. There would still be a single broadcasting system with public and private components, and the CBC would remain the dominant partner. The fifteen part-time members of the suggested independent board of broadcast governors would regulate both the private and public stations, determine broadcast policy for the CBC, and supervise CBC's management, financial affairs, and relations with Parliament. Fowler insisted that the new board would enforce broadcast regulations more rigorously among the private stations than the CBC had been doing. "Some stations may lose their licence because of a shabby performance," the commission warned.

"It is to be hoped," Fowler said, "that the long and frequently bitter argument about a separate regulatory body will come to an end and private broadcasters will accept their role as valued and essential partners with the CBC in the single Canadian broadcasting system."

It wasn't exactly what the CAB wanted, but it was a half-loaf victory. Jim Allard said that some parts of the report were "highly perceptive," but other parts "give the impression of a sermon hastily prepared by a dyspeptic clergyman after a bad breakfast."

The Liberal government agreed with most of the proposals made by Fowler and prepared to make changes to the Broadcasting Act as soon as the June 1957 election was out of the way and, they assumed, they were back in power.

One fly in this ointment, however, was Diefenbaker. He had been elected to replace George Drew as Conservative leader in the fall of 1956 and, thanks to extensive CBC radio and television coverage of the party convention, the flamboyant Saskatchewan political evangelist electrified Canadians. To Allard's delight, Diefenbaker intensified his attacks on the CBC as a way of getting at the Liberals, charging the CBC was a "mass propaganda agency" for the Liberals. Its policies, he said, were "an unjustifiable challenge to freedom of speech." Besides, he added, if private stations make a profit, why can't the CBC?

The private stations were, indeed, making money. "RIDING THE CREST OF A PROSPERITY WAVE," the *Financial Post* trumpeted, and the Canadian Bank of Commerce said broadcasting had the third highest profits of the 140 industries studied in 1957. Five years later, the government statistics showed broadcasting tenth best out of 127 industries for profits.

That June, CBC-TV cameras captured the excitement that Diefenbaker generated during his campaign, his arm-flailing histrionics contrasting sharply with Louis St. Laurent's dull-as-dishwater greyness. The result was a stunning upset victory for Diefenbaker, even if it was only a minority government. Private broadcasters were exuberant, their dreams seemingly having come true. There were persistent reports that the Diefenbaker government was considering an offer from private broadcasters to buy the CBC for $50 million, half the amount an industry magazine estimated it was worth. A popular satirical novel, *The Chartered Libertine*, by *Maclean's* editor Ralph Allan, was based on the idea of the CBC being given to a hotshot private entrepreneur. But "Dief the Chief," as the new prime minister was nicknamed, was not prepared to go that far. "No offer has been received or will be considered," he said.

Graham Spry was not reassured. "The dangers to the CBC," he wrote to a friend, "are not those of extinction, but emasculation."

Less than a year later, Diefenbaker went back to the polls and won an overwhelming majority that was watched on election night on the CBC by 7.8 million Canadians. His triumph cleared the way for him to put into place the kind of broadcasting system the CAB and its supporters had been battling for since 1936.

Signals of Tory support had been sent to the private broadcasters during the election campaign. George Nowlan, a Nova Scotia broadcaster and Diefenbaker's minister of National Revenue and the minister responsible for broadcasting, told a Halifax audience that the Conservative government would very soon license more private TV stations. Diefenbaker himself, in a campaign stop in Kenora, Ontario, promised he would introduce legislation to strip the CBC of its regulatory authority. "The time is long overdue for private stations competing with the public broadcasting system," Diefenbaker said, "that they would be judged by an independent body. . . . They should not be judged by those who are in competition with them and are, in effect, their judge and jury."

The CAB was jubilant. Diefenbaker's promises, said CAB president Vern Dallin of Saskatoon, were a result of "the consistent and vigorous information campaign conducted by your association over the years. . . . We are one of the biggest, most important and influential groups in Canada."

Under headlines such as, "LET'S CLOSE UP THIS GOVERNMENT CIRCUS" or "A NEW DAY FOR BROADCASTING," the *Canadian Broadcaster* demanded fast action on clipping the CBC's wings, calling the CBC "a highly costly public futility."

There was, however, mutiny in the ranks of the CAB. While Allard was in the midst of his pitch for cabinet support of the CAB agenda, he faced an insurrection from a group of broadcasters known as "the Rat Pack." What Allard described as "a small but vocal element in the CAB" recommended to the CAB board that Allard be replaced in his $18,000-a-year job because, they felt, his extremism was harming, not helping, private broadcasting, and that he had made too many political enemies among key people in Ottawa. The so-called rat pack included three former CAB presidents – Finlay MacDonald of CJCH Halifax, Bill Guild of the Taylor, Pearson, Carson stations, and CKCW Moncton's Fred Lynds – plus W. J. Blackburn and Murray Brown of CFPL London, Allan Waters of Toronto, and Ralph Snelgrove of Barrie. They were also uneasy about the hard-liners who supported Allard's approach. "An awful lot of the original people in private broadcasting were fairly shrill and strident in their views," MacDonald says. "They thought that the CBC was a natural enemy. They used to use expressions like, 'It's either them or us!'"

"We also wanted someone with more stature and diplomacy than Allard had," says Murray Brown. "When I was CAB president, I went to a couple of meetings with him and I was almost embarrassed by the way he did things. He didn't seem to have the stature that was required to call on ministers and deputy ministers."

Allard, who had served the CAB since 1945, notified the CAB board he would not resign and demanded a vote of confidence. "Bedlam broke loose. There was much undiplomatic language," he later said. Allard, who spoke French with an atrocious accent but an extensive vocabulary, had many friends in Quebec broadcasting, and at a stormy board meeting, D. A. Gourd, the president of the French-language station group in the CAB, said that if Allard went, all French stations would leave the CAB. Most western stations made the same threat and support flooded in from other hard-liners, including Malcolm Neill of CFNB Fredericton, Ken Soble, and Jack Kent Cooke. In the end, Allard got his vote of confidence. "They tried to get rid of me, but I survived," he said later. "Had I not watched my own back and my own interests so carefully, we would never have had an independent regulatory agency."

"It caused me to make a lot of bad friends among my colleagues," MacDonald remembers. Shortly after the failed putsch, MacDonald and Allard met at a Montreal party, where, according to MacDonald, "Allard called me 'a goddamn traitor.' He had a lot of guts. He sailed into me. He said it was too bad I was insane. That was the last time I had anything to do with Jim Allard."

Diefenbaker wanted quick action on the changes being sought by the private broadcasters, and Nowlan went to work preparing a new broadcast policy. His first move was to name as a key adviser his Nova Scotia political ally, Halifax broadcaster Finlay MacDonald. This was not what the CAB had in mind. Nowlan was not a supporter of Allard's take-no-prisoners approach, and, in fact, had been supportive of the CBC on several occasions. And, while MacDonald's appointment put a private broadcaster at the centre of government decision-making, he was hardly Jim Allard's choice. MacDonald not only was on the "outs"

with Allard, but he also had broken with the CAB by supporting the regulatory status quo. He accepted the main recommendations of the
Fowler report, including a new, single board to regulate private broadcasters and the CBC and to be responsible for supervising the CBC.

Working with a handful of senior public servants, including
Secretary to the Cabinet Robert Bryce, MacDonald recommended the
Fowler proposals and a continuation of the concept of a single system of
broadcasting for Canada, in which the CBC would remain dominant.
MacDonald says Nowlan agreed and proposed it to a special cabinet
committee consisting of himself, Finance Minister Donald Fleming, and
Transport Minister George Hees. Fleming had been a long-time critic of
the CBC, and Hees was much influenced by John Bassett, a friend and
Toronto publisher who wanted a TV licence. Bassett's financial backer,
the Eaton family, were strong supporters of Hees and had pushed him
for Conservative party leadership. Hees also had been lobbied hard by
other entrepreneurs seeking a Toronto TV station.

In late 1957, Hees had sent a memorandum to his cabinet colleagues
rejecting the Fowler commission's recommendation for one regulatory
board. That, he said, would basically change nothing. He urged the creation of two boards – one independent to regulate all broadcasting and
make licensing recommendations, and one to oversee the running of
the CBC.

Fleming and Hees fiercely opposed the MacDonald-Nowlan proposal, using the old CAB argument that there were two broadcast
systems already operating in Canada and that the CBC competed with
the private stations. In addition, Fleming wanted to tether CBC's "hog
wild" spending, and insisted the CBC's financing be based on annual
reviews and appropriations by Parliament, instead of the five-year
financing period Fowler had suggested.

The savvy CBC chairman, Davidson Dunton, saw the anti-CBC
handwriting on the wall, and after nearly thirteen years as head of the
CBC, he resigned. "He didn't have to be hit on the head," says Finlay
MacDonald. Three days earlier, on July 1, the launch of the Halifax-to-
Vancouver CBC-TV national network had been celebrated in a program
hosted by French network journalist René Lévesque and English
network TV personality Joyce Davidson. But Dunton didn't have the
heart or the energy to run a diminished CBC with a prime minister

suspicious that the CBC was trying to undermine him. Dunton's departure removed a thorn from the CAB's side.

With the cabinet arguing over the future shape of Canadian broadcasting, Jim Allard and scores of individual station operators and
owners lobbied their local MPs to support the CAB objectives. Then suddenly, Allard faced an unexpected challenge: Graham Spry was back.

His very name sent shivers through the hard-line private broadcasters,
who remembered his lobbying magic in getting public broadcasting
launched a quarter-century earlier. Spry, who had been representing the
Saskatchewan government in England, was fearful his public broadcasting dream was being destroyed and he came back to take over Professor
Lower's effort to re-energize the Canadian Broadcasting League. Calling
on his formidable range of contacts, Spry went on a whirlwind lobbying
effort, speaking with cabinet ministers, senior civil servants, broadcasters,
Liberals, and Conservatives.

Allard dismissed Spry and his new pro-CBC lobby group as "an
organization of vocal do-gooders who fail to understand the function of
broadcasting in a modern society."

Trying to exploit divisions within the CAB, Spry said in a letter to
Saskatchewan Premier Tommy Douglas, "The Canadian Association of
Broadcasters is split three or four ways. One group of private stations
accepts the Fowler Report. . . . The most intelligent of them, Finlay
MacDonald of Halifax . . . sent me a message of friendliness through an
intermediary and [said] most cordially that he was ready to see me in
Toronto or Ottawa. . . . He can be of great help. He is ready to act as a
consultant or become a member of the League or assist in any other
way we may choose. At the same time, he is a member of the much
divided CAB, the private association, and freely tells me of what happens
in their meetings."

Because of his political contacts, MacDonald was advised of the
cabinet's decision on a new broadcasting act before it was made public.
He immediately wrote to Spry, "I respect your confidence, so therefore
will advise you that the general decision respecting the new broadcast
agency has apparently been made." He then went on to describe the new
act in detail to Spry.

Having heard that the cabinet had decided against the league's objectives, Spry arranged a meeting with Diefenbaker. He put together a twenty-six member, pro-CBC delegation headed by Donald Creighton, Sir John A. Macdonald's biographer. The former prime minister was, Spry knew, Diefenbaker's personal hero. Disingenuously claiming they were "merely disinterested amateurs" concerned about broadcasting, Spry and his group urged adoption of the proposals of the Fowler report and the recommendations of Finlay MacDonald and Nowlan.

As impressive as their presentation may have been, it was, of course, too late. The cabinet had decided on July 11, MacDonald had written to Spry July 14, and Spry's meeting with Diefenbaker was July 18. Diefenbaker had already sided with Fleming and Hees in their pro-CAB arguments. Nowlan, still more supportive of the CBC than most of his colleagues, felt it was the best he could get out of the cabinet. A new regulatory board would be set up, but it would not have, as Fowler had proposed, responsibility for managing and supervising the CBC. A separate CBC board would be established to do that. However, because it was politically advantageous, Diefenbaker used the same name for the new independent board as Fowler had recommended: the Board of Broadcast Governors (BBG). Indeed, Diefenbaker said the new legislation was intended to carry out Fowler's recommendations, although that was certainly not Fowler's assessment nor that of the Liberals. Liberal Leader Lester Pearson, who had succeeded St. Laurent the previous year, said, "It runs absolutely against the report of the Fowler Commission." The name might have been from Fowler, but the spirit was from the CAB. It was much more akin to the recommendations of the minority comments of Dr. Surveyor of the Massey commission.

In the House of Commons, the badly beaten Liberals urged that the paramountcy of public broadcasting be maintained. They had little hope and less enthusiasm, since their own ranks were divided on this issue. Pearson made a bow to the effectiveness of the private broadcaster lobbying, saying, "What was once a privilege for private broadcasters has gradually become a vested interest and eventually has been invoked as a right."

The new legislation sailed through the overwhelmingly Conservative Parliament with ease. It meant a far-reaching change in Canadian broadcasting, a significant downgrading of public broadcasting, an elevation of private broadcasting, an end to the one-system approach espoused by Bennett and Mackenzie King, and at least equality between the public and private sectors. It also opened the door wide to future licensing of private broadcasters and the probability of a private TV network. A gloomy Graham Spry wrote a colleague, "Those in government hostile to the CBC gained powerful opportunities to interfere and even drastically weaken the CBC."

The private broadcasters had finally won a battle in the broadcasting war. "Private broadcasting had finally achieved respectability," said Jim Allard. "The Canadian Association of Broadcasters had a triumph without parallel in Canadian history . . . and clearly established their right to be regarded as a responsible and useful segment of Canadian society."

It was the triumph of Allard's life, the objective he had been seeking for private broadcasters for a quarter-century. "I conceived it quite simply as my duty to get it for them," he later said. "We got it because we fought hard for it. You don't get anything that you don't fight hard for, and it was a rough, tough fight." To do it, he used much the same techniques as Graham Spry and Alan Plaunt had used at the start of the 1930s in their campaign for public broadcasting. "I personally claim a great deal of credit for this," he said in an interview recorded by Walter Dales. Noting that some CAB members were hostile to the separate regulatory agency, Allard said. "I practically had to carry the ball alone because, quite candidly, most of our people were too afraid to do anything. I had a great deal of trouble with them. . . . It made me unpopular with some people and some of them have never quite forgiven me completely."

Allard was lauded by the *Canadian Broadcaster*, which described him as "the incomparable, the indispensable, the invincible Jim Allard." His boss, the new CAB president, Malcolm Neill of Fredericton, boasted to a meeting of British Columbia broadcasters, "We have attained equality of rights with the CBC. We now have new opportunities . . . and the industry has acquired a new prestige."

Thanks to their lobbying efforts, private broadcasters had gone from being supplemental to the public broadcaster in a one-system scheme to now being equal, and with domination the next target. In the number of stations alone that dominance had already been achieved. In 1957, when Diefenbaker first came to power, there were about 170 private radio stations and when he left office in 1963, there were about 240. Private TV grew in those years from some thirty stations to sixty-three. In the Diefenbaker years, the CBC had two dozen radio stations and eight TV stations in 1957, and by 1963 still had about two dozen radio stations and thirteen TV stations.

"For years now, the battle of broadcasting has been fought by the industry as a defensive operation," the *Canadian Broadcaster* editorialized in late 1958. "Now this competitor [the CBC] . . . has retired several miles back of his own lines and dug in. There he is going to stay until the forces of private broadcasting go on the offensive and blast him out of his fox hole."

The deliberate weakening of the CBC had begun. Prime Minister John Diefenbaker saluted the new CBC, saying, "Order was brought out of confusion and complaint." But the Liberals' Walter Gordon gloomily told Graham Spry, "I do not think there is much doubt that the Tories are out to wreck the CBC." Certainly what Diefenbaker wanted was the fastest possible growth for private stations and the slowest possible, if not stoppage, of CBC development.

8

Diefenbaker the Saviour

Diefenbaker was determined to hobble the CBC, and his instrument of choice was the new Board of Broadcast Governors (BBG). His first pick to lead the BBG was Allister Grosart, the national director of the Progressive Conservative party, a man who, like Diefenbaker, felt the CBC had become a propaganda mouthpiece for the Liberals. However, Grosart declined and the chairmanship went to George Nowlan's choice – Dr. Andrew Stewart, the president of the University of Alberta, who had impeccable academic and public service credentials but virtually no public profile. He was a bespectacled, pipe-smoking agricultural economist who, at the time, was leading the Royal Commission on Price Spreads for Food Products. He was also a CBC listener. "The private broadcasters feared that they could not expect much from a university professor," said Walter Dales. "[But] he was a man of real intelligence, integrity, and common sense." According to Murray Brown, "He was an understanding man and was prepared to learn about broadcasting." He also was regarded as a man who was politically unidentifiable – "a political eunuch," one colleague called him.

Privately, Stewart did have a preference. "I was not an admirer of Mr. Diefenbaker," he later confided. "I found him pompous . . . I liked

Mr. Pearson. I found him unpretentious. I am not sure that either . . . had much of a grasp of what broadcasting was all about."

At the beginning, neither did Stewart, and before taking the job he consulted Dick Rice, who was a member of the University of Alberta senate, ran CFRN Edmonton, and was one of the key players at the CAB.

The two other full-time members of the BBG were highly visible Conservatives: Roger Duhamel, a Quebec newspaper editor, and Carlyle Allison, long-time editor-in-chief of the *Winnipeg Tribune* and an ardent Diefenbaker loyalist. Allison turned out not to be such a good friend of the private stations, however, when he criticized their news-casts and advocated tougher restrictions on advertising. The dozen part-time members appointed to the BBG were also heavily tilted toward the Conservatives, including Dr. Mabel Connell of Prince Albert, a close friend of the prime minister and known as "Diefenbaker's dentist." Years later in an interview with writer-broadcaster Frank Peers, Stewart said the BBG failed to generate needed public confidence mainly because of the known political associations of most board members.

One unusual choice, however, was Dr. Eugene Forsey, a constitu-tional law and labour expert who was active in CCF politics and was anything but an ally of private broadcasters. In a letter to Graham Spry, he wrote, "Somebody should now start a strong counter attack against these miserable private broadcasters. They are, for the most part, a col-lection of bandits . . . a terrible crew." After he had left the BBG for the Senate, Forsey spoke out against the private broadcasters: "Over and over again, we got the impression that when these people spoke often in purple passages about their devotion to the public interest and their desire to promote Canadian programming and Canadian talent and so on . . . there was a lot of talk but very little action to back it up. The impression on me was that the theme song of private broadcasters could very well have been taken from that Gilbert and Sullivan opera, *The Pirates of Penzance*:

> "'Oh I am a pirate King,
> Yes, I am a pirate King,
> And it is, it is a glorious thing,
> To be a pirate King!'"

Graham Spry was deeply discouraged by the composition of the BBG board. In a *Queen's Quarterly* article he wrote half a dozen years after the Diefenbaker broadcasting legislation was enacted, he lamented "the decline and fall of Canadian broadcasting." "The CBC," he wrote, "has been outflanked, surrounded and hemmed in to a subordinate place in the structure of Canadian broadcasting. . . . The CBC has been maligned, misrepresented, savaged, nagged and subjected to meanness and indignation by hostile and sometimes greedy competitors and ill-informed politicians." He felt public broadcasting was now a "minority, subsidiary element" in Canadian broadcasting. "In a generation of conflict between the local private interests . . . and the CBC, the ordinary forces of money-making have carried the day." He told Finlay MacDonald, "The battle is lost."

Under the revised Broadcasting Act, the government had to appoint a new president and board for the CBC. With some misgivings, but anxious not to displease Quebec, Diefenbaker acquiesced to Nowlan's choice of CBC veteran Alphonse Ouimet as president. "I was not the man that the Conservatives had been looking for," Ouimet later mused, "but they were not able to find the candidate of their choice." Diefenbaker replaced the Liberal-dominated CBC board with a Conservative-dominated board, and gave them directions to rein in spending. To that end, Diefenbaker appointed Robert Dunsmore, a retired oil company president from Montreal, as chairman of the finance committee. Within a few months, however, increasingly angry at both Ouimet and CBC programming, Diefenbaker named Dunsmore as chairman of the CBC board in hopes of tightening the government's grip on the public broadcaster.

Private broadcasters, delighted by what they saw as a new dawn of broadcasting, liked the complexion of the BBG although they were uneasy with Forsey and with Stewart's lack of knowledge of the business. They were, however, pleased with Stewart's early comments: "The members of the Board have been referred to as Gods, Czars, bosses and drivers. The Board members are none of those things. Neither are they policemen nor censors. . . . They do not flex their muscles, strike menacing attitudes, practice loud noises directed at anyone or push people around."

"Happy Days Are Here Again!" the private broadcasters sang and CAB president Malcolm Neill commented, "Broadcasters . . . have had their prayers answered." Admitting that the BBG may "do things we don't completely agree with," he said, "but . . . it is definitely not their intention to shake a big stick." Station representative Bill Byles of Stovin-Byles Ltd. was joyful, "They have a sense of humour. They are democratic. They are cooperative. Their questions are intelligent and understandable." *Canadian Broadcaster* editor Richard Lewis also cheered: "Between the BBG and the [Conservative-dominated] Parliamentary House Committee, there is very little to carp at . . . what is there left to hate?"

The private broadcasters were particularly pleased with the BBG's first decision, made a couple of months after being named, to give licences to six new radio stations and power increases to eight stations. A few weeks later, they granted four more licences and power increases for six outlets. Shortly afterwards, the BBG handed out another seven radio licences and a further four power increases.

The BBG sent out feelers to see if private radio wanted to establish the permanent national radio network that the CAB had championed for so long. It came to nothing, however. "We were advised that it did not seem to be practical without assistance from the public treasury and the Board has taken no further action," Stewart said.

For years, the CAB had vigorously fought Canadian content regulations, but had reluctantly accepted that the BBG would impose some modest rules. Still they were shocked when the BBG announced much tougher rules than the CBC as regulator had ever contemplated. Stewart warned Nowlan that the private broadcasters would fight against any regulations the new BBG might impose. So the BBG chairman and the minister knew what to expect from the private broadcasters when, four months after Stewart's appointment, they sat down to discuss the matter. Stewart and Nowlan agreed on a 55 per cent Canadian content regulation for television. Carlyle Allison suggested the 55 per cent figure originated with Nowlan. Seven years earlier the CBC had proposed a Canadian content range for radio of 30 per cent to just under 50 per cent and that had made the CAB roar that this amounted to dictatorship and an infringement on freedom of speech.

Defending his proposals, Stewart said, "Board members were amazed by the admission of one station manager that he did not know what his employers had promised in the way of programming although he had been manager of the station for two years." He also said the BBG "took a serious view of radio stations which devoted most of their broadcast hours almost exclusively to recorded music and news."

Knowing that the private broadcasters would again protest, in mid-summer 1959, the BBG announced its proposed Canadian content regulations would be phased in over a couple of years.

Even more alarming to the private broadcasters, however, was a proposed regulation to have all stations set aside up to two hours of prime-time TV programming every night "for purposes to be prescribed by the Board of Broadcast Governors." This meant, the BBG said, programs of high standards, enriching, comprehensive, and essentially Canadian in character. Even in its regulatory heyday, the CBC had never dared to demand such a programming commitment from the private stations. The idea, however, met with such protest that the BBG had to withdraw it. A version of the idea came back a couple of years later when the BBG, unhappy at too much American prime-time programming on Canadian stations, ordered 40 per cent Canadian content between 6:00 P.M. and midnight, later raising the quota to 50 per cent. By the end of the century, the regulation would be even stronger, specifying the kind of Canadian programs that must be aired in prime time.

"Broadcasting," said Stewart, "is viewed as an instrument of policy designed to contribute to the national consciousness and to promote national unity." Don Jamieson disagreed. Broadcasting was, he maintained, an instrument of entertainment. "Regulation and control can do very little to improve program quality," he said. "The state cannot order audiences to listen or watch ... the state cannot command creativity."

Some private broadcasters found inexpensive ways to meet the Canadian content rule by using amateurs, low-cost game shows, and low-paid performers during the early- and late-evening hours, while devoting the heart of prime time to highly profitable American shows. "Broadcasters began to play games with the regulations, obeying the letter but flouting the spirit of the laws," said Walter Dales. As Ken Soble noted, "Why spend $3,000 or $4,000 when you can get the same credit for hiring a piano player." "While the BBG has the power to regulate Canadian broadcasters," he added, "it does not have the power to regulate Canadian viewers ... [and] I am afraid the Canadian product has its problems."

CAB president Malcolm Neill warned Stewart that there was a danger "of making the phrase 'Canadian content' synonymous with 'mediocre.'" "Good broadcasting," Neill said, "cannot be defined by regulation. . . . It would be possible to meet the percentage requirements but . . . this could be done only by the marked reduction in quality." He suggested that if content regulations were deemed necessary, they should be set at 35 per cent for the first year, rising to 45 per cent after three years.

Advertisers and ad agencies also registered their strong opposition, by saying the content rules would increase the cost of production and lead to inferior programs because there was not enough quality talent in Canada. One estimate was that it would cost fifteen to twenty times as much to produce a Canadian program as to buy one from the States. The *Canadian Broadcaster* declared that Canadian content regulation "would simply give would-be performers without any future, a completely false sense of their own abilities."

Eugene Forsey seethed with anger at the private stations' opposition to the Canadian content rules, telling a reporter, "They talk about Canadian talent and devote ten minutes a week to it." He warned against Canadian television becoming a "dilapidated annex of American television."

The BBG stuck to its 55 per cent Canadian content rule, but in light of the industry's protests, the fine print was watered down. Now the percentage could be as little as 45 per cent in the summer, an easement that lasted until 1965 after which 55 per cent was required throughout the day. The BBG also said that some broadcasts, such as an address by the president of the United States, meetings of the United Nations, or the World Series could be considered as Canadian content. The regulations were further modified to measure the Canadian content percentage over four weeks instead of one week, and later the measurement period was extended to three months, which gave stations more flexibility to slot in their Canadian content programs. Over the years, other easements were given to the industry because, as Stewart explained, "The Board always has to be conscious of the relationship between costs and revenue in a private operation. You can push them just so far and beyond that they simply could not operate."

Through the rest of the century, most private broadcasters contrived to resist Canadian content. "Lets face it," said Roy Thomson, "the best American programs are the best in the world. People want to see the best." Don Jamieson told a parliamentary broadcasting committee, "I don't think you can legislate quality. [The content regulations] may give a few second-rate piccolo players or a western band a job, [but] the material is just not there."

As CAB president in 1961, Jamieson gave the committee an example from his St. John's station of the frustration and waste of money on Canadian content: "We spent a sizable amount of money three weeks ago to produce a ninety-minute drama. We worked in cooperation with the university. We chose a classic and we wound up being criticized by the minority because they said it was a very bad presentation and a bad choice. We were criticized by the majority because we pre-empted *Naked City* and *Dennis the Menace* . . . and despite an expenditure of $3,700, we wound up pleasing no one. Even the cast were terribly disappointed because they got such a bad reaction."

But most private broadcasters grumpily swallowed the pill of Canadian content so they could load the heart of prime time with profitable American shows. It was the cost of doing business.

In some ways, at least initially, the BBG was more restrictive in its other regulations than the CBC had ever been, as Finlay MacDonald and Murray Brown had warned would happen. In the first few months, the BBG summoned seven station managers to show why their licences should be renewed. Renewal had been largely automatic with the CBC as regulator. Nobody's licence was cancelled by the BBG, but the summons sent a chill through the industry. Shortly afterwards, the BBG toughened the language in regulations on advertising and news, sports, and political programming. Stewart even mused aloud at the possibility of the BBG imposing fines on stations that violated its regulations as an interim step before a licence suspension. The CAB protested, saying it would be "tremendously unwieldy" and urging a return to the softer wording in the old CBC rules. The idea of imposing fines was dropped. It came back in 1964, however, when the BBG began to impose small fines, some as low as $25, on stations that ignored advertising limit regulations.

The CBC was also uneasy with the BBG. Alphonse Ouimet said it was designed to "cut the CBC down to size," and he anticipated what he called "a platonic enmity." In fact, he found Stewart less troublesome than he had feared, and Stewart sympathized with Ouimet's problems with Diefenbaker, who viscerally disliked Ouimet and froze his salary for five years.

But Ouimet's biggest problems came from inside the CBC, not from the BBG. First was a long, lacerating producers' strike at the CBC French network in 1959 in the middle of which Ouimet had a heart attack. "The strike," Ouimet said, "placed corporate management in a bad light in the eyes of a new and already hostile government." He was still recovering when a scandal blew up over the cancellation of a popular five-minute morning public affairs radio program, *Preview Commentary*, a cancellation blamed by the producers on interference from Diefenbaker and Nowlan, who felt the CBC was trying to embarrass the government through the program. After a blow-up in the press and a nasty House of Commons debate, the CBC reversed itself and restored the program, infuriating Diefenbaker. A parliamentary committee said it found no evidence of political interference in the program by the Conservative government, and it lashed out at CBC management for being "weak and in need of thorough revision." A royal commission was soon established to look into government agencies, and it concluded that the CBC was poorly managed. "Clean up your act," Nowlan told Ouimet.

"The CBC has been stopped in its tracks," editorialized the *Canadian Broadcaster*. "Its spendings are to be curbed; its monopoly in the TV production field is to be broken; and then, of course, second TV stations are finally on the way." The magazine said the CBC had to reduce services such as news, sports, serious music, drama, and public affairs, and these could readily be picked up by private stations. "The beginning of a new era in broadcasting," it trumpeted. It was a theme Conservative politicians repeated over the next few years as they tried to enhance private broadcasting and curtail the CBC.

Having won the battle to remove regulatory power from the CBC, Jim Allard and his CAB colleagues now set out to diminish the CBC further by restricting its expansion into television and reducing its advertising revenues. The CAB's proposals, advanced in speeches, conferences, boardrooms, backrooms, and corporate corridors, ranged from selling the CBC to private interests, making CBC a subsidized production house for cultural programs, getting CBC out of advertising altogether or out of news programming. Pleas were made, too, to loosen the CBC's ties to its private affiliates by letting them hook up with other networks on occasion.

The CAB also wanted the affiliates to be paid a larger share of network advertising revenues and for the CBC to stop forcing them to carry arts programs – "ratings killers," they said – and put on mass appeal programs that would be more attractive to advertisers. In essence, they felt private broadcasters should give the public what they believed it wants while the public broadcaster should give the public what it needs in the way of culture, documentaries, serious drama, music, and other "do-goodery." But this, they said, should not have to be carried by the CBC's private affiliates.

"At long last, the futility of state broadcasting has to be admitted," said the *Canadian Broadcaster*. "Can there be any doubt that the CBC operation has to be curtailed? . . . There is no further useful function to be performed by the CBC in the work of actual broadcasting."

Irked by many of the new BBG rules, private broadcasters demanded the elimination of all government-imposed regulations, or as many as possible. "Do-it-yourself regulation" was their battle cry. Broadcasting was more regulated than any other business in Canada, they claimed. Don Jamieson told TV executives in a Toronto speech that there was a "dire need" for a complete reappraisal and overhaul of all broadcast regulations, and he warned against do-gooders forcing élitist programs on Canadians. Former CAB president Finlay MacDonald, however, thought that broadcast regulations were necessary because, he said, "it was a farce to say that the broadcasting industry could ever regulate itself. The name of the game was profit."

Jamieson urged the privatization of the CBC and said private stations could do anything the CBC was doing and do it better. He also attacked the critics of private broadcasters, saying, "Unfairly . . . the impression is widespread that most [private broadcasters] would sell Canada down the river for an easy dollar." Nevertheless, he agreed with *Canadian Broadcaster* editor Richard Lewis that the private broadcasters' lust for money was better than the CBC's lust for power.

Eugene Forsey flatly disagreed. Broadcasting was "falling under the tyranny of the advertiser," he said. "To get rid of the CBC and turn our broadcasting over to this collection of gentlemen fills me with horror. . . . We would get American tripe dished up to us morning, noon and night."

Amid all the controversy, some of the key radio pioneers left the scene. Four veterans of the broadcasting war of the previous quarter-century died in 1959. Most notably, Harry Sedgwick, who had been the inspiration and outspoken leader of private broadcasters and head of the CAB for a dozen years, died at age sixty-four. "He led the [CAB]," said the *Canadian Broadcaster*, "through the period when its meetings consisted of a few men gathered in a back room, until it had become one of the most powerful trade associations in existence."

Another pioneer who died in 1959 was Harold Carson, the most powerful broadcaster in Western Canada. Other industry veterans who died that year were A. A. "Pappy" Murphy of CFQC Saskatoon and "Tiny" Elphicke of CKWX Vancouver, regarded by many of his CAB colleagues as one of the greatest of all Canadian broadcasters.

Private broadcasting regained an old friend the same year, when the "lovable rascal" Ernie Bushnell resigned from the CBC and went back to private broadcasting after nearly a quarter-century as a senior public broadcasting executive. "Finally . . . you came back to where you belonged, in private broadcasting," wrote Richard Lewis.

"Bush" was exhausted from the internal and external CBC battles and weakened by alcoholism, but he rejuvenated himself by planning a private TV station in Ottawa. He also spoke out, as he had thirty years before when, as a private broadcaster, he had been battling against the idea of public broadcasting as conceived by the Aird commission. In a speech to a broadcasters convention in Toronto, Bushnell said that supporters of public broadcasting were "clamouring for more and more state control and more and more regulations and regimentation. . . . Some of those who yell the loudest about the evils of private broadcasting are determined to get their hands on this electronic influencer of people's minds to control it and operate it for their own benefit, their own aggrandizement, for their profit in terms of impregnating society with their theories and their doctrines."

It was the message that Jim Allard and Walter Dales had been preaching for decades. In a later comment, Bushnell attacked what he called the élitist snobbery toward private broadcasters. "For forty years," he said, "government, its regulating bodies, and royal commissions have for the most part looked down their nose at private broadcasters as if they were trespassers or burglars or both."

But one of those government bodies, the BBG, gave Bushnell a new lease on life when he was granted permission for the Ottawa TV station, one of a number in a new round of licence granting launched by the Conservative government. In midsummer 1959, George Nowlan had announced that hearings would be held by the BBG for licences for second TV stations in bigger cities, such as Toronto, Vancouver, Ottawa, and Montreal, and four other places.

Anticipating extraordinary profits, broadcasters and their investors had scrambled to impress the BBG with glowing promises of cultural programs, community service, public responsibility, handsome spending on local talent, and detailed business plans forecasting initial losses but comfortable profits after a couple of years. As it turned out, the actual programming offered by the new stations after they got their licences bore little resemblance to what was promised at the hearings.

Bushnell won the licence competition in Ottawa, and in Winnipeg, another old-time radio operator, Lloyd Moffat of CKY, was given a TV licence. The Siftons, with big radio and newspaper holdings, lost. In Vancouver, a TV producer won a licence, and in Montreal, Canadian Marconi, which had given Canada its first radio station in 1919, got the second Montreal TV licence. Finlay MacDonald, Nowlan's old friend, won the Halifax licence, and radio pioneer Gordon Love, who ran Calgary's CFCN, also nabbed one. One surprise was the BBG award of the second Edmonton TV station to the CBC. "I was the most surprised man in the world when that happened," Nowlan said. Dick Rice, the founder and owner of Edmonton's CFRN, a CBC affiliate, was not too upset, however, because his station became independent. He thought it might make more money now that he no longer had to carry the CBC's prime-time schedule.

The Diefenbaker government, however, bent on reducing the CBC's role, was decidedly grumpy about the BBG's decision to give the Edmonton station to the CBC. Liberal broadcast critic Jack Pickersgill also complained that a CBC station in Edmonton was an "unnecessary waste of taxpayers' money." Many private broadcasters also protested the award to the CBC for being, as the *Canadian Broadcaster* noted, "a dangerous precedent."

The government tried to have the BBG reverse its decision, but when the board refused, the government acquiesced. A couple of years later, after much argument, the CBC won BBG approval for a TV licence in Quebec City, beating out a private broadcaster and again setting off complaints from Conservatives and some private stations and alarming idealogues like Richard Lewis, Walter Dales, and Jim Allard.

By far the most intense competition for a new TV licence occurred in Toronto, the most lucrative market in the country and the headquarters of Canada's advertising world. There were nine applicants, including all three Toronto daily newspapers, CFRB, Jack Kent Cooke, and Maclean-Hunter. The others were former CBC program director Stuart Griffiths, Spence Caldwell, who ran a TV syndicated film agency, and Henry Borden, representing, among others, Southam Press. All applicants promised extensive Canadian content (with Cooke, of all people, offering 64 per cent), with a heavy emphasis on culture and arts programs, including a ninety-minute drama each week. Questioned as to whether he could make a profit with all that Canadian programming, Cooke said, "I think it will be a rich plum."

The most dramatic presentation was made by the buccaneer Toronto *Telegram* publisher John Bassett, a dashing Second World War major and wounded hero. With his deep-voiced exuberance and abundant self-confidence, he could charm the pants off the devil himself. His professional ambition was driven by a ravenous desire to succeed. "He wanted to prove himself to his father and prove to Mr. Eaton, who backed him financially, that he could do something other than be flamboyant, and he did," says his son Doug.

Inside the family, Bassett was the patriarch, demanding but generous. "You always went first class with my dad," says Doug. "But I'm not sure he really understood Christmas, for example, as a family affair, opening presents together. He wouldn't stay up at night and put the electric train together or decorate the Christmas tree. But almost every Christmas he would have an old soldier from Sunnybrook Hospital down to our house for Christmas dinner."

The present he had for the BBG was a dazzling, slick film that bowled over his audience, although it got off to a rocky start when a Bassett associate, a young Ted Rogers, pushed the start button for the film. "It blew every fuse in the joint," Rogers recalled. But after five minutes of Bassett's ad lib jokes and enthusiasm, the lights came back and the show went on.

In setting up Baton Broadcasting, as he called his new venture, Bassett had surrounded himself with big-name talent, including Foster Hewitt, who would be a vice-president of Bassett's CFTO (which stood for Canada's Finest, Toronto's Own), announcer Joel Aldred, who would be president of the station, financial angel John David Eaton, as well as Ted Rogers, who was the son of a radio pioneer of the same name, and producer and performer Rai Purdy, who had been assigned by Roy Thomson to help Bassett. Thomson had been an early partner with Bassett in the CFTO application, but he withdrew when he learned that, because of his extensive media ownership, if he were a partner, Bassett would have no chance of getting the licence.

In the half-hour film shown to the BBG, a mock newscast featured snow crews clearing that day's snow, a highlight from a recent BBG hearing showing the board members in action, and previews of children's, cooking, religious, and music shows, a regular report from Ottawa, and sports programming, which would include broadcasting the Toronto Maple Leafs hockey games on Wednesday nights. The programming promised to be 61 per cent Canadian and would include productions of Shakespeare, opera, ballet, symphonies, big-time variety shows, and dramas five times a week. Bassett also promised some French-language programs, which he described in French, speaking of his love of the French language and culture. Twenty seven per cent of his station's gross revenue, he said, would be spent on Canadian writers, actors, musicians, and performers. All this was reported in great detail in Bassett's Toronto *Telegram*, which, noting support from several religious leaders, headlined one story, "CARDINAL, BISHOP, RABBI SUPPORT TV STATION BID." It was a bravura performance with hardly a word about any American programs.

Nobody had as sleek and persuasive a presentation as Bassett, who at six foot, four inches was the tallest man at the hearings and known to his colleagues as "Big John." But there were rumours that "the fix was in," arising from Bassett's ardent support for the Diefenbaker government and that of his associates, most of whom had worked hard for Diefenbaker's election victory. As well, Joel Aldred was a close friend of Diefenbaker. And, as he so often did, Bassett went too far in privately boasting that he had the licence "in the bag" and that it was "a piece of cake, baby!" With a knowing smile and his blue eyes twinkling with mischief, Bassett told a fellow applicant, writer, and performer, Mavor Moore, "I have been promised the licence by John Diefenbaker and George Hees." Hees later said he had been "very helpful" to Bassett in getting the licence for Baton.

"If only he would shut his fucking mouth!" Bassett's lawyer, Eddie Goodman, told Finlay MacDonald. "We've got it now. It's a better brief." "There is no question Bassett had the better brief," Finlay MacDonald says. "All he was doing was shooting off his mouth."

Later, according to Toronto *Telegram* Ottawa reporter Peter Dempson, Diefenbaker often said privately that he had been responsible for Bassett getting the licence. He may have said this, however, to keep Bassett indebted to the Conservative party. Bassett twice ran for the Tories and lost, and Diefenbaker had asked him to consider being ambassador to John Kennedy's Washington. Although he was a friend of the Kennedys, Bassett turned down the job on the advice of his godfather, Lord Beaverbrook.

Politics and friendship, however, likely played little roles in the BBG's decision to grant Bassett the TV licence, and even Eugene Forsey defended the award. Stewart, however, disagreed with the majority of his BBG colleagues and voted against the motion, because, as he later explained, "I felt that the owner of a newspaper in a metropolitan centre should not also own a television station."

Within a few months after CFTO was launched on January 1, 1961, Bassett found losses piling up because of high spending on programs and facilities. He wasn't the only one. Most of the new stations lost money – about $5 million in total for their first year. It would be a couple of years before most of them showed a profit. Faced with the CFTO losses, Bassett fired Joel Aldred, ordered a cutback in spending, and much of the Canadian programming fell by the wayside. Bassett brought in a U.S. network, the American Broadcasting Company (ABC), for 25 per cent of the station's equity (the maximum allowed by the Broadcasting Act) and $2 million in cash. After the BBG first approved the deal and then, under pressure, reversed itself, Bassett negotiated a new arrangement with ABC for a loan of a reported $2.5 million.

The pressure to reject any CFTO deal with ABC came, in part, from private broadcasting's old adversary, Graham Spry. He wrote to Diefenbaker, charging that TV stations in Vancouver, Kitchener, Windsor, Pembroke, Ottawa, Montreal, Quebec City, Halifax, and now Toronto all had American or British involvement. Professor Arthur Lower, president of the Royal Society at the time and another old adversary of private broadcasting, wrote a steaming letter to the prime minister. "Men who are willing to sell out and those who are parties to selling out are little better than traitors to their country," he said.

An inevitable result of the new second stations was a reduction in the size of the CBC's audience and a consequent reduction in its impact on the country. This, of course, was exactly what the Diefenbaker government and the private stations had intended. In 1961–62, the CBC also lost $10 million to $12 million in advertising to the new competition. On top of that, the government imposed a general budget cut that further reduced CBC spending plans.

All this, in turn, encouraged the CBC to chase advertising revenue more aggressively and to give greater prominence in prime time to commercially attractive shows. "The CBC is studiously selling out its original purpose," declared the *Canadian Broadcaster*. Ads and ratings dominate the CBC at the expense of private stations, it wrote. "All this is in direct contradiction to their original raison d'être. It can all be accomplished by private stations at no cost to the public." "CBC has been compelled to dilute its serious programs," *Canadian Broadcaster* editor Richard Lewis charged, "in order to attract an audience which will be numerically interesting to advertisers."

Eugene Forsey, normally Lewis' philosophical arch enemy, agreed. "The CBC is under constant attack, constant pressures to go more commercial, which means almost certainly less and less Canadian [programs]," he said. The government and private stations argued that they were not deliberately trying to damage the CBC, just giving Canadians more choice in their TV viewing.

A cornerstone of public policy for the previous three decades had been that to sustain its primacy in Canadian broadcasting, only the public broadcaster could have permanent national networks. Private broadcasters had resented this policy, pointing to it as an example of the CBC's dictatorial powers. They argued that a private network would allow them to share production expenses and therefore to produce cost-effective Canadian programming. The CBC had prevented any private national radio network, but Diefenbaker wanted to change that for television, and so did the BBG. "We have been in a sense promoting this," a BBG official was quoted as saying. The board and Diefenbaker wanted a second network in place as quickly as possible.

Spence Caldwell, who started in broadcasting in the 1920s, was the originator and first president of the CTV network, which began in October 1961. He was soon overwhelmed by infighting among the network's owners and resigned in 1965. (*Courtesy CAB*)

Pierre Juneau (*left*), chair of the CRTC, and Jim Allard (*right*), head of the CAB, were bitter enemies. Allard ferociously rejected Juneau's ideas on Canadian programming. (*Courtesy CAB*)

Jack Pickersgill (*left*), a Liberal backroom power-broker from the late 1930s to the 1950s and a senior cabinet minister in the 1960s and 1970s, and his ally, Don Jamieson (*right*), CAB president and, later, a Liberal cabinet minister. (*Courtesy CAB*)

In 1958, Dr. Andrew Stewart was named by Prime Minister John Diefenbaker as chairman of the Board of Broadcast Governors. (*Courtesy CAB*)

Iconoclastic commentator
Gordon Sinclair (*left*)
and *Toronto Star* writer
Greg Clark (*right*), a long-time
friend of Sinclair's, on a CFRB
Toronto talk program.
(*Courtesy Rogers
Communications Inc.*)

The king of phone-in radio,
Jack Webster, dominated the
Vancouver airwaves with
the bombastic but well-
informed style that he brought
to radio in the 1950s and 1960s
and later transferred to television.
(*Courtesy CAB*)

Arguments erupted when Charles Templeton (*left*) got together before a
microphone with Pierre Berton (*right*) in their daily talk show on
Toronto's CKEY. (*Courtesy CAB*)

Being honoured for bringing radio to Canadians are the broadcast pioneers (*left to right*): Lyman Potts, who started at CKCK Regina in the early 1930s at five dollars a week; Murray Brown of CFPL London, one-time chair of the CAB; Ralph Snelgrove of CKBB and CKVR-TV Barrie; and Conrad Lavigne of CFCL-TV Timmins, who gave up running a butcher shop to start a television station. (*Courtesy CAB*)

As the network's third president, Murray Chercover built CTV into a major presence but faced endless and vicious boardroom battles among the stations that owned the network. (*Courtesy CAB*)

Ted Rogers, the "king of cable," describes himself as "impatient . . . innovative . . . and not modest." (*Courtesy Rogers Communications Inc.*)

The boat-rocking, McLuhanistic Moses Znaimer of CITY-TV set Canadian television on its ear with his ideas of television with an attitude. (*Courtesy CITY-TV*)

"Big John" Bassett towered over Canada's broadcast scene for nearly three decades starting in the 1960s. A Second World War hero, Bassett was arguably the most colourful and controversial character in Canadian broadcasting of his time. (*Courtesy Douglas Bassett*)

Douglas Bassett succeeded his father in running CFTO-TV Toronto, and while not as flamboyant a character, he was even more aggressive in wanting to control CTV. (*Courtesy Douglas Bassett*)

A tornado in pants, Izzy Asper has stormed through boardrooms, courts, and corporate battlefields to establish CanWest Global as a multimedia giant. (*Courtesy* CAB)

CBC president Robert Rabinovitch has tried to bring new life to a beleaguered CBC at the turn of the century. (*Courtesy* CBC)

Seen here in a party mood in the late 1990s are CRTC chair Françoise Bertrand and CAB president Michael McCabe. (*Courtesy CAB*)

Two former CBC executives now running CTV: Ivan Fecan, president of Bell GlobeMedia (the parent of CTV), and Trina McQueen, president of CTV. (*Fred Chartrand, CP Picture Archive*)

Newfoundland Conservative MP J. A. McGrath, a long-time adversary of the CBC, told the House of Commons, "We now have second television stations in major cities, and there is the possibility of a second network which takes the exclusive national service away from the CBC; in other words, there are other people who are now capable of providing a national service . . . with no cost to the taxpayer." Even Liberal broadcast critic Jack Pickersgill had warmed to the idea, telling the House of Commons, "I think it is a very sensible thing to have a private network."

In the summer of 1960, the Independent Television Organization (ITO) was formed by the private second stations to buy, sell, and exchange programs. They did not want to establish an electronically connected network, at least not yet. At the same time, fifty-one-year-old Spence Caldwell, who had lost out at the second Toronto TV station hearings, was developing his own plans for a second network. In fact, within hours of hearing he'd lost his Toronto application, Caldwell was preparing an application for a network.

Caldwell was one of the originals of Canadian broadcasting. At high school in Winnipeg just after the First World War, he won first prize for students under sixteen for originality in producing a crystal set in a walnut shell. Later, he developed a special crystal set from a cigar box and worked with the original stations set up by the *Winnipeg Free Press* and the *Winnipeg Tribune* before going to work for Marconi. In 1944, he became the first manager of the CBC's Dominion radio network.

The BBG encouraged Caldwell in his bid for the CTV network, even though there was hesitation among many of the private stations who wanted to run their own network. Stewart backed Caldwell in part because he feared that John Bassett of CFTO would otherwise dominate any private network.

After lengthy and tense negotiations, Caldwell persuaded eight stations to take his CTV network programming: Halifax, Montreal, Ottawa, Toronto, Winnipeg, Calgary, Edmonton, and Vancouver, and in April 1961, the BBG approved the CTV network. At the same time, the stations kept alive their own ITO to buy programs, mostly from the United States, and to act as an ever-present alternative and threat to Caldwell.

As the godfather of CTV, Stewart declared on its opening night in October 1961 that it was "another tie binding Canada together." Boasting of the network's programming, Caldwell told a reporter, "We intend to prove that private enterprise can provide better entertainment than the government . . . without costing the taxpayers a cent."

During the first year, in its eight hours or so of programming a week, CTV carried three game shows (earning the nickname "The Game Show Network"), a couple of westerns, two crime shows, a barn dance, and sports programs. In contrast to the second station applicants, who had made extravagant promises about Canadian public service and cultural programs, Caldwell hadn't promised much about this, and planned to spend as little on programming as he could manage. "He produced everything as cheaply as possible," recalls Finlay MacDonald. Michael Hind-Smith, CTV's first program director, says, "We were spending around $2,500 to $3,000 on a half-hour show which wouldn't have bought the coffee on an American network production." At the time CTV was launched, Hind-Smith promised that CTV programs would be "lighter, easier to watch . . . a much more popular schedule."

"This is going to be commercial TV, an advertisers' network," the cigar-chewing Caldwell declared. "We'll carry no unsponsorable programs except for occasional public service specials . . . I think we'll make millions some day." Irrepressible and ever confident of his sales talent, Caldwell said, "I can sell programs like hotcakes." His motto was, "Nothing ever happens until someone sells something to somebody."

Caldwell's first big battle with the CBC was over coverage of the 1962 Grey Cup football championship. Together, Caldwell and John Bassett of Baton had outbid the CBC for rights to the game, but they asked the CBC to carry it as well because sponsors wanted wider coverage than CTV could provide with its small number of stations. In effect, it was an attempt to kidnap the CBC affiliates. The CBC rejected the CTV proposal. The BBG then directed the CBC to carry the CTV coverage of the game, complete with commercials. It was a directive that sprang from the BBG's support for the idea of "cross programming," in which CTV programs would be carried by the CBC private affiliated stations, thereby reaching a wider audience and producing more ad revenue. The CBC felt strongly that would weaken its control of the public network and refused to obey the BBG's directive. Eventually a deal was struck, and the CBC network carried the game, minus commercials, but with brief mentions of the sponsors' names.

With worrisome losses in his first year of business, Caldwell became increasingly shrill about BBG regulations. Even at his licence hearings,

Caldwell had warned, "I hope the Board is not going to bring about a private network in Canada and then regulate it so that it cannot function. This is a private, profit-making network – this is one of the things we do, to make money, not to bring the symphony to the people of Canada."

Noting the differences between the CBC and CTV, Alphonse Ouimet said, "The CBC is an instrument of national purpose; the CTV of commercial purpose."

The BBG had ordered CTV to carry a minimum of ten hours of programming a week in its first year, but Caldwell could manage only about eight, and the BBG had to grant him extra time to reach his commitment. (Early in its second year, CTV expanded to fourteen hours, including a nightly newscast, and reached twenty-four hours a week by the end of the year.) But Caldwell wanted much more from the BBG in the way of concessions. He requested the board help CTV by relaxing some of its advertising regulations and the Canadian content rules. He asked that CBC affiliates be encouraged to disaffiliate and join CTV. That would give CTV a bigger audience and thus more ad revenue. He complained about the amount of advertising CBC was carrying and said CBC was unfairly outbidding him for Hollywood programs.

The BBG provided some relief, moderately diluting the Canadian content regulations, easing some advertising rules, and allowing CBC affiliates to disaffiliate provided viewers in the station area could still receive CBC programs from another source. CBC supporters felt the BBG was being overly protective of CTV.

The CBC, Alphonse Ouimet said, should complement, not compete, with the second stations and CTV. "The CBC does not plan to enter into canned program competition," he said, "where western is matched by western and quiz by quiz." Still, Ouimet felt the CBC had to have programming that would maintain 40 to 50 per cent of the viewers in order to sustain its political support. Pressure to retain audience also came from the CBC's private affiliates, who constantly pushed it to program more popular shows. They said they wanted less "dictatorship" by the CBC in its placement of "mandate" programs in the schedule they had to carry. In face of the competition from CTV and U.S. networks and the need for advertising revenue, the CBC didn't quite match its competitors "quiz by quiz," but its programs did change.

The 1959, 1960, and 1961 parliamentary broadcasting committees, dominated by the Conservatives, repeatedly criticized the CBC, echoing the CAB's arguments against the public broadcaster both philosophically and in specific program terms. The CBC's programs, they claimed, were too left wing, subversive, and pornographic. Conservative MP Art Smith of Calgary denounced the quality of CBC programs, and said the private stations did a better job.

There were accusations that the CBC was overstaffed with high-priced incompetents and that the French network was filled with subversives and separatists. There was also intensive financial nitpicking by Conservatives on how the CBC spent its money, so much so that the Liberals and NDP accused Conservatives of trying to micro-manage the public broadcaster.

Key Diefenbaker adviser Allister Grosart said, "Something will have to be done about the CBC." It was a subject that came up privately among Conservative poo-bahs, many of whom, including Diefenbaker and a number of his cabinet members, gathered informally from time to time at parties in Jim Allard's Ottawa home. The cabinet, at one point, considered naming a special committee to investigate CBC programming, which several ministers felt was trying to discredit the government. Nothing was done about it, in part because George Nowlan, as he had done several times before, warded off what he felt were excessively harsh proposals regarding the CBC.

The attacks on public broadcasting alarmed the CBC's supporters. Graham Spry warned in a letter to Eugene Forsey of "letting the CBC be slaughtered by its enemies in the Parliamentary Committee." In a letter to a colleague, he fumed, "House of Commons Committees are ignorant, partisan and incompetent." CCF MP Douglas Fisher said, "I believe the government wants to destroy the CBC as a public corporation . . . in other words, wipe it out." He talked of "the niggling, nasty desire among Conservatives to junk the CBC."

"We are shocked," said the Canadian Labour Congress, "at the obviously deliberate efforts being made to undermine . . . if not destroy the CBC . . . because [private broadcasters] see in a much weaker CBC more chance of making profit." Ernie Bushnell snapped back that the statement was "the biggest heap of verbal garbage I have ever seen." Besides, he asked, "Why are broadcasters to be held up to scorn and ridicule because they have made a good profit?"

The debate encouraged private station operators to keep up their assault on broadcasting regulations. In a speech to Toronto radio and

TV executives, Clifford Sifton said free citizens were entitled to listen to programs unaffected by regulations and that broadcasters should have the same freedoms as newspapers. "Interference with programming can easily reduce broadcasters to a place where they must choose between subservience to the government or going out of broadcasting," he said.

When Don Jamieson was elected CAB president in 1961, he brought a new vitality to the group's lobbying and opened a direct avenue into the Liberal party hierarchy. He would remain CAB president for an eventful four years until politics became his principal passion. No broadcaster, except possibly for Harry Sedgwick in the 1930s and 1940s, worked harder and longer for the cause than Don Jamieson. "We must tell and sell our side of the story," he said repeatedly.

The debate and the growing power of private stations led CBC president Alphonse Ouimet to urge a major review of the industry, somewhat akin to the Massey commission or the Fowler commission and with, he hoped, the same sentiments. By this time, BBG chairman Andrew Stewart was also looking longingly at a new government examination of broadcasting to clarify the confusion in the industry. Jamieson, however, was doubtful. "Another Royal Commission, with its usual entourage of pressure groups and screwballs, could end in chaos," he said. He recommended a smaller study, perhaps guided by the BBG.

While the broadcast debate swirled with gale force, an even greater storm faced John Diefenbaker. The Conservatives had been re-elected with a fragile minority in 1962 and now faced another, much tougher election in the spring of 1963. Internal backstabbing, and his own disorganized, quixotic style of running the government, pushed Diefenbaker over the brink of political disaster. His government collapsed and voters threw him and his party out of power. Lester Pearson, a long-time supporter of the CBC and believer in the Aird, Massey, and Fowler reports, became the new Liberal prime minister. He felt private broadcasting should be secondary to the public system. Moreover, Pearson admired Alphonse Ouimet, had been a close friend of Graham Spry since their days at Oxford in the early 1920s, had had a high regard for Alan Plaunt, and had seriously considered accepting a job offer as head of CBC public relations when the public broadcaster was established in 1936.

Pearson's attitude was, as he later said, "that broadcasting should be treated as education and that there should be the greatest possible public control; that the emphasis should be on the public system and private broadcasting should be very much a subsidiary."

Suddenly with Pearson's election, everything the private broadcasters had won in the Diefenbaker years in taking primacy in Canadian broadcasting away from the CBC was endangered. Even if they had only a minority government, would the Liberals reverse Diefenbaker's radio-TV revolution? It was a nightmare possibility for private broadcasters.

9

Wooing the Liberals

"**T**hey have been getting away with murder!" That was Graham Spry's war cry as he condemned private broadcasting and demanded that the new Liberal government "re-assert the primacy of the CBC! . . . Restore the CBC to its proper position in the life of Canada!"

Private broadcasters shuddered at the prospect. CAB president Don Jamieson was so worried he sought help from CTV's Spence Caldwell in undercutting the influence of Spry's Broadcasting League. In a letter to Caldwell, he suggested, "You might be able to have some of your newspaper friends in Toronto go to work on this organization. . . . If it were possible to have some disinterested medium take the League apart this would be far more effective than anything that we could do directly ourselves."

Caldwell proposed that the CAB join the league and destroy it from within, and he and Jim Allard discussed "Trojan Horse tactics" and planting spies within the league, which he labelled "the enemy."

Alphonse Ouimet, on the other hand, was in seventh heaven, looking forward to an enhanced CBC. Soon after Pearson came to power not only was the freeze Diefenbaker had placed on Ouimet's salary removed, but his pay was doubled to $40,000. He also was given back the role of CBC board chairman in addition to his role as president, replacing R. L. Dunsmore, whose appointment by Diefenbaker was declared invalid by the Liberals.

But the indefatigable spokesman for the private broadcasters, Jim Allard, had a secret weapon in the battle against the CBC in the form of his friends Jack Pickersgill and Don Jamieson. Pickersgill was Lester Pearson's closest political adviser and Jamieson, president of the CAB, had close connections to the Liberals, and political ambitions of his own.

"I'm not happy that Jack Pickersgill will be responsible for the CBC and BBG," Spry wrote to Eugene Forsey after Pearson had named Pickersgill as the minister responsible for broadcasting. "His political future in a large measure depends on Don Jamieson." Forsey agreed, saying that he "was most uneasy about Pickersgill, especially in combination with Jamieson; both as clever as paint and neither to be trusted farther than you can kick them." Nor was Andrew Stewart entirely comfortable with Pickersgill. "I had some difficulty in following his sharp, mercurial and, as I occasionally thought, devious mind," he said later.

In 1955, Pickersgill, whose Newfoundland political godfather was Jamieson, had been instrumental in persuading the Liberal cabinet to reject a CBC-TV station in St. John's in favour of one owned by Jamieson and Geoff Stirling. He had also torpedoed CBC requests at the time for stations in Fredericton, Regina, and Saskatoon and had bitterly opposed the granting of a TV licence to the CBC for a station in Edmonton. Now, just as the Liberals came back to power, the BBG recommended that in addition to the Jamieson-Stirling TV station, St. John's should have a CBC station. Pickersgill agreed, but reluctantly. CBC-TV stations in Vancouver, Winnipeg, Toronto, Ottawa, Montreal, and Halifax, he said, were enough to produce a national service and "all the rest of this field should be left to private enterprise."

At the root of Pickersgill's actions to forestall CBC expansion was his doubt about the value of public broadcasting. In effect, he had adopted the old C. D. Howe arguments in favour of private broadcasting.

There was no one Pickersgill listened to more carefully on broadcasting policy than Don Jamieson. "Jamieson and Stirling were quite powerful in Liberal circles. They were big players," says CAB president Michael McCabe, who at the time was a key Liberal party official, executive assistant to Finance Minister Mitchell Sharp, and assistant deputy minister of Consumer and Corporate Affairs. "I used to sit on the Liberal party communications committee for elections and they were big players on that," McCabe says. "They were turned to as the people who understood communications."

As the energetic CAB president, Jamieson made it abundantly clear in speech upon speech across the country that he believed in a minimally regulated private broadcasting system, with the CBC playing a minor, supplementary role as a supplier of cultural programs to private stations. Unlike Lester Pearson, he believed broadcasting was primarily for entertainment, not for education, and best done by private enterprise.

He felt the CBC was a "potential threat to our free society," especially in its journalistic programming. The CBC, he said, could not be trusted on political stories. He strongly endorsed the idea that private broadcasters had serious responsibilities to the public but added, "Those who look to state control of radio and television as the means to bring about profound changes in our society have misread the symptoms and are prescribing the wrong cure." He thought that regulations were a "millstone" around the industry's neck. Jamieson preferred self-regulation. "We should look at government tribunals and such bodies with mistrust," he declared. "We should view every action of the BBG with mistrust because it is only in this way we can remain sharp in our analysis of what is going on."

Warning against the idea of a public broadcasting system as envisioned by Sir John Aird and set out in the 1932 and 1936 broadcast legislation, Jamieson said, "Hitler was using just such a monopoly to prostitute radio to the basest needs of his regime." Presumably with Graham Spry and Alan Plaunt in mind, Jamieson raged against "well-meaning moralists," "missionaries," "crusaders," and the "well-intentioned" who promote public broadcasting. The Fowler report, Jamieson felt, was "most unfair and biased" and filled with "naive and idealistic nonsense."

Jamieson could be, CCF broadcasting critic Doug Fisher said, "as brutally frank as any old robber baron and as piously high-minded as an archbishop."

Pickersgill and Jamieson were front and centre promoting private broadcasting, and Jim Allard knew he also had widespread but quieter support throughout the Liberal party, even if Pearson was not onside. The National Liberal Council and Young Liberal organizations in Ontario, British Columbia, and elsewhere had broken with the St. Laurent government's policy a decade earlier by urging a greater role for private broadcasters in the development of television and faster action in establishing private TV. Now the Liberal Council considered private broadcasting to be of equal status with public broadcasting, and a council resolution crafted by Keith Davey talked of the "parallel development" of the two. The idea of an all-powerful CBC with regulatory authority as it had until 1958 was not in their game plan.

Davey said that when the CBC had been the regulator, the situation was "unhappy at best," adding that "it became intolerable with the explosive postwar growth of private broadcasting in Canada." Davey, who worked with Foster Hewitt's Toronto radio station, was a growing power in the Liberal party, and was one of a number of influential Liberals who had roots in private broadcasting, including Baxter Ricard of CHNO Sudbury and Ralph Snelgrove of CKBB Barrie.

In the early days of Pearson's government, Allard and Jamieson's efforts to get local station operators to pressure their MPs in favour of private broadcasting seemed to be paying off. Graham Spry worriedly wrote to Tommy Douglas, "The Members are terrified of saying anything that may upset their local private stations. Private broadcasting, in fact, is the most powerful lobby in recent Canadian history." These were impressive words from a man whose own record made him a clear rival for that title.

Although sensitive to Pearson's philosophical commitment to the CBC, Pickersgill felt he was on safe ground when he announced in the House of Commons within days of the Liberals assuming office that, "It is our position that there should be scope for the parallel development of both public and private initiatives in broadcasting with an impartial agency of control."

That clearly ruled out a return to Mackenzie King's 1936 legislation. "That was an unholy situation," says the CBC's current president, Robert Rabinovitch. "The CBC should never have been both the regulator and a service." Even such a staunch public broadcasting supporter as Ian Morrison, currently head of the Friends of Canadian Broadcasting, says, "The undoing of the dominance of the CBC was good for Canadian society in promoting pluralism and other voices, even though the pendulum may have swung too far off on the private side today." One-time Standard Broadcasting senior executive Ross McCreath says that it would have been impossible to return to the pre-Diefenbaker, CBC regulatory era, especially when Pearson had only a minority government. "They just couldn't go back," he says. "I don't think the Canadian people would have seen it as a smart move by the government."

Pickersgill wanted a new study of Canadian broadcasting and named a "troika" to provide guidance: Andrew Stewart of the BBG, Alphonse Ouimet of the CBC, and Don Jamieson of the CAB, a trio, said Pickersgill, who had "the greatest experience in broadcasting." Experience, yes, but the trio's clashing perspectives also made the troika highly combustible. For private broadcasters, though, the mere presence of the CAB on such an important governmental advisory committee gave them new status and ensured them a key voice in any new broadcast policy. Their new role resulted from Don Jamieson's intensive lobbying, especially his private discussions with Pickersgill.

In a whimsical mood, Andrew Stewart wrote a poem to mark the occasion:

> "The 'Troika' is surely a 'queer'
> Three horses, no lead, no rear,
> A stud CAB
> And a mare CBC
> But the BBG's gelded I fear."

There was nothing whimsical about the troika's deliberations, however. "An exercise in futility," Ouimet told broadcaster and author Frank Peers, complaining that Jamieson was too rigid a defender of private broadcasting objectives. Jamieson felt, with some justification, that Ouimet wanted the BBG to regulate the private industry and leave the CBC on its own. After a year of on-and-off discussion, the troika produced a joint nine-page report, but each of them also produced lengthy individual reports. Jamieson's was by far the longest, and he used it later as the basis of a book that was highly critical of public broadcasting, *The Troubled Air*.

One thing the three did agree on was that there was no longer a single system of broadcasting in Canada. "Virtually meaningless . . . a complete myth . . . highly unrealistic and impractical," said Jamieson, dismissing the policies of prime ministers Bennett, King, and St. Laurent. The troika also agreed that Fowler had been wrong to recommend a single board to regulate both the CBC and private broadcasters.

But they did not agree on much else, and so the government appointed yet another advisory committee, headed by Robert Fowler, who had talked a great deal with Pearson and presumably reflected much of his thinking about the role of private and public broadcasters. Joining Fowler on the advisory committee were Marc Lalonde, a Montreal lawyer, an acquaintance of Pierre Trudeau, and a future Liberal cabinet minister, and Ernest Steele, a deputy minister responsible for cultural affairs. Jim Allard anticipated the new advisory committee with dread, noting that "Communists, for example, have appeared at almost every hearing [in the past] opposing our views."

Allard and Jamieson were furious when the new Fowler committee produced a stunning indictment of private broadcasters, brutally rejecting most of Jamieson's and the CAB's ideas and castigating private station programming. Regarding private TV, it stated, "The systematic mediocrity of [most] programming is deplorable." As for private radio, it reported, "In many cases radio has become a mere machine for playing recordings of popular music with frequent interruptions to carry as much advertising as can be sold." There was far too little Canadian programming in prime time on private TV stations, the report concluded, and far too little paid to Canadian performers and writers. American shows dominated the heart of prime time, and the licensing of more private stations had led to more viewing of American programs.

So what? responded the *Canadian Broadcaster*. "It is not true ... that Canadians want Canadian broadcasting. . . . This is shown clearly by the overwhelming popularity of programs and program material brought in from the United States." Jim Allard thought that Canadians were not influenced by American programming: "It may well be that Canadians need protection from American influence in the industrial area. It is obvious we did not require that protection in the cultural area."

The committee also worried private broadcasters with its recommendation that the CBC should capture 25 to 30 per cent of Canadian TV advertising. But their biggest worry was the recommendation that a single board run broadcasting in Canada, setting regulations for both the CBC and private stations and also overseeing management of the CBC. The new agency would eliminate both the BBG and the CBC board of directors, replacing them with something called the Canadian Broadcasting Authority. In any conflict between public and private broadcasting, the desires of the CBC would prevail. This was much the same approach Fowler had taken in his royal commission report eight years earlier, and it defied the central recommendation of the troika to maintain two boards.

Rubbing salt into the private broadcasters' wounds, the Fowler report noted that a new broadcast law "should make it clear that no one has an automatic right to renewal of a licence." The old bugaboo of expropriation – however unlikely – was back to haunt broadcasters.

The report criticized the CBC for its management, but the broadcasting philosophy it enunciated was a stunning throwback to what private broadcasters considered as the pre-Diefenbaker "bad old days." Fowler, however, viewed it as a last chance to bring back the Aird-Mackenzie King concept of broadcasting in Canada.

Seething with fear and resentment at this possibility, Allard, Jamieson, and private broadcasters across the country lashed back with accusations that what Fowler advocated was "dictatorial," "communism," "repugnant to our sense of democratic freedom," "sinister," "frightening." Looking back on their campaign about ten years later, *Canadian Broadcaster* editor Richard Lewis said, "Robert Fowler was torn apart limb from limb and coast to coast . . . for the dark foreboding clouds this man has cast over the industry." Lewis suggested Fowler had a conflict of interest because he was president of the Canadian Pulp and Paper Association and therefore had a pro-newspaper and anti-broadcast bias. In private, Allard went further, calling Fowler "the kept bastard of the Liberal Party."

Jamieson scoffed at "inexperienced amateurs" meddling with the business of broadcasting. "Unquestionably there are some private broadcasters who are money-grabbing opportunists and fast-buck artists . . . but these are a very small minority," said Jamieson.

In addition to its public anti-Fowler campaign, the CAB privately enlisted its friends in the Liberal party, notably Jack Pickersgill, to dilute or, better still, kill the committee's recommendations. The CAB already had Conservative support, but deep divisions within the party over the issue of Diefenbaker's leadership left it too weak to do much. So the private broadcasters focused on gaining Liberal support.

The CAB said the recommendations were "potentially more dangerous than the system that existed between 1936 and 1958. "The proposed Canadian Broadcasting Authority . . . Chairman would be virtually a broadcasting Czar empowered to determine what Canadians would see and hear from Canadian broadcasting stations." The Fowler proposals, the CAB added, "would seriously damage the ability of Canadian broadcasters to provide programs Canadians . . . want, [would] result in an inferior and less acceptable standard of programming and drive a majority of Canadian listeners and viewers to U.S. stations."

Jean Pouliot, who replaced Jamieson as the association's president, said the system brought in by Diefenbaker "is the best system the Canadian public has yet had." He claimed that the Fowler proposals would be worse than the 1936 legislation because "the Canadian Broadcast Authority would, in addition to the powers of the former CBC Board, have the power of granting and taking away licences." Even the CBC objected to establishing Fowler's single board of broadcast authority, saying, as had the CAB, that it would give "Czar-like powers" to the chairman.

Before Pearson's cabinet could take any action on the Fowler report, another election was held, in late 1965, returning another minority Liberal government. Private broadcasters felt Pearson's lack of a majority in the House would force him to be more prudent in his broadcasting proposals. It also gave more leverage to Don Jamieson, who, in a by-election within a year, joined Pickersgill in the House as a Liberal MP from Newfoundland. The *Canadian Broadcaster* saluted his entry into politics, saying, "No person alive could duplicate the work Don Jamieson has done for the industry."

Sensitive to both the private broadcasters' concerns about the Fowler report and the opposition to it among many Liberals, Pearson was unsure how much of the report he would able to implement.

In the spring of 1966, the cabinet and Pearson's enthusiasm for the CBC was severely tested when a very public explosion occurred over the CBC's public affairs TV program *This Hour Has Seven Days*. CBC management had demanded major changes in the controversial and confrontational program hosted by Patrick Watson and Laurier LaPierre. When the producers refused, verbal barrages were hurled by both sides in public and in emergency parliamentary committee hearings, and Pearson himself got personally involved before the issue was messily resolved with the program's demise.

"[There is] uncertainty and chaos in the affairs of the Canadian Broadcasting Corporation," cried John Diefenbaker in the House of Commons. "Let's stop the rot at the CBC," said the *Montreal Star*. The *Canadian Broadcaster* chimed in with a proposal to have the CBC focus only on "good" programs and "rid the country of the qualities of needless waste, dictatorial thought control and arrogant authoritarianism."

Pearson was fed up with the fiery debate over *Seven Days*, with the CBC in general, and probably with broadcasting overall. At the same time, the newly named secretary of state responsible for broadcasting, Judy LaMarsh, was preparing a white paper on broadcasting. Like Pearson, she was also fed up with the CBC, although her anger was aimed not at the *Seven Days* producers, but at Alphonse Ouimet, whom she despised and held responsible for what she called "rotten management."

Pearson had initially taken a significant role in his government's deliberations on the new broadcasting policy, sitting as chairman of a cabinet committee on the subject. He also addressed the annual CAB meeting in 1967. But his interest waned as time went on, although not fast enough for Judy LaMarsh, who resented what she considered to be Pearson's interference with her responsibilities in developing broadcast policy.

The cabinet committee met with Fowler himself, and with officials of the BBG, CAB, and CBC. Both the CAB and Ouimet reiterated their opposition to the "one board" idea. At the same time, many newspapers ran editorials that were highly critical of the Fowler recommendations, especially those papers that owned radio and television stations.

LaMarsh later said that Pickersgill played a key role in the discussions because he had more experience in the field than any other minister and because he had "many friends in broadcasting and was always highly solicitous of the interests of his friends." Indeed, some ministers nicknamed Pickersgill "the champion of private broadcasting." Don Jamieson, as a new MP, was also talking to various cabinet ministers, and Judy LaMarsh quoted him as saying it was "notorious" that the CBC unfairly outbid private stations for American programs, leaving only "the dogs" for the private stations.

While puzzling over the future of broadcasting policy, Pearson faced charges of political favouritism in an application the BBG had approved in June 1967 to move CKVR Barrie's transmission tower to the Toronto area, a move that would enormously enhance the value of the station. The trouble was the station was owned by Toronto radio operator Allan Waters, an acquaintance of Pickersgill, and two well-known Liberal supporters, Geoff Stirling from Newfoundland and Ralph Snelgrove from Barrie, who had twice been an unsuccessful Liberal candidate in federal elections.

The Conservatives charged that this move to Toronto was Liberal revenge for the granting of the CFTO TV licence to Tory John Bassett in the Diefenbaker era. Diefenbaker himself told the House of Commons, "This deal is so smelly it requires no olfactory excellence in order to understand it. It has got all the appearances of a plan to make millions under cover of secrecy and concealment." Even LaMarsh described the pressure brought to bear on the deal as "underhanded action." "There was certainly political influence from some quarter," she said. "In Cabinet I made my charges against the ministers I felt were involved in this underhanded action. I did not have the proof, however, and those charged heatedly denied it."

BBG chairman Andrew Stewart, who voted against the proposal, said that Pickersgill had phoned him to say that while he did not want to interfere, he hoped the board would "deal kindly" with Stirling, Snelgrove, and Waters. LaMarsh said in her memoirs that the "swarming agents" of the three broadcasters had been vigorously lobbying cabinet. After a political storm, and much embarrassment to the government, cabinet rejected the BBG's approval of the move.

Fowler's proposals were doomed to sink under the weight of Pickersgill's and Jamieson's persuasive talents, the dogged lobbying of the private broadcasters, and the largely negative reactions of the CBC and BBG unless Pearson was willing to fight hard for them. Although philosophically inclined to do so, he had none of Mackenzie King's political skills, and he faced considerable opposition both within the Liberal party and cabinet. He also faced the reality of a minority government, with the Conservative Opposition noisily opposed to Fowler. He would have to spend a great deal of political capital to make a fight of it, and he reluctantly concluded that he would rather invest that capital on other issues.

In the final days of the *Seven Days* controversy, LaMarsh had presented her white paper on broadcast policy. It differed substantially from the thrust of the Fowler report and was shorn of most of the Fowler recommendations and rhetoric. The act that followed largely kept the structure of two boards, one as a more powerful successor to the BBG and one for the CBC.

The new regulatory board would be called the Canadian Radio and Television Commission (CRTC), a tougher, more activist board than the private broadcasters had faced in the BBG. Andrew Stewart would be replaced as chairman by Pierre Juneau, a long-time National Film Board executive. LaMarsh felt Stewart had been too soft in dealing with the private stations. Other members of the new CRTC included former CBC producer Harry Boyle; a Montreal newspaper broadcast columnist; a former special assistant to Pearson; and others who knew far more about radio and TV than the original BBG members had when they were appointed. Juneau was "a new Caesar," said John Diefenbaker, who described the CRTC as "the Star Chamber."

"It was a tremendous difference in style, with the CRTC being much more structured and less friendly than the BBG," says Murray Brown. "The BBG had been quite casual and rather informal."

LaMarsh said the act "tilted" toward public broadcasting, but almost all of the Fowler report's recommendations were gone. "The idea of a Czar of broadcasting is dead!" said CAB president Jean Pouliot. The fire had gone out around the Liberal cabinet table by the time LaMarsh finally presented the proposed act. "Most of the ministers couldn't care less," she later said. "They didn't read it and sat through explanation and discussion with their minds on other things in their own departments."

The fire also had gone out of Graham Spry and his followers, who saw their last, best hope for a return to Aird's principles go down the drain. The original concept of one public broadcasting system for the whole country was now clearly kaput. Never again would there be any doubt that the private sector dominated Canadian airwaves. The cabinet's decision to tinker with, but not fundamentally change, Diefenbaker's downgrading of the CBC a decade earlier was confirmation that henceforth private broadcasters would play the primary role in Canadian radio and television.

The Liberals' new Broadcast Act sailed through the House of Commons and the Senate, where it was introduced by Keith Davey, who said public and private broadcasters would be better off thanks to the act.

Most of the credit for the dramatic change from the heyday of Bennett, King, Spry, and Plaunt goes to the CAB's relentless Jim Allard, as private broadcasting's point man, CFRB's shrewd Harry Sedgwick, the avenging thunder of John Diefenbaker, and the persuasive powers and political agility of Don Jamieson and Jack Pickersgill. It may also have been inevitable.

"Private stations won the battle with the CBC because the Canadian people wanted choice," says Michael Hind-Smith. "They had logic on their side. The politicians were prisoners of that public demand for choice."

But "choice" was little more than a euphemism for American programs, and private broadcasters were poised to exploit the age-old Canadian love affair with Hollywood, reaping big profits and audience share by featuring American programs and Canadian advertising. This outcome was reinforced by three waves of government policy that encouraged private broadcasters: widened privatization; program importation; and fiscal deprivation. Add to that the CBC's predilection for self-mutilation and masterly Ottawa lobbying by the private sector and you have the answer to how private broadcasters retook the high ground in their war with the CBC.

A triumphant Jean Pouliot told a parliamentary committee that the government's broadcast policy "represents the most thoughtful and objective public statement on broadcasting so far produced." From his seat in the House as a new Liberal MP from Newfoundland, Don Jamieson said that the new act was "the best piece of broadcasting legislation we have had. It is far better than any of its predecessors."

These were booming days for private broadcasters, who reaped total profits of $10 million in 1964, $22 million in 1965, and were heading rapidly toward $100 million. They also had four times as many radio and TV stations as the CBC.

While private TV broadcasters may have been happy about their growing profits and influence, they were increasingly unhappy with Spence Caldwell's CTV. They had kept alive the CTV's shadow rival, their own Independent Television Organization (ITO), through which they bought mostly American shows and produced and exchanged some Canadian programs. Don Jamieson was especially happy with ITO because CTV would not pay for a microwave link to Newfoundland, and ITO provided the programming he needed.

By 1965, the stations had decided Caldwell's network wasn't really needed and they injected new life into the ITO. "Gradually, the ITO squeezed and squeezed and squeezed the network," says Michael Hind-Smith, who was CTV program director at the time.

The rivalry between CTV and ITO had led the Fowler committee to castigate the private broadcasters in its report. "A private hassle between two competing groups is going on with little regard for the public interest," it had said. "This unsavoury feud between private interests in Canadian television should somehow be brought to an end."

Fowler had been against the private stations taking over CTV. "They have not shown themselves to be competent or responsible enough," his report read. He was especially uncomfortable with the thought that John Bassett of CFTO Toronto was the power behind ITO and would dominate any new private network, an apprehension shared by BBG chairman Dr. Andrew Stewart.

The eleven stations involved in ITO ignored Fowler and Stewart's concerns and took over CTV in early 1966. Ken Soble from Hamilton proposed a different network to the BBG, but Stewart and his colleagues reluctantly felt that between CTV and Soble, the new CTV was the better option. It would be a cooperative network, owned by the stations, each station having one vote and sharing expenses on the basis of audience size and revenue. This meant, said then CTV president Gordon Keeble, "Bassett had de facto control." The stations raised their network programming from twenty-four hours a week to sixty hours. Prime time, however, remained dominated by American shows such as *The FBI*, *Gunsmoke*, and *Mission Impossible*. Inevitably there were boardroom flare-ups – especially between Bassett and Ray Peters, who represented British Columbia Television (BCTV), which ran CHAN Vancouver – over programming, over which stations would produce what shows, over personalities, and over where the network "anchor" station would be located.

"My dad didn't like Peters," says Bassett's son Doug. "For one thing, John Bassett was tall and Ray Peters was short. Peters was in the West and my dad was in Toronto. . . . The West was always so goldarn jealous of the East, and so was Ray Peters." Reflecting his Toronto-centricity, John Bassett told author Peter C. Newman, "You get out to Western Canada for Christ's sake, you know, Vancouver and all those places, and you're away from the action. This [Toronto] is where it's at." He also was critical of the quality of programs produced at western stations. At one point, Bassett told the CRTC that he didn't want to air inferior programs just "because they're made in the West."

Because of all their troubles with Bassett, Spence Caldwell and Gordon Keeble tried to switch the CTV anchor station from Bassett's Toronto outlet to CHCH Hamilton, owned by Ken Soble. "Caldwell and Keeble tried very hard to set up Soble as the anchor so we could do without Bassett," says Michael Hind-Smith. "But it didn't work out."

Bassett was forever loudly pushing programs he wanted to produce for CTV, and so was Stuart Griffiths of CJOH Ottawa, whom Finlay MacDonald describes as "another arch enemy" of Bassett. Downplaying his power within the CTV board, Bassett said, "I'm just one vote among all the others, but I vote louder." He also argued louder. "Bassett was very difficult," Hind-Smith says. "We had some monumental battles over how much time Bassett was prepared to yield to the network as we built up the network hours. He yielded ground very reluctantly. He also played hardball in terms of getting production into his studios, and he hated the notion that we contracted independent producers. John Bassett was a very overbearing, tough, opinionated person. I recall a lot of very bitter stuff."

"We were eleven prima donnas. . . . What a rattle this was," MacDonald told author Susan Gittins. For the rest of its life as a cooperative into the 1990s, the CTV boardroom was a bullring of big, competing egos, self-interests, and confrontations, which Gittins graphically portrays in her 1999 book *CTV: The Television Wars*. The epic boardroom feuds between Peters and Bassett, and between Peters and his successors in Vancouver and Bassett's son Doug, who succeeded him, were filled with plots and counterplots, secret deals, and obscenity-riddled accusations. "There are a lot of people in the broadcasting business who didn't like me, didn't like me because I was John Bassett's son, and the press was always writing about how loud I was. But the people that counted, respected me," says Doug Bassett. At one point, Jean Pouliot of CFCF Montreal was warned by his doctor not to attend CTV board meetings because they were too dangerous for his health. "It was a circus with the lions in charge," says Tim Kotcheff, CTV news head at the time.

Faced with bedlam during board meetings of the 1960s, with daily yelling phone calls from Bassett, and with CTV's debts piling up, an exhausted Caldwell finally surrendered. "We knew damn well that it was only a matter of time before this thing was going to collapse. . . . It just didn't work and was doomed to failure," says Finlay MacDonald, a CTV director at the time.

Former CBC producer Murray Chercover, who began in broadcasting at age fifteen at CFPA Port Arthur, Ontario, moved over from Bassett's CFTO to run the new CTV, replacing Keeble and firing Hind-Smith. Although he was called "Bassett's man" at first by some station operators,

Chercover, who was used to coping with Bassett's tirades, soon earned high marks from most board members for deflecting Bassett's more pyrotechnical outbursts. He paid a price, however. A long-time pill-popping hypochondriac and heavy smoker, Chercover was in hospital for a triple bypass a couple of months after he finally retired from CTV in 1989. "We never thanked him enough," Finlay MacDonald says.

"Bassett really gave birth to the CTV network," MacDonald says, "if only because he was never inhibited by any knowledge of broadcasting. It was his ego and daring and his sense of nationhood."

MacDonald recalls one confrontation over programming between Ray Peters of Vancouver and Bassett: "Peters said, 'Why in the name of Jesus did we pre-empt shows last night and put on the election in Quebec?' Bassett screamed back, 'Because, you stupid prick, the election in Quebec has a hell of a lot to do with the whole country!'"

A few years later, Bassett was again raging at his fellow broadcasters when they bitterly opposed revised Canadian content regulations from the new CRTC, setting a minimum of 60 per cent Canadian content for TV and 30 per cent for music on radio. "A rampage . . . aimed at the total subjugation of the Canadian broadcast media," declared the *Canadian Broadcaster*. Chercover said the stark economic reality was that the new regulation would "destroy" CTV by costing the network and CTV stations about $15 million a year. At a CRTC session, he complained about "élitists who believe they know better than the Canadian public" what programs they want to watch.

Other private broadcasters trotted out their oft-used epithets about Canadian programming, calling the CRTC content proposals "fascistic," "communistic," "dictatorial," and "isolationist." "No, Virginia, a Canadian is not free to decide what he will watch on television . . . or listen to on radio," wrote the *Broadcaster*. In another editorial, the magazine claimed that "worthwhile" American shows would be replaced by "mediocre" Canadian ones.

In a seven-hour harangue at a 1970 CRTC hearing, the CAB declared that Canadian freedom was endangered by the content proposals because they "abrogated" freedom of speech. Canadian newspapers are not regulated for Canadian content, said the CAB, so why should broadcasting be singled out for such a restriction? Charging that Canadian content regulations would establish a "cultural ghetto," Raymond

Crepault, owner of several Quebec stations, warned, "They hope vaguely to build some kind of wall across the U.S.-Canada border."

Jim Allard claimed that implementing the regulation would be outrageously expensive. "There is no talent in Canada," the then CRTC chairman Pierre Juneau recalls Allard telling him privately. "And when there is talent," Allard added, "they prefer to go to California." The CAB told the CRTC, "It is high time the gut issue was on the table: many Canadians really want and actively seek out U.S. programming." CAB president W. D. McGregor of Kitchener warned Juneau, "What do you want to turn out – quality meat or sausages?" He added that there was no cultural problem about American programs on the Canadian airwaves. "Canadian identity," he said, "is not a fragile thing. It is a tough, flexible cord which has bound us coast to coast for a hundred years."

McGregor remembers one particularly vituperative session with the CRTC. "It was smelly, hot, and just awful in the hearing room," he says. "There was a big fight between Allard and Juneau, we just let Juneau have it. Juneau went ballistic and so did Jim [Allard]. That was the problem. They were real adversaries. Some of our folks were upset with Jim and felt we weren't going to accomplish anything with these two at each other's throat. Some felt Jim was a loose cannon who felt everything was a conspiracy."

An exasperated Juneau attacked what he called "the prophets of doom, the messengers of mediocrity" and said, "We're just getting a whisper of our own material into the picture. We're just trying to breathe, for God's sake, in an atmosphere completely dominated by U.S. material." He noted how the U.S. motion picture industry had "bled Canada" by dominating Canadian movie screens and taking almost all the revenue. "They never did anything to help Canada get films of its own, a bit of itself, on the screen," Juneau said. "They're not going to do the same thing to Canadian television now that they did in Canadian movies in the past. We won't allow it."

All this was dismissed by Allard, who called them "vague, fearful, alien threats."

However, John Bassett agreed with Juneau, saying he had "absolute disgust" for the arguments of his fellow broadcasters. The CAB's position on Canadian content was, he said, "foolish" and "something beyond my comprehension." It was the beginning of a highly improbable, longtime friendship between the straight-laced, idealistic Juneau and the swashbuckling Bassett. Juneau later said, "I like interesting people, and Bassett was very interesting!"

Stuart Griffiths of CJOH Ottawa also disagreed with the CAB's attacks on the Canadian content regulations. Both he and Bassett resigned in protest from the association. "My dad didn't want anyone else to talk for him," says Doug Bassett. "He was an individual . . . his own man. That's why he didn't like the CAB." There was a certain amount of self-interest in their arguments because both Bassett and Griffiths had hoped to produce more programs for other private stations in meeting their content needs. In the end, Bassett wound up providing about half of the CTV Canadian programming.

Despite the tidal wave of vitriol, the CRTC stuck to 60 per cent Canadian TV content and 30 per cent for radio music, but softened the regulations by letting the percentage for television be averaged over a year instead of three months. Later, it reduced the prime time commitment to 50 per cent, then it gave stations a further break by lengthening the definition of prime time to 6:00 P.M. to midnight, from 6:30 to 11:30 P.M.

In response to the CRTC's easement, the private stations agreed to spend more money for CTV programs and to strengthen the network. The stations obeyed the letter of the law on Canadian content by airing inexpensive shows and largely avoiding costly productions such as Canadian drama. Half a dozen years after the Juneau content rules were proclaimed, the CRTC conducted a survey that showed, as writer Susan Gittins has noted, that when news, public affairs, and sports were taken out of the CTV schedule, 90 per cent of its broadcast day consisted of U.S. shows. In 1986, the Task Force on Broadcasting Policy observed that of 52,000 hours of English television programming available to the average Canadian, barely 370 hours were Canadian drama and most of that was on the CBC.

With variations, the basic Canadian content rule of 60 per cent overall and 50 per cent in prime time has stayed. In 2000, the CRTC said broadcasters still had to air 60 per cent Canadian content all day and 50 per cent in prime time and ordered major broadcasters such as CTV and Global to air eight prime-time hours a week of what the CRTC calls "priority" Canadian-made programming. Previously CRTC had put special emphasis on Canadian drama, but "priority" was now broadened to include comedy and variety shows, music programs, documentaries, entertainment magazines, and regional programs other than news and sports.

In the 1970s, radio station operators were almost as unhappy with their 30 per cent Canadian music content regulation as their TV colleagues were with their 60 per cent content rules. They complained they not only would lose money, but that there simply were not enough Canadian recordings to meet the quota. Veteran broadcaster Lyman Potts had taken a different view back in 1962 by establishing the Canadian Talent Library. At the time, there was no Canadian recording industry to speak of. Under the wing of his employer, Standard Broadcasting, which operated CFRB Toronto and CJAD Montreal, Potts provided recordings of Canadian musicians to radio stations, for a small fee. An ardent nationalist and believer in Canadian talent, Potts had been frustrated by political complaints about private radio failing to promote Canadian talent. "I sat through so many sessions of parliamentary committees where the broadcasters were absolutely lambasted by the politicians for their lack of support for Canadian talent," he says.

In the first year, Potts produced one hundred musical selections in ten albums with musicians as varied as Mart Kenney, Howard Cable, Wilf Carter, and later The Boss Brass, Lucio Agostini, and Denny Vaughan. By 1981, the library had brought out about 225 albums, including the first albums of performers such as Gordon Lightfoot and Tommy Hunter.

"We were showing what radio could do without a regulation," Potts says. "If everyone did what we were doing, there would be no need for a regulation. However, some people did nothing and ten years after we introduced the Talent Library, the CRTC initiated the 30 per cent Canadian content rules."

In 1998 when the Canadian radio content was raised to 35 per cent, broadcasters again warned they'd lose money. "We had a mini-revolt on our hands with broadcasters saying, 'We're not going to obey the regulation ... our listenership will go down and our revenue will go down,'" says CAB president Michael McCabe. "No they won't," said the CRTC chair Françoise Bertrand. She told the radio executives, "I've heard you, and the therapy is over. Let's get on with it. You're all big boys and you'll figure it out." And figure it out they did, as former CRTC chairman Pierre Juneau has noted, "None of them has handed back their licences."

Today, the CAB has donned the mantle of Canadian nationalism in its public rhetoric, with McCabe saying that private radio wants to develop more popular Canadian music and music stars. The CRTC is pushing radio to develop and carry more Canadian programming not only through the content rules, but also through a "benefits" policy that directs that anyone buying a profitable new station must spend 6 per cent of the value of any deal on the development of Canadian talent. On top of that, the CAB has launched the Radio Starmaker Fund, which plans to spend more than $26 million over the next eight to ten years creating Canadian music stars. But, without the Canadian content requirements originally imposed on radio, and the earlier efforts of Lyman Potts, Canada likely never would have established its own record industry or developed homegrown music stars such as singers Bryan Adams, Anne Murray, Burton Cummings, or Céline Dion, and bands such as Rush, Barenaked Ladies, or The Tragically Hip.

This battle over Canadian content was the last one fought by Jim Allard, the man who had run the CAB for a quarter-century. Obsessed by what he considered were the evils of government interference in private broadcasting and its exasperating instrument, the CBC, the pugnacious Allard had grown increasingly shrill over the years. He worried about spies infiltrating the CAB and once, riding an elevator in a downtown Toronto hotel with Lyman Potts, he hushed him, saying as they got off, "There are spies everywhere, even perhaps the elevator operator . . . anybody. You have to be careful talking around people." Potts says, "He nursed grudges, and he never gave up on anything. He was very aggressive, almost driven, a man of strong opinions who in the end just wore himself out working like a dog. He sacrificed everything."

"He made friends and he made enemies," Potts recalls, and in 1973 Allard's enemies finally ousted him from the CAB leadership. "He was crushed," Potts says. Fifteen years earlier, his adversaries had tried and failed to expel him, but this time Allard was worn out from all the infighting. Most private broadcasters now wanted a diplomat, not a pit bull, to run the CAB. "He lacked subtlety and wasn't sophisticated," says Allard's CAB colleague William McGregor. "He felt everything was a conspiracy, he always saw plots. But he was a fellow who made things happen. Jim saw it all as a cause."

One of Allard's earlier adversaries, Murray Brown of London's CFPL, remembers when he was CAB president, going to New York with Allard and spending an evening with him. "It was very depressing actually because he was sort of against everything," Brown says. "He was against most of the established things in our lives and very negative. I got along with him in talking business, but on a social basis I was not comfortable with him. I was happy to get away from him."

"He drove himself too far in the politics of broadcasting, in fighting the CBC," says veteran broadcaster Ross McCreath. "He was just going after it tooth and nail. That was always up there in big red neon letters insofar as Jim was concerned. You started a conversation with him and you wouldn't be into it more than five minutes and he'd be off on a tangent. That was his whole point in life. He alienated a lot of private broadcasters." One of them was Murray Brown, who says, "He had a marvellous brain, but it wasn't well-controlled and he let his emotions run away with him. He was good at working behind the scenes but was not a good front man. As CAB president, I was sometimes almost embarrassed by the way he did things. He didn't seem to have enough stature."

"He was a workaholic and could be quite confrontational at times, but he certainly had an incredible knowledge of how government works and who the key players were," says Gerry Acton, who worked with Allard as a CAB vice-president.

"He was a gunfighter," says Michael Hind-Smith, who, after he left CTV, became a "gunfighter" himself for the cable industry in Ottawa. "Allard was very tough, determined, opinionated. He was much feared for the intensity of his argument. The owners he represented were perhaps too cautious or inarticulate and fearful of the regulatory agency and so they hire gunfighters like me and Allard."

Allard was a bundle of contradictions. Strongly pro-civil rights, pro-abortion, anti-Vietnam War, married to an artist, and a frequenter of Ottawa's élitist Rideau Club, he nevertheless felt that senior civil service mandarins had too much power and that the parliamentary system was not working. "He was a very strange guy," says Murray Brown. "You never really knew who Jim Allard was. You never knew what made him tick."

"He was a likable anarchist," says William McGregor, one-time chairman of the CTV board and president of the CAB.

Looking back, Allard commented, "Behind the powerful façade, CAB was badly underfinanced, faction-ridden, and overextended. The association policy objectives were achieved by political, personal, and publicity campaigns executed by its chief executive officer [Allard himself] and supported by a thin red line of members."

Ironically, most of those who followed Allard as leader of the CAB came from the Ottawa élite that Allard had so deeply feared and resented, including Ernie Steele, who had been a deputy minister and a member of the Fowler committee that was so critical of private broadcasting. None, however, would so dominate the broadcast policy scene as Allard.

In his final years, Allard described himself as a "communications consultant," working on projects for the CAB, among other things, and devoting more time to his hobby of researching famous old crimes. With a sour view of Canadian governance, a few years after his forced retirement, he wrote to Newfoundland Conservative MP J. A. McGrath, "In my brief thirty years in Ottawa, I've seen real power pass from the hands of Parliament into the executive, from there into the hands of the bureaucrats and then into the hands of small groups of special advisers who are not really part of the public service. Right now it would almost appear that effective power is passing into the hands of various pressure groups."

Allard died in 1982, embittered to the end and, as Lyman Potts says, "He was just mad at the world and t'hell with everyone. It was sad because, for me, he was a hero."

A hero to some, a villain to others, Allard played a key role in changing the character of Canadian broadcasting. He had fulfilled the promise he made to his friend and ally Walter Dales in Edmonton's Cecil Hotel beer parlour in 1936 when he vowed to cripple the CBC and make private broadcasting dominate Canadian airwaves.

A poignant irony in the story of Canadian broadcasting is that the architect of the private broadcasting triumph, Jim Allard, is largely forgotten today while the loser, the gregarious élitist Graham Spry, the father of public broadcasting, is honoured and remembered.

10

The Dazzling Transformation

A key part of Jim Allard's successful strategy had been to turn criticism of CBC programming to the private broadcasters' advantage. The louder the complaints about the CBC, the more sympathy and political clout went to the private stations, especially as they escaped most such criticism by offering only uncontroversial programs. They tut-tutted and gained allies as the CBC was accused of being a "monster" out of control, particularly in its public affairs and drama programs.

Vancouver Liberal MP Grant Deachman attacked the "morbid preoccupation of the CBC with the dregs of society, the pornographers . . . the Nazis, racists, prostitutes, addicts and characters of doubtful sex." The CBC concentrated on "only the negative, only the filthy, only the ugly," said Alberta Conservative MP Frederick Bigg. Ontario Conservative Percy Noble got carried away in telling the House of Commons, "It is time to halt the headless horsemen of the CBC. The CBC [is] a Trojan Horse in our midst, attacking, destroying, and spreading filth and disease in the nation." Toronto Liberal MP Ralph Cowan called the CBC "a cancer on the body politic of Canada."

Charges of disloyalty to Canada on the part of CBC producers and performers echoed through the House of Commons as well. Urban Affairs Minister Andre Ouelette said he had "a list" of separatist sympathizers within the CBC who were trying to "destroy the country." John Diefenbaker warned the House of Commons that the CBC may be filled with communists and separatists.

All the while, CBC Radio was sinking into oblivion in the face of competition from private radio. CCF broadcast critic Doug Fisher described the CBC as "a middle-aged and rather frumpy institution which has lost a great deal of its zest." CBC Radio was a deflating balloon with old-fashioned and increasingly irrelevant programming, and its audience was fleeing for private radio's popular music programming, garnished with news, weather, sports, traffic reports, and the occasional interview and phone-in show.

In 1970, the CBC executive vice-president at the time, Laurent Picard, ordered up a "radio revolution" that redefined CBC Radio, transforming the radio schedule from mush to zest with such programs as *As It Happens* with Barbara Frum, *This Country in the Morning* with Peter Gzowski, and seven hours a day of early-morning, noon, and late-afternoon local news and current affairs. It now offered a distinctively different fare than was being heard on the private stations, even though private radio continued to win the popularity contest.

Not long afterwards, CRTC chairman Pierre Juneau believed that CBC-TV could achieve the same distinction by dramatically cutting back on commercials and maybe, in time, getting rid of them altogether. "We do not want broadcasting to be only an extension of the marketplace," he said. That pleased CTV and the independent stations, as they anticipated picking up some of the dropped CBC commercial revenue. It distressed the CBC's private affiliates, however, who would lose revenue on network programs.

This age-old battle over commercial revenue had begun in the late 1920s with the Aird report's recommendation of "indirect advertising" for public broadcasting. Spry, Plaunt, and their supporters encouraged this approach, saying that the government could not pay all the cost of a public system. This had led to the contradiction of, in the words of the BBC's first head, John Reith, trying to satisfy both "God and mammon." Through the years, arguments raged between the purists who believed there should be no commercials on the CBC, the private CBC affiliates who felt that it must take on substantial advertising, and frustrated pragmatists who said *some* commercials were okay, but not too many. The CBC's private affiliates, who got a share of all network advertising, have always pressed for more commercials, including advertisements during the national news, which, they said, would make the news seem "more successful." Pressure for more commercials also came from the Fowler report, from a number of MPs, from the Treasury Board, and from many a cabinet minister.

This led some CBC executives to seek more commercial revenue as a measure of success. Even so, all CBC presidents bemoaned their dependency on advertising. "The ideal commercial policy for the CBC is to be out of commercials," said Alphonse Ouimet. Al Johnson, head of the CBC in the late 1970s and early 1980s, spoke of commercials "polluting" public broadcasting, noting, "We at the CBC were always trapped with the tensions between commercials and public service." Ivan Fecan (pronounced Fet-zan), former head of CBC English TV programming, agrees: "The most difficult job for anyone at the CBC is balancing between the commercial interests and needs and the public service interests." But even well-intentioned CBC presidents and executives could not end the dependence on commercials, so CRTC chairman Pierre Juneau tried to force their hands. At the 1974 CRTC hearings, he demanded that the CBC cut its TV ads by one minute per hour each year for the next five years, a total cut of 50 per cent, and then he said the CBC should consider more cuts.

"There is a contradiction between the CBC's public service preoccupations, which are the reason for its existence, and its marketing preoccupations," Juneau said. But Laurent Picard, who had become CBC president, flatly refused to make the cuts, and he won the confrontation with Juneau when the cabinet took no action to force the issue. At the same time, Picard did give up commercials in children's TV programming, at a cost of $1.5 million a year, and on radio.

The CBC private affiliates were not only unhappy about giving up any commercial revenue at all, but they were becoming increasingly restive at the CBC's efforts to Canadianize its prime-time TV schedule. While most of them understood the public policy reasons behind the CBC's efforts, their objective was more profit, and that meant they mostly favoured popular American shows, not Canadian programs. They protested at meetings with CBC program officials, and a few stations threatened to disaffiliate because of "Canadianization." They saw greater profits in being an independent or a CTV affiliate rather than a CBC affiliate with "mandate" obligations.

Bob Elsden, president of the Blackburn broadcasting division in London, Ontario, which included CFPL London and CKNX Wingham, explained succinctly the dilemma facing the private station CBC-TV affiliates. "The move of *The National* to ten o'clock and the creation of *The Journal* were great moves for the CBC," Elsden said. "But, if you look at the other side of the coin, it took five hours of prime-time programming and revenue right out of the affiliates' pocket." Elsden said that it cost too much money to be a CBC affiliate. "Over the years," says Lyman Potts, "stations that had fought for CBC affiliation originally were doing their darndest to get off the network."

The first to go in 1961 was CHCH Hamilton and, as a result, the CBC share of the rich Toronto-Hamilton area slipped. Then stations in Kitchener, Sudbury, Barrie, London, Wingham, and Calgary followed, again reducing the CBC's audience and widening the gap between the audiences for private and public broadcasters.

It was not only the growing strength of CTV and the powerful private sector lobbyists in Ottawa that gave private broadcasters domination over the CBC. In some cases, the CBC itself inadvertently helped the private broadcasters' cause, such as the CBC's 1992 "repositioning," which shifted the news from ten o'clock to nine, a rushed move that saw a large chunk of the CBC news audience switch to CTV and never return. Another self-inflicted wound was the decision to abandon the CBC parliamentary channel in 1991. It was promptly picked up by the cable companies and repackaged as CPAC. With its focus on live and recorded coverage of Parliament, major political events, Supreme Court hearings, royal commissions, and conferences, it has been not only a valuable public service, but also of great political benefit to the private cable operators, much as the *Report from Parliament Hill* was to private broadcasters forty years before. "Surrendering that channel to the cable companies was the biggest mistake of all," says Ian Morrison of the Friends of Canadian Broadcasting.

Over the years, there have been other CBC missteps that led to the loss of its once dominant position, including the long, mishandled Montreal producers' strike in the early years of TV; the near-fatal attraction to Hollywood shows that infected CBC prime time until the 1980s; the badly managed *This Hour Has Seven Days* crisis in 1966, which exposed internal CBC chaos; the tactically flawed effort in 2000 to kill local news programs; and in the late 1990s tensions between the president and chair of the CBC, which lessened CBC effectiveness.

The damage caused by these stumbles was aggravated by weakening financial support for the CBC on the part of government, whether Liberal or Conservative. Draconian budget-slashing started hurting the CBC in the Trudeau days. A $71-million cut in spending for its 1979–80 budget began a couple of decades of blood-letting that severely hurt the CBC's ability to fulfill its parliamentary mandate.

Convinced he had been misrepresented and mistreated by the CBC news, Brian Mulroney stepped up the cuts while he was prime minister, and his cuts were followed by Jean Chrétien's more vengeful slashing. Confronted with what he considered intolerable reductions to CBC financing, Tony Manera resigned as president in 1995. It was nothing short of a miracle that in the late 1990s, his successor, Perrin Beatty, while accepting further cuts, was able to push through an almost 100 per cent prime-time Canadian content schedule. It made a dramatic contrast to the money-making, heavy American schedule on private station prime time, but there was so much water in the soup because of the cuts that the quality of many programs suffered, in everything from news to drama. There was less research, less staff, fewer production resources, less room to test and experiment, less willingness to take creative risks, fewer original programs, and more repeats.

The Chrétien government had ordered the cuts to help eliminate the federal government's annual deficit, but the CBC was disproportionately harder hit than other areas.

Chrétien's attitude toward the CBC appears to stem from his resentment for the contempt he feels many in the French network hold for him. Added to this was his conviction that separatists abound in the CBC's French radio and TV networks. "I am frustrated every night by it," he said when he was a Trudeau cabinet minister. When he became prime minister, he got his revenge. "There has never been a prime minister more hostile to the CBC than Jean Chrétien," says Ian Morrison. Over the years both the CBC's budget and its staff have been reduced by about 40 per cent.

The cuts were so deep, even some private station operators voiced alarm. Veteran broadcaster Doug Bassett is one of them. "For God's sake, give them the money," he says. A close friend of Brian Mulroney, Bassett had urged him to provide more funds to the CBC. "When the party that I supported was the government, I pleaded with friends of mine in the government to give them the damn money," he says. "It only amounts to a case of beer a year for each Canadian."

"The 'kick me!' sign had to come off the CBC," says current CBC president Robert Rabinovitch.

The Friends of Canadian Broadcasting launched a vigorous campaign to stop the CBC budget hemorrhage, targeting cabinet ministers and Liberal backbenchers. Author-philosopher John Ralston Saul, husband of Governor General Adrienne Clarkson (a former CBC star herself), lent his support to the battle for more CBC resources. "The need for public broadcasting is greater today than it has been since the 1930s, 1940s, and 1950s . . ." Saul said. "Public broadcasting is one of the most important remaining levers that a nation-state has to communicate with itself."

At the beginning of the new century, even Prime Minister Chrétien privately admitted he may have gone too far in slashing the CBC funding and began restoring some of the CBC cuts. "It's clear," says Rabinovitch, "that the government now understands that we have gone through a significant amount of pain."

The change in Chrétien's attitude stems in part from public concerns and in part from Rabinovitch's careful cultivation of his high-ranking Liberal friends, and his stronger control and leadership within the CBC. But perhaps most of all, the change came because of the widely praised series *Canada: A People's History*, produced by Mark Starowicz, who, earlier, had successfully launched *The Journal* with Barbara Frum. "The history series really did it because people in power were saying to each other, 'This is the kind of thing the CBC should be doing,'" says one highly influential Liberal.

To produce the kind of quality programs he wants, Rabinovitch knows he needs more money, but at the same time, he's leery of more money. "In 1980 when the government said if you sell more ads you can keep the money, they didn't do the CBC a favour because that began to pervert the programming," he says. "I'm also fearful of money because I'm worried it will relieve people of the need to understand the necessity of changing the way we think and the way we work." Nevertheless, he will gladly take whatever additional funding the government provides.

While the CBC was being squeezed, the government was seeking ways to alleviate some of the private broadcasters' growing pains. In fact, the value of the benefits provided to them almost equal the cuts to the CBC. "Ottawa has provided a whole range of things that have helped the private sector immensely, protecting it against American competition," says Ian Morrison.

The unspoken deal between successive Canadian governments of the last half-century and private broadcasters has been abide by the Canadian content and advertising rules and we'll help you be economically viable. "From my perspective, you have to be realistic," says Françoise Bertrand, who resigned as CRTC chair in early 2001. "What are the paybacks you can get out of the system in terms of Canadian content to serve the Broadcasting Act. We want to make sure they have their flow of revenues for which we expect more hours of Canadian content. The more flow they have, the more content. On radio, for instance, we now allow multiple ownership in one market, more concentration of ownership, but on the other hand you'll give us 35 per cent Canadian content rather than 30 per cent."

While broadcasters chafed under the rules, they profited from the government's favours. To help subsidize Canadian programming, Ottawa established a fund of about $200 million a year, half paid for by cable and satellite companies. It funds the production of Canadian programs to be aired by both private and public Canadian broadcasters. For private broadcasters, says CAB president Michael McCabe, "the Canadian Television Fund has become the single most important funding source for Canadian television programming." Grants from the fund to producers are conditional on their having a licensing agreement with a broadcaster, and approval triggers about four times the grant's value in other funding. This has enabled CTV, Global, and others to do much more Canadian programming than they otherwise would. Since the fund was established in 1996, it has meant more than 8,500 hours of Canadian programming and jobs for thousands of production personnel. There is now a vibrant independent production industry, made up of a handful of major companies and about 540 smaller production houses.

Robert Rabinovitch, however, says the fund is an instrument of an industrial policy, not a cultural policy, because the fund seeks to recoup its investments from producers. That, in turn, encourages the making of programs that have few, if any, Canadian references and so can be sold to the United States and other countries.

The government's push for the CBC to buy programs from independent producers rather than make entertainment shows in-house has resulted in the dismantling of most CBC arts and entertainment production. "This place is a shell of its former self," says Rabinovitch.

Successive governments have also helped private broadcasters lessen the damage caused by their American competition. When American border stations began chasing Canadian advertisers, private broadcasters complained they were losing a fortune to stations such as KVOS, in Bellingham, Washington, which was targeted at Vancouver, KCND in Pembina, North Dakota, aimed at Winnipeg, and Buffalo, New York, stations that scooped up Toronto advertising. Ottawa stepped in with a tax law that made advertising placed by Canadian firms on U.S. border stations aimed at a Canadian audience non-deductible as a business expense.

A CRTC rule that directs Canadian cable services to substitute a Canadian signal for an American one when the same program is being broadcast at the same time on both stations has also been of extraordinary value to Canadian stations. Commercials secured by the Canadian station replace the commercials of the U.S. station, and the Canadian signal shows up on both cable channels. As president of All-Canada Radio and Television in the 1970s, Ross McCreath was a key participant in the effort to get the cable substitution regulation. "It saved our industry," he says. "It resulted from intensive lobbying by us commercial types, done under a CAB umbrella. It's made a very big difference."

One estimate is that this rule, together with the tax law initiative, brings Canadian stations about $150 million a year in what's called repatriated ad revenue. "It certainly was immensely valuable to the private stations," says Michael Hind-Smith, president of the cable lobby organization at the time cable substitution began. "I used to make a regular point of enraging John Bassett," he says, "by having surveys done showing the millions of dollars going to private stations because of the substitution. It used to drive him crazy because it gave leverage for the CRTC to ask how much of these extra profits was being spent on Canadian content."

The drawback has been that with the Canadian station carrying an American program at the same time as the U.S. network, New York has a great deal of influence in setting Canadian TV schedules. "The private broadcasters have had to be really very much in line with the American broadcasters, taking their schedules," says Françoise Bertrand. The value of cable substitution, however, may be diminishing in the new technical world. "With satellites and the Internet and every-thing else," says Ivan Fecan, "how sustainable is a business model based on simultaneous substitution? [It] is, I think, a non-starter a few years out. Therefore, you better hurry up and begin to develop your own brand of content. It is a strategic imperative that we have reasons for people to watch us other than substituting an American signal."

Cable's arrival was a key factor in expanding the presence of American programs in Canada, transforming the face of Canadian television, and, in the process, further diminishing the role of public broadcasting.

"Cable was the thing that really killed fortress CBC," says Finlay MacDonald. "I can understand the government using Canadian content rules to try to prevent a complete cultural annexation of Canada and all that good stuff," he says. "But suddenly, for Christ's sake, they give hun-dreds of cable licences to people who are bringing in every goddamn American program. Why then should we be surprised that the audience for Canadian stations is fragmented?"

That sentiment is echoed by a contemporary titan of broadcasting, Izzy Asper, chairman of CanWest Global. "Canadian television has been fragmented more than any other market in the world," he says. "The greatest mistake we made in this country," he told TV interviewer Pamela Wallin, "was made when they allowed the untrammelled access of the American networks into Canada." Privately, he adds, "That was just outrageous, outrageous!"

CITY-TV president Moses Znaimer, however, argues, "There never was a mass market except by compulsion." Only the handful of stations and networks that existed before cable call it fragmentation, he says. "That's a prejudicial word," he adds. "From where I sit, that wasn't frag-mentation, that was democratization, that was amplification, that was modern society. People want alternatives and when options arrive, the mass quickly breaks down into its underlying truth: a zillion tastes and opinions. Sooner or later the group struggle is replaced by the individ-ual's struggle for identity and meaning and self-improvement."

Fecan thinks it's a waste of time to bemoan the arrival of cable TV. "You're not going to stop technological change. You just can't stop it, and you look pretty silly trying," he says. "You should try to use the energy of change and be in the forefront."

The political argument for licensing cable companies to carry American programs was that since Canadians living near the border could get the American networks via their antennas, it was unfair to deprive other Canadians living farther from the border of the same access.

This dilemma for the government had been brewing since the beginning of cable in Canada in the early 1950s. Cable had been developed in the United Kingdom and several European countries, and by 1948 nearly 900,000 homes were getting radio by cable. A few years later, rudimentary cable systems were delivering television shows to homes in the United States. At the same time, in Montreal, an experimental cable service delivered static-free radio to subscribers, and in 1951, in a makeshift, two-camera studio in the same city, Rediffusion Ltd., a British company, started sending out films and panel discussions, the first cable system in North America to originate its own programs. In September 1952, the system was carrying the bilingual programs of CBC-TV in Montreal, and by 1953 it had six thousand subscribers.

London, Ontario, was the site of the first commercial development of cable outside Montreal, led by the owner of a local dry-cleaning business, Edwin Jarmain. Fascinated by amateur radio and by the possibilities of television, in 1952 he set up an antenna in his and a neighbour's backyard, picking up TV stations in Cleveland. He persuaded thirteen neighbours to subscribe to his cable service, each of them paying $150 for installation and $4 a month for the service.

In its early years, cable was not regulated by the BBG because it wasn't considered to be broadcasting. But by 1960, there were two hundred community cable systems in Canada (half of them in Quebec), and both the private stations and the CBC protested that cable had an unfair advantage because it was unregulated. "The broadcasters were bleating about possible competition and looking to legislation to protect themselves," said pioneer cable executive K. J. Easton. Cable began to replace the CBC as "the enemy" for private broadcasters. "They make money," says Asper of his cable rivals, "selling our signals which they take for nothing."

The cable systems responded by forming a lobby group, which argued that regulating cable would amount to state interference with freedom. "It is not the prerogative of the government to force the Canadian public to watch Canadian programs," the lobby group said.

"The basic unfettered right of the public to receive stations of its choice should be recognized and any action to curtail this is censorship," said cable association president Gilbert Allard (no relation to Jim Allard). This was more or less the same argument made over the years by private radio and TV operators. Also following the lead of private broadcasters, the cable industry is now seeking tax breaks and less regulation by Ottawa.

But regulation actually benefited the cable operators. "If people are honest with themselves, without regulation, cable would never have grown the way it did," says Michael Hind-Smith, who in 1975 started a fifteen-year career with the Canadian Cable Television Association after more than two decades with the CBC and CTV. "It was protected, one licence per area, a licensed monopoly. Who knows what kind of chaos might have ensued without regulation."

Jack Pickersgill, ever protective of private broadcasters, developed an advisory role for the BBG on cable in the mid-1960s, and the new broadcast legislation approved by Parliament in 1968 brought the 445 cable systems then operating across Canada under CRTC regulation. A couple of years later, Canada had the highest cable subscriber-to-population ratio anywhere in the world. By the end of the century, cable had become a billion-dollar business, with about two thousand cable systems in the country, most of them small operations. About three-quarters of the 8.5 million cable subscribers were being serviced by a handful of big companies such as Rogers, Shaw, and Vidéotron.

Ed Jarmain's objective in setting up cable in London in 1952 had been to bring in clear signals of American stations. That, he figured, was what the public wanted. He was right, and cable operators were in business to provide network shows taken from American border stations. As private broadcasters had known for decades, cable entrepreneurs quickly learned that the road to profit was paved with American shows. This was especially so with pay-TV, which featured American movies and the occasional Canadian film at off hours. Thanks to Pickersgill, Don Jamieson, and Jim Allard, its arrival was delayed but not stopped. "The private broadcaster lobby delayed the introduction of pay-TV for more than a decade," says Ted Rogers. In the end, public pressure for more movies on television, ably abetted by the cable industry lobbying, won out.

Ironically, it was the champion of Canadian cultural nationalism, CRTC chairman Pierre Juneau, who made this happen. He faced the age-old contradiction of Canadians saying they wanted Canadian TV programs, while turning their dials to American programs.

In a melancholy comment on this phenomenon, writer Robert Fulford said in a 1973 *Saturday Night* article, "When presented with the best that the CBC had to offer, the people of Canada, on the whole, yawned. They yawned and then they switched their dials to Bellingham if they lived in Vancouver or to Buffalo if they lived in Toronto."

Hollywood has always seemed more glamorous than Canada, with its vast publicity machine churning out stories about the stars and whetting Canadian viewing appetites. Canadian shows and stars have had a hard time even getting noticed amid the flood of American showbiz gossip and news that pours out of our papers and magazines.

"There is no question that cable brought in a lot of American television," says Michael Hind-Smith. "That's what the people wanted. The cultural nationalist argument is a tiresome one in the sense that it really doesn't have very much support other than a small group of self-appointed guardians of Canadian nationhood. The growth of cable was a very direct response to consumer demands for greater viewing choice. Juneau didn't really have an option about licensing cable. He was faced with inevitability."

Nevertheless, Juneau did come under fire from cultural nationalists for the licensing of cable companies. Writer Morris Wolfe condemned Juneau as the architect of increased Canadian viewing of American TV shows. "He established a pattern of CRTC decision-making that has succeeded over the years in undermining the central role of the CBC in the Canadian broadcasting system," said Wolfe.

Juneau also was attacked by the cable industry itself, which felt that, even though he had approved widespread cable licensing, Juneau was no friend. Hind-Smith recalls Juneau once referring to cable as "a cancer on the broadcasting system." "He was part of a generation that really feared that our Canadian identity would be swallowed up by watching American programs," Hind-Smith says. "That's an old-fashioned emotion."

With his sophisticated aggressiveness and political know-how, Hind-Smith helped make millionaires of many a cable operator. He was so effective in getting licences, negotiating with the CRTC to ease regulatory pains, and arguing against what he calls "the cultural warriors," that Communications Minister Jeanne Sauvé told him, "I hear you're the most dangerous lobbyist in Ottawa!"

Cable had been introduced to meet the constant call for more choice, and in the late 1980s, the demand was appeased again by the arrival of specialized channels. Most private broadcasters had missed the boat when cable first came on the scene, but they were at the front of the line of licence applicants for specialized channels in such areas as music, sports, science, news, history, women's interests, and other subjects. These channels took audience away from the regular TV stations, but the private broadcasters realized that if they owned the new channels they could profit rather than suffer from the audience fragmentation. "We became our own fragmenters in owning specialty channels," says Izzy Asper, "but we have to because otherwise we won't survive."

CTV was given a number of specialty channels, as were other big TV groups such as CHUM, Shaw, and CanWest Global. Between 1983 and 1999, the CRTC issued licences for about sixty specialty channels, pay-TV, and pay-per-view channels. The scope of the specialty channels was seen in 2000 when the CRTC sat down to consider applications for digital specialty cable channels. On the table were 452 applications offering a multitude of choices including all poetry, all sex, all biography, all horror, all martial arts, all soap operas, all fishing, and all local or regional news. The latter underlined the trend toward localism that CITY-TV president Moses Znaimer has championed for decades.

In 1990, specialty channels had 14 per cent of the TV audience and revenues of about $226 million: $60 million from advertising and $166 million from subscriber fees. In 2001, with English Canadians watching an average of about twenty-two hours of TV a week, the audience had grown to nearly 40 per cent and revenues had ballooned to $880 million, including $300 million from advertising. Znaimer predicts that the audience share will rise to 50 per cent and then level off.

In the 1980s and early 1990s, the arrival of specialty cable channels touched off a round of acquisitions, as the private broadcasters scrambled to maintain their footing. There was a whirlwind of deal-making, spinning the heads of old-timers as they watched a new generation of swashbucklers take over Canadian radio and TV.

Doug Bassett of CFTO Toronto, while not as colourful as the father he succeeded, was more aggressive in wanting to control CTV. His father had purchased CFQC Saskatoon from the family of pioneer broadcaster A. A. "Pappy" Murphy in 1972. "It gave him more clout at the CTV board meetings," Bassett says. Fourteen years later, Doug went on a buying spree, picking up CKCK Regina and three other Saskatchewan stations for $61.5 million. Critics say that he overpaid for the Saskatchewan stations, but Bassett says, "I did it because I wanted to expand Baton and I wanted to get control of CTV. It was something my father wasn't able to achieve and something I probably would be remembered for," he says. "Dad would have liked to have control of CTV, but without buying any more stations." Within a few years, Bassett paid out around $200 million to buy stations in Ottawa, Sudbury, Timmins, North Bay, Pembroke, and Sault Ste. Marie. In 1992, he took over London's CFPL and Wingham's CKNX.

When Bassett decided to step down as head of Baton, his successor, Ivan Fecan, who had been recruited by Bassett from the CBC, exuberantly carried on the campaign to get control of CTV, buying still more stations, merging with some and exchanging others. Fecan transferred his fascination with television programming to a fascination with big business deal-making. "I was a financial virgin when I came here," Fecan says. "And I've been really surprised at how creative business is and what an interesting collection of personalities there are," he adds. "I really enjoy it."

Carrying on Bassett's expansion, Fecan took over stations in Kitchener and Calgary, won a licence for a Vancouver station, and exchanged the Baton properties in London, Wingham, Pembroke, and Wheatley for four Maritime stations owned by CHUM. That deal gave Baton a majority of votes in CTV and enabled Fecan in 1997 to orchestrate the Baton takeover of the whole CTV network, fulfilling John and Doug Bassett's long-time dream. It also meant the departure of John Cassaday as CTV president and the arrival of Fecan in that role. Cassaday became head of Corus, the radio-TV arm of Calgary's Shaw cable dynasty, which by 2001 owned, or had a share in, a dozen specialty channels and about fifty radio stations.

As the twentieth century ended, CTV paid about $400 million for a controlling interest in NetStar Communications, which, among other things, owned the sports channel TSN, the biggest audience-winner of any specialty cable channel, and its French-language equivalent, as well as the science and nature channel Discovery. The owner of eighteen conventional TV stations, CTV also began a news headline specialty channel and had interests in a television satellite service in the Maritimes, in a number of specialty channels, including a comedy channel, a history channel, a talk channel, and an outdoor life channel. The squalling baby that Spence Caldwell had given birth to four decades earlier had grown into a billion-dollar business.

Bassett and Fecan were not the only ones buying up stations. In 1989, Maclean-Hunter paid $600 million to buy the stations of Selkirk Communications and then spun off $217 million of those assets to Western International Communications (WIC), which controlled, among other stations, CHAN in Vancouver. Five years later, Maclean-Hunter itself was bought by Rogers Communications, which, in turn, sold off much of the broadcasting properties Maclean-Hunter had owned.

All these breathtaking buying binges paled, however, when the deep-pocketed BCE, the parent of Bell Canada, came along in the winter of 2000 with an offer the CTV owners could not refuse: $2.3 billion for the whole thing. BCE president Jean Monty says he wanted CTV for its "distinctively Canadian product" and, looking at the new media future, he says, "The convergence of television and the Web opens unlimited opportunities." Like many others, he believes that in the future, content will be king, and repackaging content for different media – a broadcast channel, cable channels, the Internet – plus sales to the United States and other foreign markets, can mean profit for Canadian productions. BCE is betting this is where the future lies.

CTV and its stations were not enough for BCE. Even before hearing the CRTC ruling on the purchase of CTV, Monty startled the country with a convergence deal merging CTV, the *Globe and Mail*, and BCE's Sympatico-Lycos network into a $4-billion media corporation to be run by Ivan Fecan and called Bell Globemedia. It has four thousand employees. The new media giant includes CTV's specialty channels, such as TSN, Discovery Channel, Talk TV, The Comedy Network, and half a dozen others, Sympatico, Canada's leading Internet portal, a number of local Web sites, and the *Globe and Mail*'s nine Web sites along with its electronic databases. BCE owns just over 70 per cent of the new company and the Ken Thomson interests have the rest. Monty talks of "connectivity, content, and commerce" as the driving forces behind BCE's strategy.

Izzy Asper shares Monty's ambition to lure more people to use more platforms. After years of often bitter confrontation and negotiation, in 2000 Asper finally achieved his dream of a national network for Global, a network to rival CTV. His triumph grew out of an immensely complicated and controversial deal that divided up the hundreds of millions of dollars' worth of radio, television, cable, and other assets of WIC of Vancouver.

At one time, WIC had been Canada's largest private broadcaster, with holdings in radio, television, cable, pay-TV, and satellite communications, and had competed with Baton for domination of CTV. Its downfall began with the death of founder and patriarch, the silver-haired, one-time chartered accountant, Frank Griffiths, Sr. Without his steadying presence, the company was suddenly overwhelmed by boardroom battles and family feuds, secret deals, takeover attempts, and lawsuits. Griffiths' widow finally sold a block of stock to the Allard family of Edmonton (no relation to Jim Allard), but a verbal brawl broke out between the families. When the dust finally settled, Izzy Asper's CanWest Global of Winnipeg and Shaw Communications of Calgary carved up the WIC empire. Shaw, through its broadcasting offspring, Corus Entertainment, took over WIC's dozen radio stations and most of its cable specialty channels. CanWest Global gained television stations in Alberta, British Columbia, and Ontario, which, added to his other stations, gave Asper the national network he wanted. When all the spending to acquire the WIC stations and other assets was added up, the bill to Asper was around $800 million.

Asper's dream of a network had begun more than a quarter-century earlier, when he and a couple of colleagues picked up the corporate remains of the short-lived fantasy of a genial broadcast hustler by the name of Al Bruner, a former CFTO and CHCH Hamilton sales executive who bet on the commercial success of an Ontario TV station featuring prime-time Canadian programming. He lost his bet.

His station, Global, was licensed to serve seven million viewers in the Windsor-to-Ottawa region. Under Bruner's whirlwind and often chaotic leadership, Global went on the air amid much fanfare in January

1974, with studios in Toronto and transmitters across its broadcast area. Within three months, Bruner's dream had become a financial nightmare, losing $1.5 million a month and putting Global on the rim of ruin. "It was one mother of a business disaster," says Asper, a close friend and admirer of Bruner. "His backers pulled the plug and we came in. I loved the guy and his program ideas, but he was no damn good at putting the dough together." Bruner was forced out, and the idea of a private station featuring Canadian programming went out with him.

The aggressive new operators of Global – radio mogul Allan Slaight and broadcast consultant Seymour Epstein of Toronto, and Winnipeggers Paul Morton and Izzy Asper – were determined to take Global from rags to riches. They did it by firing much of the staff, cancelling most of the costly Canadian programming, and airing American shows, so many that Global was nicknamed "*The Love Boat* network."

"Global was in bankruptcy," Asper recalls. "It was going to go off the air. We had hour-by-hour longevity. Hundreds of jobs were going to be lost. We had to survive and so we programmed anything that would keep the station alive, *Charlie's Angels* and crap like that which had mass appeal." He defends the heavy use of American programs, saying that Canadians would tune in to American networks if Canadian stations did not run Hollywood shows.

Within a couple of years, Global was making a profit, but it was also making trouble among the owners. Slaight was managing Global, but resented Asper's incessant questioning, and the combination of Slaight's exasperation and Asper's frustration blew up into nasty legal warfare. After persuading bankers to lend them the money, Asper, Morton, and Epstein bought out Slaight and, in time, brought in David Mintz as president. His answer to demands for more profit was to air more high-rated American shows. Mintz, an effervescent salesman, had used that approach successfully in running KVOS Bellingham, Washington, which was aimed at the Vancouver market, and he substantially fattened Global's bottom line. In 1987, Global hit $100 million in revenue, the first English-language TV station to reach that level, with a profit of $20 million.

Despite the money rolling in thanks to Mintz's super salesmanship and program strategy, Asper and his partners, Morton and Epstein, fell out over their differing visions of the future for CanWest Global, with Asper having much more ambitious plans. Once again boardroom

warfare erupted at Global and more than ten thousand pages of testimony and documents were strewn over a legal battlefield involving
suits and countersuits, charges of misrepresentation, breach of con-
tract, and corporate oppression. "You couldn't go to a board meeting
without everybody pulling out their tape recorders," says Asper. "There
was a lot of yelling and screaming. . . . We were in [a] gun-at-our-head
court battle."

At one point Asper had to get a court order just to ensure that he
would be invited to Global management meetings. The boardroom
drama was every bit as pyrotechnical as the CTV board meetings had
been in the heyday of the Bassett-Peters clashes. After five years of legal
mayhem, Asper forced his one-time friends and partners Morton and
Epstein into a court-ordered auction – a high-noon financial shootout
over who would own Global. The corporate drama lasted seventy
minutes with fourteen bids and counterbids before Asper finally won
full control of Global in late 1989, buying out his partners' slightly under
40 per cent ownership for $150 million. The battle may have seemed to
be over, but a dozen years later, Epstein and Morton were back in court
suing Asper for $325 million over their deal.

Amid all the legal huffing and puffing and the Byzantine intrigue,
Asper was working on his dream of a nationwide Global network, the
"third force" he and Al Bruner had envisioned almost twenty years
earlier. He bought stations in Vancouver, Saskatchewan, Quebec, New
Brunswick, and Nova Scotia, and tried but failed to get CRTC approval
to buy stations in Alberta. The failure was reversed in 2000 when
CanWest Global bought the WIC stations in Ontario, Alberta, and
British Columbia. Asper now had his national network, even though, as
he says, "There were a lot of bumps along the way."

Asper now owned several cable specialty channels, Internet sites, and
a number of TV and film production companies as well as Global, but it
wasn't enough for him. He had also become an international broadcasting entrepreneur with operations in New Zealand, Australia, and Ireland.
In 1991, he took over the money-losing New Zealand network TV3 and
ran it with the same high intensity that had moved Global from big losses
to big profits. Within a couple of years, he was making money with TV3
after cutting costs and staff and reshaping the network to be more adver-
tiser-friendly. "When I was first there, I got all the staff together and

asked them to tell me what business they thought they were in," says Asper, who was dubbed by the New Zealand media as "Prince Izzy." "Some said news, some said entertainment, and some said education. 'No you're not!' I told them. 'You're all wrong. You're in the business of selling soap. You're in advertising plain and simple. This is a commercial business we're in,' I said. It was a whole new approach for them."

Asper, who once said, "TV stations are gigantic advertising machines there to be filled with product," took that conviction next to Australia, where he bought another money-loser – The Ten Television network – and turned it into a cash cow. A venture in Chile TV was less successful, bringing a small loss to the company, and Asper was affronted when his licence application for a British TV operation was rejected. He moved on to Ireland, where he ran that country's first private national TV network and began looking at other European properties.

In Canada, no sooner had Asper fulfilled his dream of getting a national network for Global than he was off chasing another vision designed to give him more platforms for his content. "The more cluttered the world gets, the more you have to have bazookas and neutron bombs to get your message across," says Leonard Asper, Izzy's son and successor as president of CanWest Global.

Within weeks of getting the CRTC's approval to swallow the WIC stations, the Aspers got their "bazookas" and "neutron bombs" overnight by becoming media barons, paying $3.2 billion to buy up most of Conrad Black's Canadian newspaper empire, including thirteen of Canada's biggest papers, more than one hundred others, and a 50 per cent share of the *National Post*. Leonard spearheaded the deal as part of a convergence strategy to marry print and television, which would see product "repurposed" for individual TV stations, for the Global network, for his newspapers, for his specialized channels, and for the Internet, as well as being sold outside Canada. The deal made Global a multimedia giant and was, says Leonard, "the ultimate convergence transaction." Izzy says, "We don't intend to be one of the corpses lying beside the information highway." "The content that the print people have the capacity to generate, it would take generations for the television industry to be able to do the same thing," Leonard says. Perhaps even more important to the Aspers, their converged media giant offers one-stop shopping for advertising deals covering the whole range of media.

With a network, individual stations, specialty channels, newspapers, and Internet sites, Asper wants to be Canada's most comprehensive advertising service provider. "We're no longer just looking for how much advertising we can sell in one broadcast or a program," Leonard told author Peter C. Newman. "We are constantly looking for ancillary revenue streams and multiple platforms – Internet, special channels, and so on." With those platforms, Global also increases its program-buying clout because it will be buying for more than one service. At the end of its 2000 business year, revenue from Asper's operations in Canada, Australia, New Zealand, and Ireland was $404 million, up 51 per cent from the previous year.

Also in love with the idea of corporate convergence was Pierre-Karl Péladeau and his Quebecor media empire. In 2000, for about $5.5 billion, he scooped up the Quebec cable and broadcasting mammoth Groupe Vidéotron Ltée. with its 1.5 million cable subscribers. His intention was to create out of this an integrated media powerhouse that includes the world's largest commercial printing operation, magazines, the *Sun* newspaper chain, and scores of other daily and weekly newspapers, the French-language television networks TVA and TQS (which the CRTC ordered Péladeau to sell) and other TV activities, a film development company, an Internet portal, music operations, and cable. "We can today count Quebecor as a player that has solid-enough foundations to rate on a global scale," forty-year-old Péladeau said in announcing the acquisition of Vidéotron. Péladeau's flamboyant, controversial, and separatist-leaning father, Pierre, had started the empire in 1950 with the purchase of a Quebec weekly newspaper for $1,500. Quebecor now has more than sixty thousand employees in fifteen countries.

A few months after Péladeau bought Vidéotron, Jim Shaw joined the élite club of cable moguls when Shaw Communications of Calgary spent $1.2 billion to buy Moffat Communications of Winnipeg, giving Shaw 2.6 million cable and Internet customers, rivalling Ted Rogers' customer base. Like Péladeau, the forty-three-year-old Jim Shaw is the son of a communications pioneer and, after taking over as CEO, has dramatically expanded the company.

Patriarch J R Shaw, who changed his name from Jim to J R to avoid confusion with his son, founded his company in Edmonton in 1966, and under his son's spur, it has grown to an enterprise valued at more than $7 billion. Jim Shaw has a quiet intensity, loves fast cars, motorboats, and speedboats, and is somewhat more aggressive than his father. "We like to work hard and we like to play hard," he says. He started in the family cable business at the bottom, doing home installations and, like the sons of Asper and Péladeau, has endorsed the potential of modern media convergence more enthusiastically than his father.

While the birth of vertically integrated media giants is considered by many to be revolutionary, it is, in fact, old hat. Three-quarters of a century ago, William Randolph Hearst pioneered the concept with the synergy of his corporate family of newspapers, news agencies, syndication services, magazines, newsreels, radio stations, and a Hollywood movie studio. A Hearst newspaper feature was often translated into a magazine spread, which in turn was repurposed for his newsreels, discussed by his radio commentators, and ultimately made into a motion picture, and Hearst movies were always highly praised by Hearst newspapers, columnists, reviewers, and magazines.

The dazzling transformation of Canadian broadcasting from the storefront operations of its early days to the multibillion-dollar big business behemoths of today is illustrated not only by the mega-deals of BCE-CTV, Pierre-Karl Péladeau, Izzy Asper, and Conrad Black, but also by the myriad of smaller deals that have whirled around the broadcasting business in recent years. The outburst of deal-making partly came about when the CRTC changed its rules to allow multiple radio ownership. In the first couple of years after that rule was changed in 1998, 166 radio stations changed ownership in deals worth $400 million. The major players on Canada's radio scene are no longer locally owned stations, but broadcast conglomerates that own stations across the country, such as Astral Media of Montreal; Telemedia Communications of Montreal; CHUM of Toronto; Corus Entertainment of Toronto; Slaight Communications of Toronto; and Rogers Broadcasting of Toronto. In Newfoundland, one company, Newcap, now controls fifteen of the province's private radio stations.

Meanwhile, other deal-making was going on: Shaw bought television operations in Atlantic Canada worth nearly $450 million, and its broadcast arm, Corus, bought seventeen radio stations and four TV stations from Power Broadcasting for more than $100 million. Corus then paid $540 million to buy the animation production company Nelvana, and spent $165 million for half a dozen Quebec radio stations. Astral Media paid $225 million to buy Radio-Mutuel's radio stations and specialty channels and another $225 million for nineteen Telemedia radio stations in Quebec and Atlantic Canada, and Rogers bought up Cable Atlantic for $232 million. A whole new burst of deal-making undoubtedly will spring from the June 2001 CRTC decision to allow cable companies to own specialty channels.

"Big Is Better!" was the broadcast industry's motto as the new century began. "You either grow or you die," says Calgary's cable and broadcast goliath J R Shaw. "Bigness is a trend around the world," says Ivan Fecan. "It's really important to have strong resourced Canadian companies that can compete." The result is that more and more TV and radio outlets are falling into the hands of fewer and fewer people. "That worries governments because bigness threatens governments and all the British socialists in Ottawa," says Izzy Asper. "They're suspicious and scared of it because it threatens them. They want to keep corporations small to minimize their power." But bigness doesn't worry former CRTC chair Françoise Bertrand, whose commission approved the broadcast deals. "The CRTC has recognized," she said, "the importance of consolidating the Canadian radio and television industries. The stronger our companies, the more they can contribute to achieving the cultural objectives set out in the Broadcasting Act."

Still, there are doubters who question the benefits of merger mania and warn that Internet people are different from entertainment people and content people are different from line company people. "I am not convinced there are the synergies that people are talking about in the BCE-CTV case," says Robert Rabinovitch. "Vertical integration not only reduces competition, but can also stifle creativity and innovation," says broadcast critic Matthew Fraser. "It's the way of the world, but there is a danger it will be overdone," says Ted Rogers. "There is a great danger of bureaucracy. I'm having a lot of trouble in getting it to work, getting people to work together. But we'll get it." Rogers also thinks BCE and the

Aspers will have a hard time making corporate vertical integration work. "It's easy for Fecan or Monty to decide on it, but it's the guys down the line who will make it work or not. They'll integrate it and then in some cases they may unintegrate. Do you really think the *Globe* and the *National Post* can both survive? I don't. Do you really think a management team that is experienced in running television stations is going to find it easy to run newspapers? I don't. Izzy's a wonderful man, but he's going to have to come out of retirement." Leonard Asper says, "What the players are doing is gathering up all the assets to be able to bring this new world to us in five, ten or fifteen years. But it will not happen overnight."

Izzy Asper himself is concerned about merging the cultures of television and newspapers as he aspires to do since buying Conrad Black's papers. He points to the merger problems of Canadian and Air Canada as an example of the difficulties. "Putting two different cultures together effectively and without abrasion in a harmonious way is a very delicate surgery," he says. "But even so, to fear convergence is ludicrous."

Watching the print and broadcast convergence mania from the sidelines, CITY-TV president Moses Znaimer cautions, "Historically, those cultures have not meshed at all."

But for all the perplexing futures facing the likes of Izzy and Leonard Asper, Ted Rogers, Ivan Fecan, Moses Znaimer, and Pierre-Karl Péladeau, as the new century dawned the private broadcasters were on a giddy roll. Sparkling with excitement at the opportunities and challenges of convergence, new technology, and their growing political and economic power, private broadcasters had entered a new era. Their success was beyond even the wildest dreams of Jim Allard, Harry Sedgwick, Spence Caldwell, and the other pioneer broadcasters.

11

Rinky-Dinks to Billionaires

The pioneers of Canadian broadcasting, with their rinky-dink stations, would look in astonishment at what's happened to their fun little business since that day in 1926 when Jacques Cartier of CKAC Montreal led his band of radio colleagues into the King Edward Hotel boardroom to chart the future of Canadian broadcasting and form the Canadian Association of Broadcasters. Their fledgling business grew beyond imagination. At first, though, most of high society had disdainfully sniffed at them as small-time lowbrows to be seated well below the salt.

"To embark upon a broadcasting career was to risk not only the scorning of the business community which regarded [radio] as a frivolous toy destined for quick oblivion, but to gamble one's social acceptance," Jim Allard once said of the early days. As writer Donald Jack noted in his book on CFRB, *Sinc, Betty and the Morning Man,* "Private radio men in the Thirties . . . were not socially acceptable. . . . The social arbiters considered that the people involved in it were frivolous and undignified."

The radio pioneers were dreamers and shopkeepers of the 1920s, like Keith Rogers broadcasting from his living-room studio in Charlottetown, Pappy Murphy in his studio at the back of his Saskatoon electric store, Harold Carson, who won his Lethbridge station in a poker game, Bert

Hooper, who was the only CKCK Regina employee, announcing, managing, and sweeping up, and George Chandler, who bought his station in Vancouver for $300 down and $25 a month for a year.

None of them could ever have imagined that their broadcasting descendants would be billionaires: CFTO co-founder and cable king Ted Rogers with estimated personal wealth of about $3 billion; Izzy Asper with about $2 billion; Pierre-Karl Péladeau and his brother, Erik, of Quebecor with about $800 million; Standard Broadcasting's Allan Slaight, who started out as a news reporter at CHAB Moose Jaw, now worth about $745 million; J R Shaw, the cable mogul who built Shaw Communications into a giant radio-TV player, has about $745 million (in 1999 alone, Shaw earned more than $30 million in various kinds of compensation); Winnipeg broadcast entrepreneur Randall Moffatt with about a billion; and, the richest of them all, although only part of his money came from broadcasting, Ken Thomson, whose father, Roy, began the Thomson empire in the 1930s with his Northern Ontario radio stations, and whose assets are estimated at about $24 billion.

Whether billionaires or mere millionaires, one consistent theme among the titans of broadcasting is that they're hooked on hard work. "Work in this very competitive, creative, and incredibly changing environment is as addictive as I'm told crack cocaine is," says CTV president Trina McQueen. "It gives you the same kind of high and the same kind of needing to have more – a sense that you're on a wild ride and it's pretty hard to get off. A good example is Ted Rogers and the story that when he was being wheeled into the operating room for a heart bypass, his cellphone was with him and they had to pry it from his anesthetized hands."

McQueen says it's not so much how high the stakes are as it is how passionate you are about the job. "Putting on *The National* every night as I did for years at the CBC was as intensive an experience as being involved in the BCE takeover," she says. "The intensity comes from within, not from without."

Broadcasters graduated from being socially and economically questionable in the 1920s and 1930s, to prosperous parvenus in the 1950s and 1960s, and, finally by the end of the century, to corporate colossi, sophisticated, cocksure, and running the most powerful cultural force in the nation. And no one personifies the new titans of broadcasting more than the wavy, white-haired, baby-faced boss of CTV, forty-seven-year-old Ivan Fecan.

Tall, slim, with a sophistication tempered by a touch of gee-whizery, Fecan knows more about television programming than anyone else in Canada, watching and critiquing it morning, noon, and night, with little or no time for hobbies, vacations, social life, children (he has none), or feet-up relaxing. Personally a bit shy but professionally aggressive, when his calculating eyes are not on a TV screen, he's wheeling and dealing his way through meetings, negotiations, or presentations about TV or print, more recently the latter as the new BCE-owned media corporation that he runs includes the *Globe and Mail*. At home with his wife, Sandra Faire, a successful TV producer in her own right, conversation focuses on the media, and Fecan listens closely to her professional advice.

Over the years, his voracious, almost lustful, appetite for television has been even more intense than that of the early broadcast pioneers such as Ted Rogers, Sr., Harry Sedgwick, or David Sarnoff. Like a baseball addict who knows the ERA of every pitcher and the batting statistics of every slugger, Fecan knows the performers, writers, producers, the program schedules, the strengths and weaknesses of individual shows, the deals made and pending, the program demographics, and the gossip of the industry. And he's been taking a crash course to gain similar knowledge of the world of print in his new media role as president of Bell Globemedia, whose annual revenue is about $1.2 billion. "I love it," he says. "I just love it. I'm not the smartest guy around, but I can work pretty hard."

He worked hard as a child, too, helping to support his Russian immigrant mother who had fled the Soviet Union virtually penniless. Born and growing up in the tough ethnic neighbourhood of Toronto's Kensington Market, Fecan worked, among other places, for an ethnic radio station and did sports freelancing for the *Globe and Mail* and the Toronto *Telegram*.

After graduating from Harbord Collegiate, he spent three years at York University in Toronto, leaving before getting a degree. "I was too impatient," he says. His first taste of television was at age nineteen, while working at CKBI-TV in Prince Albert. He wound up in Prince Albert because he was trying to see the country during his summer break from York and had got as far as Melfort, Saskatchewan. "I was almost out of money," he says, "and there were only two ways of getting out of Melfort, one was the bus to Saskatoon and the other was the train to Prince Albert. The train left first, so that's what I took."

His first job at CKBI was producing commercials for the station. While in Prince Albert, he also did a TV feature on a penitentiary inmate and tried to sell it to the CBC without any luck. Using just the audio track, he "repurposed" the feature into a radio story and sold it to CBC Radio. The CBC was impressed with the young, creative hustler, and he was soon working on the program *Identities* and sharing an office with Barbara Frum and Geraldine Sherman. In 1975, he became the first producer of the science radio program *Quirks and Quarks* with David Suzuki as host. Later he was hired by producer Mark Starowicz to work on the current affairs program *Sunday Morning*. "I credit CBC Radio with my real education in journalism," Fecan says. "You learn how to write in radio, how to structure and get to the story essence. It was fabulous to work there. When I think about the foundation of everything I've done in media, I think about CBC Radio."

In 1976, CITY-TV's Moses Znaimer, also a former CBCer, took Fecan away from the public broadcaster first to produce and later to run CITY-TV news in Toronto. For a while, he worked at CITY during the week and spent his weekends moonlighting at the CBC, producing Nancy White's cabaret material for *Sunday Morning*.

A couple of years later, the CBC rehired Fecan to run its local Toronto station, and he soon was promoted to be in charge of CBC-TV variety programming. In 1985, Hollywood beckoned and he went to work for NBC as a program vice-president. He nursemaided shows such as *Saturday Night Live* and *Late Night with David Letterman* and kept an eye for the network on *The Johnny Carson Show*. After a couple of high-octane years shuttling between Hollywood and New York, the CBC lured Fecan back to Canada to be CBC-TV program director and then vice-president in charge of English network television.

Ironically, at the same time, Trina McQueen, who is now Fecan's corporate right arm, was vice-president in charge of CBC news and current affairs, and she and Fecan were institutional rivals, fighting each other for budget and air time. Uncomfortable with CBC president Gérard Veilleux's management style and "bone weary" from handling CBC budget cuts, McQueen quit the CBC in 1993 to set up and run the new Discovery Channel Canada. In 1999, she left there to join Fecan at CTV as executive vice-president. Fecan has held CTV's door open for a large number of former CBC executives as well as McQueen, such as communications head Tom Curzon, programming president Susanne Boyce, business affairs vice-president Roman Melnyk, comedy and variety chief Ed Robinson, and Bob Culbert, vice-president of documentaries.

At the CBC, Fecan coped better with Veilleux than did McQueen. "I seemed to be able to deal with him," says Fecan. "I didn't find it a chore or troubling. I've been able to work well with people others consider difficult. Brandon Tartikoff at NBC had a tough reputation. So does Moses Znaimer, and Starowicz, too."

Veilleux himself quit the CBC presidency shortly after McQueen left, and within weeks, Fecan followed them out the door. Wooed by Baton Broadcasting head Doug Bassett, Fecan became Bassett's senior vice-president, moving to the executive vice-presidency less than two years later. In 1996, Bassett retired and Fecan took his place as president and CEO of Baton, where he orchestrated Baton's takeover of CTV and became the network president.

Along his meteoric career path – "My outside limit in jobs was three years until I was CBC vice-president," he says – Fecan had more program successes and admirers than he had failures and enemies, but he also had a substantial number of the latter. His aggressive, sometimes micro-managerial style offended numerous CBC producers, who resented his intrusions into what they felt were their creative areas. His CBC successes included the comedy programs *Kids in the Hall*, *Codco*, *This Hour Has 22 Minutes*, and the drama series *The Road to Avonlea*. His failures included an attempt at late-night variety, with *Friday Night! With Ralph Benmergui*, and the sitcom *Mosquito Lake*. But failures are part of doing business in television, he says. "You have to take risks if you're going to do anything worthwhile. What I really like a lot is talent-spotting and being able to develop people – developing a team."

Fecan also enjoys the financial rewards of being on the throne of a media empire. He has an elegant new home in Toronto's tony Rosedale area and personal wealth soaring into the stratosphere, with his multi-million-dollar compensation in salary, bonuses, incentives, and stock options. Even so, he lags far behind the $2 billion in assets of his brash, combative rival, Izzy Asper of CanWest Global.

If television for Ivan Fecan has been "the show," for Izzy Asper it's been "the deal." Storming through boardrooms, banks, courts, and corporate battlefields over a quarter-century, Asper has taken a floundering TV company from the edge of bankruptcy to being the richest TV operation in Canada and now has transformed it into a media giant. He did it with hurricane ferocity and relentless tenacity, a style he's had all his life.

"The Minnedosa Kid" is a nickname he likes for its suggestion of a Horatio Alger story of an ambitious, super-confident kid from the frontier town of Minnedosa, Manitoba, nestled on the Little Saskatchewan River with a population of two thousand. His Russian-born father, a classically trained violinist and orchestra conductor, owned the town's only movie house. Asper was introduced to showbiz by working as an usher in the theatre, the Lyric, seating fans and scraping chewing gum off the seats.

At the University of Manitoba, Asper became the campus debating champion, wrote a jazz column for the student newspaper, and was class valedictorian. He graduated with a law degree and in 1957 launched a successful corporate law practice, and on the side, he wrote a syndicated tax and legal column for newspapers.

But his competitive nature craved more challenge and excitement, and he gave up a $200,000 annual law income for the daredevil life of an entrepreneur. His first venture was to set up a distillery to export liquor, which made money from the start and was bought out at a handsome profit eight months later by a Montreal firm. With cash in his pocket and a political itch in his heart, his next target was the office of the premier of Manitoba. The son of what he has described as "a pathological Liberal," Asper won the leadership of a moribund Manitoba Liberal party in 1970. It had just three seats in the legislature. He was dubbed "Landslide Asper" when he won his own seat in a general election by just four votes and brought Liberal representation in the legislature from three to five. Asper says he's a middle-of-the-road Liberal, but friends and colleagues call him a right-wing Liberal along the lines of C. D. Howe, the one-time Minister of Everything for Mackenzie King and Louis St. Laurent.

Bored by mundane local issues and realizing he had little chance of winning the premiership, Asper's political fires quickly cooled. "I wasn't any good at it," he says. "I didn't enjoy it. It needed more patience than I had." He headed back to the battlefield of business, particularly television. At the time, Winnipeg had CBC and CTV stations, and an American station, KCND, serving the area from Pembina, North Dakota. The CRTC was prepared to licence a third Winnipeg station, so Asper, with his political colleague Peter Liba, put together a small group of investors, including Winnipeg theatre owner Paul Morton and Toronto broadcast engineer Seymour Epstein.

The would-be station owners quickly realized that four stations were one too many for the Winnipeg market and they decided to buy KCND and move it to Winnipeg. The owner, a rich Texan, was reluctant to sell until the Canadian government indirectly persuaded him. Asper let the Texas tycoon know that the Canadian government was about to take action that could destroy KCND's advertising revenue from Winnipeg, its main source of income. The new policy would deny Canadian businesses a tax deduction for the cost of ads they put on American stations that were aimed at a Canadian market. The combination of Ottawa's move to protect Canadian broadcasters and Asper's persistence wore down the Texan, who finally sold the station to Asper for $750,000. The CRTC gave Asper the licence, and what was now called CKND began broadcasting to Winnipeg on September 1, 1975, from a converted Safeway supermarket store with equipment trucked up from Pembina and offering glitch-strewn local programming.

CKND soon overcame its initial production gaffes and began threatening its local rivals. The CBC station's six o'clock local news had long been number one in the market, but was soon knocked off its pedestal by CKND's six o'clock airing of *The Gong Show*. Asper had found a money-making formula for success: prime-time American shows, tight cost controls, and advertiser friendliness. It was a prescription that he effectively applied later to his entire broadcast empire.

As the biggest financial success story in Canadian broadcasting and the industry's Peck's Bad Boy, Asper lives by the rule: Never be afraid to attempt to do things that people tell you can't be done. Other advice he gives in what he calls Asper's Axioms include: Never do a little deal; Never forget where you came from; Never forget the system is built on greed; and Never start a war, but if you're in one, take no prisoners.

His restless, workaholic nature, his fourteen-hour working days, his chain-smoking, his heavy coffee drinking, late nights, and his aggressive style caught up with him at age fifty in 1983 when he was felled by a heart attack. He had a quadruple heart bypass and in 1999 had a pacemaker implanted. Twice he announced to colleagues that he was going to retire, only to keep on delaying the day. Finally, in 1998 he moved upstairs to be executive chairman of CanWest Global, which allows him to focus on corporate strategy. Being in one job too long weakens leadership, he believes. "We all have a tendency to grow more conservative, even defensive, the longer we remain in the same post," he says. His new role away from daily operating responsibilities gives him more time to plan his philanthropy and to indulge in his lifelong passion for jazz. In fact, his business philosophy borrows from his love of jazz. Both, he says, are based on improvisation and the challenge is "making beautiful harmony out of cacophony. . . . I've been accused of running my company like a jazz combo."

Asper is an accomplished pianist, a fan of Duke Ellington and Dave Brubeck, and a devotee of George Gershwin. His Gershwin memorabilia includes the seventeen pages of brown paper on which the libretto to *Porgy and Bess* was written and which is kept in what is known as "The Gershwin Room" in his Winnipeg home. "I've always said," he told Winnipeg theatre critic Kevin Prokosh, "that if I could die and come back, I'd come back and finish Gershwin's life. He was only thirty-eight, man."

Asper owns a Palm Beach mansion, a Winnipeg home, a summer retreat at Falcon Lake northeast of Winnipeg, and a posh Manhattan apartment where he stays on trips to New York for business meetings by day and to visit Manhattan jazz clubs at night. One of Asper's fantasies, he says, is to live in New York in the Roaring Twenties: "Gershwin would come to play the piano, Robert Benchley would be there, and Igor Stravinsky and F. Scott Fitzgerald would drop by with bagels and cream. . . ."

Asper feels he's "the luckiest guy in the world," even if he does tote his briefcases wherever he goes and ODs on hour-long 2:00 A.M. business phone calls. But his travels always bring him back to his beloved Winnipeg, and he refuses to move his corporate headquarters to Toronto. "I live ten minutes from the airport, ten minutes from my office, ten minutes from my friends," he tells everyone who asks. "It's a small city. I love it." But he frets that his career has been all business. "When I went into TV I thought I was going to have a lot more fun in it than I did," he says. "I wanted to be in the content side, not the business side. But we had no money, so when you have no money you spend twenty-four hours a day begging banks. I'm pissed off that I spent my life in financial trench warfare. So I never got to do what I really wanted to. But my last hurrah will be in the creative field. Now I've got a chance and I've got licences from the CRTC for a specialty channel in jazz and one called *The Canada Channel* with political debate, documentaries, current issues for those who really care about Canada. I'm a history and public affairs buff and it'll be fun, but first I've got to get the cable companies to carry them and I've been kissing butts from Toronto to Calgary to do that." It's an improbable but not impossible aspiration for the sixty-nine-year-old, hard-nosed dreamer and self-made billionaire, "The Kid from Minnedosa."

Asper believes he'll have more time for that aspiration now that his thirty-seven-year-old son, Leonard, has responsibility for most day-to-day operations. The dimpled, boyish Leonard is not quite a chip off the old Asper block. He's more open to compromise, but he has his father's combative competitiveness, hard work habits, and fierce determination. He's also more attuned to the new media than his father. Former CRTC chair Françoise Bertrand says, "Izzy himself didn't really believe in the Internet, but today the company seems to have changed its mind. Now that Leonard has more authority, I can hear different things."

The driving ambition and single-minded workaholism of the Aspers and Ivan Fecan are qualities shared by their arch rival, TV titan Ted Rogers, whose communications empire encompasses everything from cable to cellphones, broadcasting to magazine publishing, the Internet to video stores and sports franchises, including the Toronto Blue Jays. Where they differ, however, is that while Izzy Asper has focused on deals and Ivan Fecan on shows, Ted Rogers is a visionary fascinated by technology. They differ, too, in that while Asper and Fecan grew up in Russian immigrant households, Rogers is the descendant of wealthy Anglophone ancestors who reportedly came over on *The Mayflower*, made fortunes, were heaped with honours for civic contributions, and gave him an establishment pedigree as a quintessential Toronto WASP. "But," he smiles, "we also had a relative who was hanged."

He was a mischievous rebel in his years boarding at Toronto's exclusive Upper Canada College, frequently getting caned by his teachers for pranks and rule-breaking. He took up boxing at school and says, "I've always been a fighter." In his last year at UCC, he lived at home and was chauffeured to school every morning. At the University of Toronto, he honed his entrepreneurial skills in a dozen money-making schemes, including booking dance bands and selling photographs of students and their dance dates. He was president of the U. of T. Progressive Conservative Student Federation and was once detained by U.S. immigration authorities as a suspicious political character when he declared he was a member of the Progressive Conservative party. That led to a campus demonstration with U. of T. students protesting and waving signs saying, "Release Our Ted" and "Save Rogers." He also led the Youth for Diefenbaker student movement, travelling the country in support of John Diefenbaker.

Rogers' hyperactivity springs from an almost desperate determination to honour his father, who died at age thirty-eight in 1939 when Ted was just five years old. "He just worked himself to death," Rogers told writer Bruce McDougall. "He was my hero and role model and I think I was very motivated by that because I felt cheated that he died. . . . If you have a feeling you've been robbed, you have a touch of bitterness and it really propels you. . . . It has always driven me."

Because of his father, Rogers also has deeper roots in broadcasting than either Fecan or Asper, as Ted Rogers, Sr., was one of Canada's broadcast pioneers, a founder of Toronto radio station CFRB, the inventor of batteryless radio in 1925, and was experimenting with television in the early 1930s and radar in 1936, three years before his death. "His memory . . . has provided me with incredible inspiration," says Rogers. "I would have liked to hug him." Rogers adds, "I inherited from him through my mother impatience to get the job done, and determination, focus and I guess I'm innovative . . . I'm also not modest. If I was, I wouldn't have to work so hard!"

Rogers has always worried that like his father he, too, would have a short life. "He died so young and I've always thought I would die young," he says. At thirty-five, he bought a lot of life insurance and put his assets in a trust. "Now I'm sixty-eight," he says, "and I've had bypasses, heart attacks, and a lot of operations, so I don't think I have a lot of time."

His entrepreneurial skills and his gambler's instincts were evident when, in 1960, while still a law student, he used the last $85,000 of his inheritance to buy Toronto FM station CHFI, managing the station while pursuing his studies. Around the same time, he and the famous TV announcer Joel Aldred raised $1.5 million in a scheme to get a Toronto

TV licence. When they couldn't raise more money, Rogers made "a cold call" to John Bassett and wound up in a partnership with him to run CFTO. Rogers and Aldred owned about one-third of the station and Aldred became company president and Rogers vice-president, but Bassett remained the boss. Bassett became close to Rogers, recognizing a bit of himself in the tall, slim, precocious young man. "I liked Bassett very much," he says. "We had the same approach. We didn't give a damn. . . . We were both bullshitters. . . . Our style was to invade, attack . . . move forward."

During a 1967 holiday in Australia, Rogers read a book about cable TV and was immediately seized by the potential of the new industry and formed a cable company that would, in time, be worth billions. Within a year, he had a licence and soon he was able to offer ten channels to his Toronto customers along with channels for music from CHFI and CKEY. Three years later, he raised his service to twenty TV channels. By buying up his competitors, Rogers was the largest cable company in Canada by 1981 and today it remains number one.

In 1985, his restless business style took him into the cellphone business, expanding it to include paging and high-speed data transmission. In 1994, Rogers again moved into new technology, selling his cable subscribers access to the Internet. That same year, Rogers bought Maclean-Hunter, becoming Canada's biggest magazine publisher. Along the way, he has picked up about thirty radio stations across Canada, some TV interests, including The Shopping Channel, and a couple of hundred video rental stores. His company's assets are about $7.8 billion, with an operating profit for 2000 of $918 million on revenues of $3.1 billion.

Rogers' frenzied buying and selling and his ever-expanding universe have intrigued and frightened associates and observers. British Telecom and AT&T were so intrigued they recently invested a total of $1.4 billion for a one-third interest in Rogers' cellular telephone network, Cantel, and Microsoft invested $600 million in Rogers Communications. These infusions helped allay some of the alarm that shareholders and observers had felt over Rogers' foundering share values and the massive debt load he was piling up to fuel his expanding empire. With those investments and rising profits, Rogers cut his company's long-term debt from a terrifying $5.3 billion to $3.4 billion.

Rogers is philosophical about his daredevil financing and his close calls with bankruptcy: "You don't deserve to be called an entrepreneur unless you've mortgaged your home to the business. Four times I've been within a hair's breath of losing my house and my business. It's not fun, but you just have to have faith and pray and work hard."

He also is a tough customer to deal with in business negotiations. A colleague of Rogers once told writer Matthew Fraser that "Ted has the skin of a rhino and the balls of a hippo." Ron Osborne, who was head of Maclean-Hunter and tried to stop the Rogers takeover of the publishing company, reportedly told friends after the fiery negotiations that as a negotiator, Rogers was "a Detroit knee-capper." One of his ancestors, back in the 1500s, was an English minister, the Reverend John Rogers, who was known as "Roaring Rogers." According to historians, "Rogers" is a war name, meaning "renowned spearman." Early in his career, Rogers was described in a Toronto newspaper headline as, "THE YOUNG MAN WHO GETS WHAT HE WANTS."

An example of his tough style can be seen in his effort to buy Quebec's cable conglomerate Vidéotron. He'd made an agreement for the purchase but had also made a deal for a kill fee if the purchase didn't go through. It didn't when he was later outbid by Quebecor, and he collected a kill fee of $241 million, more than twice what he paid to buy the Toronto Blue Jays.

In a tense boardroom showdown with John Bassett one time, Rogers recalls, "John stood up and said, 'Ted, I've always thought of you as a son.' Senator Stanbury, who sat next to me, whispered, 'Yeah, like a son of a bitch!'" Rogers dismisses the tough-guy image, saying with a grin, "In negotiations, I believe in love, not war."

A high-intensity, risk-taking visionary, Ted Rogers slam-bangs his way through eighty-hour work weeks, sometimes sleeping at his office and taking little time to enjoy the coddled life of the billionaire that he is. "I never keep track of how many hours I work," he says. But with salary, bonuses, and other compensation adding up to about $3.5 million a year and a personal worth estimated at $3 billion, he can easily afford such millionaire's toys as a lavish summer home in Muskoka, the warm-weather playground of Toronto's rich and powerful, a private jet to fly him in three hours to his luxurious winter home in the Bahamas, where he enjoys sailing his multimillion-dollar yacht, and a mansion in Toronto's ritzy Forest Hill area, where he bought and demolished a neighbour's home so he could have a tennis court.

Wherever he is, Rogers, the overachieving salesman, is always working on new deals, investigating potential ventures, often outraging and frequently inspiring his colleagues. Faxes, phone calls, couriers, and e-mail follow him whether he's on the yacht or the tennis court. Five briefcases travel with him when he takes a so-called holiday. Rogers seldom takes time to rejoice in his conquests. He says, "I've never given up. . . . Never give up. Never, and keep trying. I learned that from my father and my mother. I'm not mechanical because I'm too impatient. I don't read the instructions. But I am a technological visionary." Former Ontario premier David Peterson says, "He just never relaxes. He's the only guy I know who does three things at one time." This is underlined by Rogers' colleague Phil Lind, who told a CBC interviewer, "Ted always has a million and one ideas, and they've always got to be implemented right then and there."

Rogers has had to pay the price for his hyperkinetic business and lifestyle, including a quadruple heart bypass, aneurism surgery, and eye surgery, and little time to savour family life. Whether in Muskoka or Nassau, Rogers doesn't see much of the sun because, "I get all these skin cancer things and then they stab you and carve them out. I also only have one eye, it sometimes turns all red. I have to be a little careful. I'm just lucky to be here." But as he heads toward seventy, he wonders if he should slow down a bit. "I enjoy what I do, but as you get older you can get too involved in the work, and you want to have more fun. Maybe I can be more balanced and slow down to a gallop." He has told colleagues that he plans to leave his job in 2004 and become a consultant to his company.

"Rogers is a genuine entrepreneur, perhaps the most daring Canada has," says Peter C. Newman, chronicler of Canada's rich and famous. ". . . He is the great Riverboat Gambler of the Canadian Establishment."

If there is anyone the exact opposite of the whitebread tycoon Ted Rogers, it's the brash Russian immigrant and iconoclastic TV philosopher king, Moses Znaimer of CITY-TV in Toronto. In his own way, Znaimer, with his cocky little station that grew, has had as big an impact on what we see on TV as Rogers, Fecan, or Asper.

Born in Kulab, Tajikistan, to parents fleeing the Nazis, Znaimer arrived in Montreal as a child in 1948 and became a breathtakingly self-confident TV visionary. He has revolutionized the industry with his tradition-busting philosophy that what's important is "the flow, not the show . . . the process is the product." He has translated his controversial McLuhanistic perspective into a unique TV success story, broadcasting a downtown, hard-edged, youthful, and open concept of television. What he produces is television with an attitude. "Television with character," he calls it.

Fifteen TV sets, including one with a six-foot-wide screen that stares at him across from his desk, flank Znaimer in his office, where he puts in fourteen- to fifteen-hour days, usually ending at midnight or later. He uses an office cot if he spends the night at work. "The title I gave myself," he says, "is president–executive producer. I work intensively at the beginning of a program or channel to establish its look and feel. I have conceived every one of our channels, written every one of their mission statements, configured the original schedule, hired all the key creative staff, including the on-air casting. I am a producing president. I am not a financial president. I am not a sales president. It is my conceit that you can recognize a Moses Znaimer channel. I don't know of any other producing president in the world."

Znaimer has been rocking boats all his life. After graduating from McGill and Harvard, his first job was producing a CBC commentary program called *Metro Byline.* "On my first day, I clashed with a guy called Peter Gzowski, who was a freelancer and who was not used to having his scripts edited. I said, 'I'd like to see your script.' He said, 'What do you mean, you'd like to see my script?' I said, 'I'm the producer!' and he grudgingly handed it over. I proceeded to make some corrections and he was quite horrified. He couldn't believe my cheek. But he accepted my editing."

Shortly afterwards, Znaimer and producer Andrew Simon launched *Cross Country Check-up* on CBC Radio and then he did a program advocating abolition of the Crown. "The shit hit the fan," he says. He was "exiled" to Ottawa, where he worked on, among other projects, the daily morning radio program *Preview Commentary.* He also did a radio documentary series about Jews and gentiles, which, he says, "got me into more trouble," and he was transferred to the local current affairs program *Twenty Million Questions.* On the side, during Canada's Centennial year, 1967, he produced a TV series on the fiftieth anniversary of the Russian

Revolution. It, too, was controversial, and he was getting known for being an "enfant terrible." "When the powers that be found out what I was doing, they were stunned and thought they should punish me," he says. They sent him to Toronto to work on the afternoon TV program *Take Thirty*, hosted by Adrienne Clarkson and Paul Soles. Later he joined the Sunday-night TV current affairs program *The Way It Is*, run by a fellow creative disturber of the peace, Ross McLean. Znaimer was a reporter and producer, who covered everything from the civil war in Biafra to student riots in Mexico. When the CBC rejected his proposal for a high-tech phone-in show to poll Canadian attitudes on current issues, he resigned in frustration and took his talents to the venture capital business. Lawyer, and now senator, Jerry Grafstein, a friend from Znaimer's Ottawa days, suggested that he join a small group of colleagues to launch a new television station in Toronto.

Znaimer's heart had been in television ever since he had bought his family's first set with money from his bar mitzvah. (Today, he has one of the largest collections of vintage sets in the world.) Intrigued by Grafstein's suggestion, Znaimer eagerly joined Grafstein, Phyllis Switzer, and Edgar Cowan in seeking a licence. They were competing against the *Toronto Star* and Standard Broadcasting. "The *Star* and Standard said Toronto was too important a licence to be given to a kid. I was twenty-eight," Znaimer recalls. "But we got the licence for CITY, and our style of storefront openness evolved from necessity. I didn't have the money to go with a Rolls-Royce style. Besides, I had a taste for cinema verité, and we developed a video verité. So my needs and my tastes intertwined."

In keeping with his hip style of television, Znaimer set up shop in the former Electric Circus nightclub in the heart of downtown Toronto. Later, as CITY expanded, he moved the station a dozen or so blocks to a 1915 five-storey Gothic building, which originally had housed the Methodist Book and Publishing Company.

What the Methodists would think of what comes out of the building now is intriguing to contemplate, for it includes not only CITY-TV, but also a whole range of specialty channels, showcasing the arts on Bravo, music on MuchMusic, science fiction and fact on SPACE, and showbiz gossip on STAR, as well as an eclectic range of individual programs on sex "in all its diversity" that show "the lives and loves of gay, lesbian, bi, trans, and open-minded straight people around the world."

Znaimer says, "CITY has no game shows, no cooking shows, no exercise shows, no kiddie shows, no religious broadcasts. You simply narrow the amount of material you touch on."

Money was a challenge for Znaimer in CITY's early years, but soon the Bronfman family provided needed cash, and in 1978, Allan Waters' CHUM Ltd. added CITY to its growing media empire, making Znaimer the creative leader of its TV domain. By 2001, the CHUM realm included twenty-eight radio stations; seven local, independent TV stations in southwestern Ontario, Ottawa, and Victoria-Vancouver, four regional and six national TV specialty channels; Internet operations; and an international arm that sells the CITY style to stations around the world, including Argentina, Colombia, Finland, Romania, and Spain. MuchMusic is seen in eighteen million American homes, some via cable but mostly by satellite, and television stations in more than 130 countries buy many of CITY's programs.

Znaimer likes to quote Albert Einstein: "Imagination is more important than knowledge." He believes in short, sharp jabs of programming. "My view is that brevity is the soul of television. The intelligentsia take the view that long is deep and short is shallow. But there is a lot of flatulence in great length and a lot of brilliance in pithy construction. Not every eight-hundred-page novel is better than a Guy de Maupassant short story. Video is the short-story form."

Znaimer also turns on its head the notion that local news is the least significant. "We inverted that agenda," he says. "There is not much I can do about Washington. There is even less I can do about the Middle East. But I'm a factor in my city. I'm a force in my neighbourhood. I'm a power on my street. And I'm a fucking king in my house." Accordingly, *City Pulse News* shows the action in the streets rather than the discussions in the boardrooms and corridors of power.

"Moses is a brilliant niche broadcaster," says Robert Rabinovitch. "He's the only one who's really focused on that Canadian market because it makes him distinctive. He understands the logic of being a niche." Znaimer's ideas are catching on, and many among the veritable flood of new channels spilling out of TV sets these days are using local programming to sharpen their identity. "There is everywhere a powerfully felt need for local culture," Znaimer says.

One of Znaimer's concerns is that copycat rivals may soon challenge him on his own turf, especially Global, which, since Izzy Asper bought the Southam chain of newspapers from Conrad Black, now has access to enormous amounts of local news generated by the newspapers. "Ouch!" says Znaimer. "That's tough. If they have the wit to marshal that, they will be a powerful adversary."

Just as Izzy Asper has his axioms, Znaimer has his "commandments" that encapsulate his approach, although, while Asper's are for the world of hard-headed business, Znaimer's comments are more philosophical. "Television is the triumph of image over the printed word," is his first commandment. Others include: "TV is as much about the people bringing you the story as the story itself"; "The best of TV tells me what happened to me today"; "TV creates immediate consensus, subject to immediate change."

Although he is denounced by many in the intelligentsia for zapping eyeballs instead of enriching brain cells in his mad dash to entertain people, Znaimer looks to TV as a future instrument of education. He's considering a bouquet of educational channels. His company already owns the provincial educational channel in Alberta, having bought it when the Conservative government there wanted to privatize it. "It's time to bring education to the people fully in an electronic way," he says. "Television has transformed the lives of every man, woman, and child on the planet. We rely on television for our knowledge of the world, our work, our play, our social interaction, our democracy. Now for the first time, history is moving inexorably toward total dependence on a single core technology. Ours is the central business of the age, a powerful force for good."

How we use that force in Canada is essentially up to Moses Znaimer, Ivan Fecan, Izzy Asper, and Ted Rogers, along with other private broadcasting luminaries such as Trina McQueen, Jim Shaw, John Cassaday, Allan Slaight, and Pierre-Karl Péladeau. They, with a still-to-be-defined helping hand from public broadcasters, will control most of what we hear and see on the air in the years ahead. Our viewing future is in their hands.

12

A Whole New World

"**W**e are on the verge of something entirely new and unpredictable, something that is transforming Canada's broadcasting landscape. It's a whole new world out there, so hang on to your hat!"

When CAB president Michael McCabe says that, he's talking about revolutionary technologies, colossal media conglomerates, boundless choice for viewers and listeners, and the erasure of national and cultural borders. He's talking about a tornado of change – corporate change, creative change, policy change – and about digitalization, interactive TV, audience fragmentation, demassification, and the decline of networks. He's talking about the future of the CBC, the CRTC, of regulation, and about a handful of corporate leviathans with a mind-boggling array of media pipelines, including TV stations, networks, radio, cable, specialty channels, the Internet, books, magazines, and newspapers, as well as a cornucopia of product spilling out of their own production houses, their own sports teams, events they own or control, and a myriad of other product producers. McCabe himself, however, won't be representing private broadcasters when all these changes occur, having decided to retire as CAB head in November 2001 after thirteen years at the helm.

"I predict," says Moses Znaimer, "the continuing proliferation of channels and choices – more channels, more methods of delivery – and there will be no end to it."

What McCabe and Znaimer are talking about will bring either a new Jerusalem or a new Babylon, depending on what comes down the multitude of media pipelines. Those pipelines aren't worth a damn without content the public wants or needs flowing through. The Fowler report's comment in 1965 is as valid today as then: "The only thing that really matters in broadcasting is program content. All the rest is housekeeping." That's especially true now there are so many channels that the need to stand out is paramount. "When you go from scarce television, when there was just a handful of channels, to multi-channel television, the focus goes to the programming," says Znaimer.

The most successful of the new media titans will be the ones who realize they are not in the pipeline business, but in the content business. The pipeline is only a means to an end. If their TV shows are boring, if their baseball or football teams are losers, if their news is unreliable or dull, or if their music is outdated, all the pipelines in the world will be useless because content is king. Paraphrasing an old American political slogan, Robert Rabinovitch says, "It's the programming, stupid!"

"Ultimately," says Izzy Asper, "it comes down to the product. With so many new technologies like the Internet and satellites, programming rules the roost. . . . If your content is no good, the delivery systems won't help you." That's why he bought the Fireworks Entertainment production house in 1998, which gave him six hundred hours of program content, and why he spent $140 million to buy a Dutch distributor, giving him, among other things, another library of six hundred hours of TV programming. It's also why Ivan Fecan spent $49 million buying a half-interest in the movie and TV production company Landscape Entertainment run by powerful Hollywood producer and former CBC-TV star Robert Cooper.

The big issue throughout the history of Canadian broadcasting has been the airing of Canadian programs. For decades, the BBG and then the CRTC, as well as cultural nationalists galore, have pleaded, demanded, and threatened private broadcasters about airing more Canadian programs. The CRTC states that its primary objective is to "maximize Canadian content in all communication media." With anguished reluctance and dire warnings about the cost, but knowing their licences depended on it, private broadcasters have grumpily aired a few Canadian programs, in addition to news and sports, all the time continuing to fill their prime time with highly profitable American shows and complaining about losing money on Canadian programs.

"All Canadian broadcasters lose a considerable amount on the Canadian drama programming they exhibit," says Asper. "The private industry hasn't got the money to do popular drama," says former senior broadcasting executive Ross McCreath. "When they do put it on, because they haven't got the money, they do it on a shoestring budget and they end up with a show that doesn't get any ratings and they don't sell any time. If you have three or four of those, you're out of business."

The arithmetic is simple. Ivan Fecan has noted that the average American series generates about $200,000 an hour in revenue and costs $80,000 to broadcast, for a net profit of $120,000. Canadian productions aired by conventional broadcasters, he says, generate about $125,000 in ad revenue per hour, but cost $200,000, for a net loss of $75,000.

But the transformation of the Canadian broadcasting landscape that Moses Znaimer and Michael McCabe talk about has awoken new interest in Canadian productions. The endless argument about Canadian content might soon be over. "The future for Canadian private broadcasting is in its Canadian programming," McCabe says. "It's what sets us apart." "Canadian can be profitable," says Fecan. Repackaging programs for different media pipelines, including the Internet and specialty channels, and selling overseas to a product-hungry media world brings in extra revenue that can make Canadian content profitable. For the first time, there might soon be a business incentive to produce Canadian programming. Rabinovitch, however, remains skeptical that private broadcasters will make more Canadian programming. "At this point," he says, "it's rhetoric. I've got to see it to believe it. None of the private broadcasters can survive and make money without being just rebroadcasters of American programs." In a discussion with York University students in Toronto, Rabinovitch said of private broadcasters, "They see Canadian content as the cost of a licence and if they had their way they would sell out to NBC or ABC in five seconds. Don't expect them to have a social conscience. It's antithetical to what they are all about." As for most of the specialty channels, Rabinovitch says, "Their programming is basically repeats or programs done on the cheap. If you want quality

Canadian programs, the only one who can afford to do it is the CBC."

However, among a few private broadcast executives, especially those who once worked at the CBC, there is a strong desire for more Canadian shows. One reason why Doug Bassett and his Baton boardroom colleagues enticed Ivan Fecan to leave the CBC was Fecan's background in Canadian programming. "They're now pushing the Canadian envelope at CTV as far as they can, recognizing that at the end of the day they have to show a profit," says independent consultant Pauline Couture, who has worked with CTV and other broadcasting and production organizations. "I've always seen Canadian programs as really important," says CTV's Trina McQueen, "not so much so that artists could be employed, but because of what it means to the individual viewer's ability to dream and imagine and connect."

Former Quebec TVA boss Daniel Lamarre agrees. "The future of Canadian television in the new millennium will be built on Canadian content," he says. "With the new global Internet, we'll have no choice but to distinguish ourselves with our own culture [and] create Canadian content that can attract domestic audiences and also have strong export potential."

Attracting those Canadian audiences, however, will mean a big increase in private network spending on Canadian programs. CRTC figures for 2000 showed that of its on-air revenue, CTV spent 32.9 per cent on Canadian shows; TVA, 32.2 per cent; and Global, 19.4 per cent. For Global and CTV, most of that expenditure went to news and sports. For the key drama-comedy area, Global spent 4.5 per cent of its total revenue on Canadian content, CTV, 8.4 per cent, and TVA, 6.1 per cent.

The distance the private networks have to go in getting Canadians to watch Canadian programs is shown in CRTC viewing statistics. While almost all of CBC's prime-time viewing was of Canadian programs, the private English networks in 1999 attracted only a tiny share of viewers to their prime-time Canadian programs. For Global, 5 per cent of its total audience was for Canadian programming, and for CTV it was 12 per cent. TVA had 68 per cent.

Thus there is a big gap, particularly for the private English networks, between their rhetoric and actually increasing Canadian programming and viewing.

Another reason why Canadian private broadcasters are beginning to look seriously at airing more Canadian programming is that, within the next half-dozen years, American producers could decide not to sell their shows to Canadian networks and stations because they might be able to make more money distributing them themselves. "Down the road, the Americans are not going to sell their programming to us," says Michael McCabe. "They're going to say we want to drive our brand name all over North America so we want this program exclusively. For example, *Schindler's List* was not available for sale to Canadian TV because the U.S. network said they wanted it exclusively. They had an advertising advantage that outweighed what they would get from a Canadian network in a sale. The more that happens, the more you have to turn to Canadian programming. And the availability of programming on the Internet and through the satellite means we are going to have to have more Canadian programming. So Canadian broadcasters are no longer resisting Canadian production and, in fact, believe that it is the key to their survival. We are going to have to make money with our Canadian programs, and in the 500-channel universe, what will make us distinctive is our Canadian programming."

Former CRTC chair Françoise Bertrand agrees with McCabe. "Now there is going to be a business reason for Canadian programs that was not there before. The business reality has been such that it was easy to buy American content. But now, the Americans – Mr. ABC, Mr. Fox, and Mr. Disney – won't need you any more because they'll be able to send their product through to the viewer themselves. So this changes the economics of programming. There soon may be a new motive and a new incentive for the broadcasters to air Canadian programs."

There are, however, some industry executives who feel an American refusal to sell programs to Canadian broadcasters is a long way off. "I've been hearing about that for years," says Trina McQueen. "I'll be collecting my pension before it happens." Ted Rogers is similarly skeptical. "I've heard the theory, but my radar doesn't have the Americans withholding their product and providing it themselves. I'm not sure it's a realistic theory," he says. "I think it's a lot of flim-flam," says Rabinovitch. "The evidence is not there yet."

The incentive for private broadcasters to air Canadian programs has been, for more than forty years, the government's broadcast regulations requiring Canadian content and, more recently, the government's annual television fund subsidy for Canadian programs, worth about $230 million.

In the past, the fund's millions have gone to independent producers who make and own the programs, not to the networks and stations that, in effect, rent them for showing. But now, the TV operators want to have some of that government money go directly to them. They already own the news, sports, and local programming, and they want a chance at owning the entertainment programs produced with money from the government's television fund, but right now that's not allowed. However, looking ahead, Trina McQueen thinks, "That's a barrier that will come down."

Michael McCabe would like to see not only that barrier down, but also an increase in the fund to subsidize private broadcaster productions. "We have to have our programming out there making money. We must be developing distinctive programs that we own. We've got to talk to the government about giving incentives to us to achieve this because we can't make enough money on our own."

Some support for this viewpoint comes from Françoise Bertrand. "More and more you see it is in the interest of broadcasters to do either in-house production or to own production companies, or to share distribution rights with production companies," she says. With profit from distribution rights becoming more important to the TV industry, Bertrand believes broadcasters should have a larger share of them.

"Distribution rights will become maybe not as important as advertising revenues, but will become more and more, very important," she says. "If those revenues are strictly going to production companies, then the broadcasters will be impoverished. Going into the digital world, owning content, having proprietary rights, is important. If broadcasters want to grow and move and sell, they need to own rights." Besides, if the broadcasters increase their distribution profits, Bertrand says, "then we would expect them to offer more hours of Canadian content to help fulfill the purposes of the Broadcasting Act."

What kind of Canadian content is produced may become an issue, however. The emphasis on profits from exporting Canadian programs means "industrial" Canadian shows will be the focus of private production – generic shows shorn of most, if not all, Canadian reference points, place names, experience, and issues.

"In order to have an industrial base, we will need to do a whole range of generic programming, keeping writers and directors working," says McCabe. "A lot of this programming is going to be generic because the economics won't work otherwise. For those Canadian dramas that tell our Canadian story, the CBC should be doing them."

That's something Rabinovitch agrees with. "The type of Canadian content that the private networks will generate will be Canadian content that ultimately can be resold to third parties – distinctively not Canadian. To be economically viable, they need a sale to an American network or European network. And the only product that will sell in the States is a product that is not distinguishably Canadian. The CBC's job is to make distinguishably Canadian programs."

Bertrand says, "I think you can be successful with strong Canadian content and still be capable of exporting." She believes that while "industrial" drama will not echo Canadian values, it will provide a creative base. CBC drama, however, she says, should be strongly reflective of Canada.

Bertrand gives the cable industry poor marks for its encouragement of Canadian programming. "The broadcaster has to be the driver, not cable companies," she says. "Cable companies, frankly, have been much more keen to have more American services. They don't believe in Canadian content. I haven't seen any proof that they do. What they believe in is packaging for their customers."

In the past, private broadcasters repeatedly complained that there was not enough talent in Canada to produce quality programs, but that attitude is changing. "There is a huge pool of Canadian stories and talent to draw on from across all the arts," says Ivan Fecan. "There is no scarcity of Canadian content," says Asper. And, adds Susanne Boyce, CTV's head of programming, "People will watch Canadian. The audience is there."

One route to more Canadian programming is the CRTC requirement for a "benefit" package associated with new deals requiring CRTC approval. The new owner of a TV operation must pledge to spend 10 per cent of the value of the deal on development of Canadian programming. Seeking a regulatory okay for its $2.3 billion takeover of CTV, BCE promised to spend $230 million to develop Canadian programming, talent, and culture, including $56 million on new series and specials and $53.5 million for expanded news coverage, foreign news bureaus, and a current affairs series for young adults. Global, in its $800 million buyout of WIC, promised the CRTC that it would spend $84 million of new money on Canadian programming, documentaries, funds for western

Canadian producers, spots on famous Canadians, and support for aboriginal producers.

With commitments like these, with the need to differentiate themselves among the multitude of television choices, and with the threat that American producers might not continue to sell their products to Canadian TV stations, Canadian private broadcasters may have no choice but to concentrate on Canadian programming. "The more you control your own schedule, the better you're going to be in the long run," says CHUM Television president Jay Switzer.

"Technology has always outstripped government. The power of government to control anything is diminishing rapidly."

It was diminishing when CAB president Jim Allard made that comment a quarter-century ago, but now the issue is whether that control is disappearing, not just diminishing, at least so far as CRTC regulation is concerned. Around the same time, Don Jamieson went one step further, saying, "The day may have come when even as great a power as the state will have to abandon its efforts to shape broadcasting deliberately as an instrument of national policy."

Allard and Jamieson may have been ahead of their time since, today, a large number of people believe the end of broadcast regulation is in sight. "Regulation, in due course, is just going to wither and die," says Michael Hind-Smith. "I don't think it has the support of the people." Ivan Fecan says, "Over time, regulation has diminished and will continue to diminish because it is simply impossible to regulate the same way one did years ago, although you will still want to make sure there is benefit to the country as a whole."

Izzy Asper, a long-time combatant with the CRTC, says, "Governments and regulators must take off the shackles and understand that . . . it is the viewer, not the regulator, who sets the programming agenda. . . . Regulations against foreign ownership and cross-media ownership will vanish, as will the CRTC and content quotas as we know them."

Ted Rogers agrees. "We're seeing the death pangs of dying, interfering regulations. With increasing globalization and competitiveness and moving from monopoly to competitive service, regulation will fade. The CRTC can't say you can package this way and not that way when the customers all want it that way. You can't have Rogers Cable run by the customers and run by the CRTC. If we do a poor job, our customers will leave us and our stock will go down."

Nor does the CRTC have many friends in the media. "The CRTC is toast," *Marketing* magazine has said. "Kill the CRTC," urged the *Windsor Star*. "The CRTC hangs on for dear life [in a] swelling sea of change. Its grip is slipping. Good," the *Globe and Mail* has pronounced. "The CRTC should be scrapped," read one editorial in the Moncton *Times-Transcript*.

But wait a minute, says Françoise Bertrand. "I don't see it being obsolete. Accessibility, universality, the importance of cultural sovereignty and cultural diversity are all values so dear and important to Canadians that the market forces will not apply. There still will be a need for a certain regulatory response." Former Baton Broadcasting head Doug Bassett agrees, "CRTC regulations will still be there because people are still concerned about their own identity. If there were no regulations, we'd just be a mirror of the U.S."

Bertrand, however, says new technology makes a difference. "Technology drives us to look at the world differently," she says, "but the public purpose remains the same. For instance, we were driven by technology to look at the world differently for digital licences."

The CRTC also took a different view of radio when it eased the regulation that had prevented multiple radio station ownership in the same market, and it also took a different view of the Internet. There are around 5,000 radio stations on the Internet worldwide, including many set up specifically for the Internet. Online in Timbuktu, you can listen to a Toronto Maple Leafs hockey game or in Kelowna hear the BBC. With the convergence of computer and television screens and with digital technology capable of providing an unlimited supply of viewing options, the 500-channel universe, at which so many have scoffed, could readily turn into a 5,000-channel universe. It would be something like those superstore magazine racks that, in Canada today, offer about 5,000 different magazine titles, most of them American.

With technology shifting the ground under the CRTC's regulatory feet, the agency decided not to impose any regulations on the Internet, allowing Internet operators to work under self-regulation. The CRTC defended its position by saying, "any attempt to regulate Canadian new media might put the industry at a competitive disadvantage in the global marketplace."

There was loud support for the non-regulation of the Internet. The cable industry lobby group, the Canadian Cable Television Association, saluted the CRTC for its approach and asked for the same exemption from regulation to apply to interactive TV. The CAB's Michael McCabe also welcomed the CRTC's hands-off approach for the Internet. One reason is that it offers an opening for private broadcasters to argue against regulations they still have to live with on Canadian content, foreign ownership, advertising, and other areas. "The Internet is not licensed, unlike us, and . . . will not have any Canadian content restrictions and they will not have to pay many of the royalty fees for music as we do," Izzy Asper says. "The CRTC should monitor the situation."

But CTV's Trina McQueen is not so sure the Internet will remain unregulated, and she likens the Internet today to the old Wild West. "It's just cowboys shooting each other and there's no sheriff in town," she says. "Once they start making money, then there will be a sheriff because where there's a lot of money being made, there will be regulation."

Michael McCabe suggests a number of "triggers" that should lead the CRTC to re-evaluate the regulations under which the private broadcasters operate. The triggers might include, McCabe says, if the Internet takes too much advertising – say 10 per cent of the total broadcast media ad revenues – or if there is a rapid and significant drop in TV viewing or radio listening.

The CRTC's decision on the Internet may well have given the CAB a lever to force re-examination of something it has been seeking for three-quarters of a century – a loosely regulated business, similar to that in the United States. That's a factor in the current parliamentary review of Canadian broadcasting, a review that, ironically, produced identical reactions from two sworn enemies in the battle over broadcasting: "Long overdue," said Friends of Canadian Broadcasting spokesperson Ian Morrison and CAB head Michael McCabe.

P rivate broadcasters have no shortage of ideas about reshaping their old nemesis, the CBC. No one is certain about its future, not even CBC president Robert Rabinovitch. "It's not written in stone that it will survive. With the choice of channels that we now have, a lot of people believe the CBC is redundant; it's done its job and it's history. I personally don't believe that."

But a lot of people do believe that. The Canadian Alliance party would like to privatize all or part of the CBC, and so would many Conservatives. Michael Hind-Smith says, "I just don't see a future for the CBC. I don't think it has significant public support any more, nor does it have a significant raison d'être. The CBC doesn't produce anything much that this country would miss. It was important in its time, but its time has passed."

"In the late 1930s and 1940s, when I was a kid," Izzy Asper says, "my entire family would sit around in our living room just glued listening to CBC Radio. But it became narrow and obsolete, and then when cable television came along they began to give up on their mandate. I still listen to CBC Radio in Florida, though."

"Today, the CBC is attempting to function in a world that no longer exists . . . CBC Television no longer has a constituency," Asper told Toronto businessmen. "Yet it still receives nearly $1 billion of government grants and funding from Telefilm, which is used to compete for advertising with the private, taxpaying sector." Asper thinks that the CBC's annual government funding should be replaced by voluntary subscription fees, public donations, and grants. "Its programming should be 100 per cent Canadian. It should be the broadcaster for Canadian intellectuals. There should be no commercials and it should not be competitive with the private sector. That means no cartoons, no sports, no local news, and . . . the CBC should ultimately get out of national news programming."

Moses Znaimer also has a radical prescription for the CBC. He suggests the CBC federal grant of about $1 billion be cut in half, with $500 million going to private broadcasters for the production of Canadian programs and $500 million to the CBC, while telling the CBC to narrow its programming range. "Tell them, 'Don't dance at every wedding,'" he says. Rabinovitch dismisses Znaimer's idea of giving half the CBC budget to private broadcasters. "There's a lot of nonsense in saying, 'Well, just give us the money and we'll do better programming.' Look at the tax breaks the private stations already get, look at the subsidies, at the write-offs and the grants."

Asper and Znaimer's concerns are reflected in Quebec by private broadcasters there who view the CBC as a dangerous rival. Radio-Canada is a more aggressive competitor of private broadcasters, with a much greater audience impact than its English counterpart. The CBC English TV network prime-time audience for the 1999–2000 season was 8.4 per cent. Radio-Canada's prime-time average was 25.8 per cent.

"The public broadcaster should not be playing the ratings game," says Pierre-Karl Péladeau, who, among other things, runs rival network TVA. He calls the CBC French and English networks "dangerous dinosaurs" and says they "should not be hustling for the same sort of films or other U.S. programming that commercial stations already offer to Canadian viewers." Contrasting his private broadcaster responsibilities with those of the CBC, Péladeau told a CRTC hearing, "I'm not dealing with taxpayers' money. I'm dealing with private money, the money of the shareholders, and I've got shareholder value in mind and that's where we're ruled."

These alarms about the CBC are not reflected, however, among most of the English-language private broadcasting executives. With a few exceptions, they no longer regard the CBC as a worrisome competitor.

"We used to fight the CBC all the time," says Michael McCabe. "But we won that battle. Who's our enemy now? Cable! We do battle with cable because they control access to the viewers."

Incensed at what he considered the CAB's bias against cable, Ted Rogers resigned from the CAB in the winter of 2001.

Trina McQueen regards cable more as an uncomfortable partner than as an enemy. "It's like a really unhappy marriage, but it's still a marriage where you need each other," she says.

"I'm a great believer in the CBC," Doug Bassett says. "The people in the private sector should get up and fight for the CBC." His recipe for a future CBC is no commercials and all-Canadian programming. "Give them the money to do it!" he says.

That sentiment is also reflected in COMPAS surveys on public attitudes toward the CBC, which have consistently shown strong public support. A recent survey showed 82 per cent of Canadians felt the CBC was doing a good job.

Even McCabe calls himself a CBC supporter. "The CBC has got to be there to tell our stories," he says. "Private broadcasters are in the business of making money, so I don't think we will be able to do enough product that is distinctively Canadian." The CBC's job, McCabe has told the CRTC, is in "providing truly indigenous Canadian programming that might not otherwise cover its costs . . . taking a leading role with risky and experimental programming that pushes the creative envelope, and incubating Canadian creative talent and technology."

Trina McQueen supports McCabe's idea of the CBC taking a leading role as a risk-taking program innovator. "We grew up thinking the CBC had to be the mainstream of broadcasting instead of it being more like a cultural organization such as a museum, an art gallery, or a university. Former CBC president Juneau always said he wanted the CBC to be a highway, not a pathway. But there aren't many eight-lane highways in television these days. Everybody's a niche now, and there is a tremendously exciting, unique, and innovative role for the CBC as risk-takers.

"Right now," McQueen says, "the CBC vision is to be pretty much what it used to be. But the CBC has to unchain itself . . . redesign itself . . . even though many people who work for the CBC hate that idea and will fight it forever because they see the CBC as being dominant and mainstream. But as a viewer I'm hungry for ideas, hungry for programs that make sense of the welter of information around us. I want to be stimulated, challenged, and maybe even offended at times. The CBC should be part of the nation's intellectual and cultural treasure."

"The CBC's role will change like all our roles have changed," says Ted Rogers. "But there is a function for the CBC in promoting Canada and Canadian programming that the private broadcasters can't afford to do. It'll be a smaller role, but that's true of everybody with market fragmentation."

To differentiate itself from private stations, Rabinovitch says CBC programming must be distinctive, high quality, and reflect Canadian voices, experiences, history, and reference points. But it's one thing to say that and another to make it happen.

"We have to be honest with ourselves in dealing with limited resources," Rabinovitch says. "We're going to have a lower audience share and we're going to have to be more specialized on the main channel. We have to focus down in some ways and have the courage to get out of some areas that the private sector can do as well as we can." That means, he says, more news, documentaries, investigative journalism, comedy, quality arts and entertainment programming, and children's television. "But I think we'll be doing less drama, maybe fewer but larger, and less light entertainment, especially as we have less access to the Canadian Television Fund," he says.

But getting out of some program areas is a high-wire act, as Rabinovitch found out in 2000 in his frustrated effort to eliminate local dinner-hour news programming. "I want my old CBC back," declared an editorial writer in the *West Prince Graphic* on Prince Edward Island. But in the reality of the new media world, that won't happen, especially as Rabinovitch searches for distinction from private TV. The CBC can never again be all things to all people.

Rabinovitch is also determined to cut some advertising, especially in news programs, and find new ways of presenting it. The CBC gets about $330 million a year from advertising, and Rabinovitch figures that initially his plans would cost about $21 million in lost advertising. "There is a role for a distinctive, qualitative broadcaster that is not dominated by advertising. If I had my way, I'd love to be out of ads completely, except for sports, but I can't afford to go any further. Still, I'm using this cut as a symbol."

The past budget cuts and less advertising revenue forced the CBC to slash, prune, and sell almost everything in sight to find replacement money. It sold its two specialty networks in the United States; it sold its headquarters building in Ottawa; it's selling its transmission assets including twenty-five hundred transmitters and hundreds of transmission sites and towers; and it's renting out surplus space in CBC buildings. All this in addition to firing several thousand employees over the last few years, chopping back programs, and slicing administrative support.

While government rhetoric still emphasizes the importance of public broadcasting, the net effect of past government decisions, budget slashing, and CRTC rulings inevitably undermined that rhetoric, lessened the CBC's role, and enhanced that of private broadcasters. Clearly, what the government said it wanted the CBC to do and what it financed it to do were two very different things.

Meanwhile, the lions of private broadcasting such as Asper, Rogers, Fecan, Péladeau, and Shaw have grown stronger, exuberantly leaping into the new media, combining the latest sophisticated technical tools with what's been called everything from corporate vertical integration to convergence, consolidation, mega-mergers, bulking up, clustering, critical mass or "tall trees." The result: giant conglomerates with huge economic, political, and social power far outdistancing public broadcasting in impact on the country, and a very far cry from what Messrs. Spry, Plaunt, and Mackenzie King had dreamed about so long ago.

The loss of CBC dominance was inevitable because of technological advances, according to Rabinovitch. "The reality of technology change made that dominance artificial and not maintainable, especially with cable and specialty channels," he says.

Perhaps all this was forecast by the political godfather of Canadian public broadcasting, Prime Minister R. B. Bennett, who said seventy years ago when launching public broadcasting, "It may be that at some future time, when science has made greater achievements . . . it may be desirable to make other or different arrangements."

The "greater achievements" Bennett referred to have now occurred and those "different arrangements" are being put in place.

13

Idealists Versus Swashbucklers

The private broadcasters' success in achieving dominance over the public broadcaster may have been inevitable because the new technology, and because of the growing political clout of business and the diminishing influence of those who believe government should play a role in making broadcasting an instrument for public good. "If there is a political trend where a country tends to be more on the left, the public broadcaster tends to become dominant," says Trina McQueen. "In the same way, we're now living through a period of what I call aggressive capitalism in which the individual wants more choice, wants more than a public system, and wants to feel in charge or empowered."

In the 1920s, private broadcasters ruled the airwaves, but in the 1930s, the pioneer radio operators almost lost their birthright as the government made public broadcasting responsible for everything on the air. The idea was, in time, to eliminate private stations altogether. But private broadcasters would not willingly lie down and die. They staged a remarkable comeback. They did it through the extraordinarily effective lobbying by broadcast icons such as Harry Sedgwick and Don Jamieson, and the bullheaded persistence of Jim Allard; by consistent government failure to provide the money necessary to achieve the parliamentary mandate given to the CBC and the CRBC; by the granting of high power to a large number of private radio stations; by the licensing of so many private radio and TV operations; by the CBC's arrogance in relations with the private stations, especially in its early years; by the CBC's haughty patronizing in dealing with the Conservative party in the 1940s and 1950s; by the arrival of CTV, Global, cable, and the specialty channels; and, especially, by the defanging of the CBC by the political patron saint of private broadcasting, John Diefenbaker, when he was prime minister in the late 1950s. Through it all, the private broadcasters began to flourish while the CBC lost political leverage, lost much of the missionary zeal of its creative broadcasters, and lost audience.

The glory days of CBC broadcast dominance are now long gone and, without a rebirth, the CBC will dwindle into irrelevance like an old soldier fighting past wars. Although there have been several valiant attempts over the last quarter-century, the CBC has not yet designed its role in the new world of television, which is dominated by a handful of private media goliaths. The survival of public broadcasting in Canada depends on the CBC giving up its supermarket of programming and narrowing its range. It will have to be less dependent on advertising, be clearly distinctive from private broadcasters, and be more effective at exploiting the reservoir of public support it still has. If the CBC has the wit and willpower to do this and the government has the inclination to support it, a reborn CBC could become the premier network of quality, relevant Canadian programming. It may no longer be the biggest stage in the country, but it could be the most prestigious.

The great political fear about broadcasting has been that the Americans would take over Canada's airwaves. To the credit of the private broad-casters and the government, Canada won that battle in a corporate sense. The American networks have not taken possession of our broadcasting stations as they once threatened to do. In another sense, though, Canada lost the fight. We kept the pipeline Canadian-owned, but what has flowed through it has been mostly American programs wrapped in Canadian advertising, especially in the heart of prime time on the private stations. We escaped New York ownership but fell into the hands of Hollywood and became an American cultural colony.

New technology, corporate morphing, "repurposing," and the possi-bility that Americans will become disinclined to sell their programming to Canadian broadcasters give our private stations a chance to start reversing that cultural colonization in the next few years. Whether they take it remains to be seen. But, in a universe of unlimited digital options, it may well be, as Ian Morrison of the Friends of Canadian Broadcasting says, "that the only way Canadian private broadcasters can succeed in the twenty-first century is to be Canadian."

In a painful paradox, however, just as we may see private broadcasters begin turning to Canadian programming in a substantial way, there is on the horizon a possible return to the old American effort to buy control of major Canadian broadcasters. There is pressure on Ottawa to ease foreign ownership restraints as part of North American free trade. If that happens, it would open the door for U.S. communications giants to turn their current minority interest in key Canadian broadcasters into ownership.

Allard, Sedgwick, Jamieson, Spry, Plaunt, and all the Canadian broadcast pioneers would be agog if they could hear the winds of change now howling through Canadian broadcasting, bringing in the mystifying and sometimes terrifying wonders of multibillion-dollar convergences, interactivity, digitalization, vertical integration, and endless choice. They lived in a different world and would look on with amazement at the entangled and dazzling future of Canadian radio and television, and at the brutal jungle broadcasting has become. "It's killer warfare in that jungle now. They're out to destroy each other," says Izzy Asper. "The Marquis of Queensbury must have died."

"It's the end of an era and I would not want to be in it today," says old-time broadcaster Murray Brown. "It's complex, it's very rough and very tough.

"It used to be a nicer business."

Sources

Primary Sources

Personal Interviews by Author

Abbott, Roger (Toronto); Acton, Gerry (Ottawa); Asper, Izzy (Palm Beach, Fla.); Bassett, Douglas (Toronto); Boyle, Harry (Toronto); Brown, Murray (London, Ont.); Bertrand, Françoise (Ottawa); Davey, Sen. Keith (Toronto); Fecan, Ivan (Toronto); Hind-Smith, Michael (Niagara-on-the-Lake, Ont.); Johnson, Al (Ottawa); Kotcheff, Tim (Toronto); MacDonald, Finlay (Halifax); McCabe, Michael (Ottawa); McGregor, William (Kitchener); McQueen, Trina (Toronto); McCreath, Ross (Toronto); Morrison, Ian (Toronto); Pickering, Edward (Toronto); Potts, Lyman (Burlington, Ont.); Rabinovitch, Robert (Ottawa); Rogers, Ted (Toronto); Znaimer, Moses (Toronto)

Oral History Tapes

Allard, T. J. (Selkirk Collection); Avison, John (British Columbia Archives); Baker, Bill (Canadian Communications Foundation); Bass,

Fred (British Columbia Archives); Beardall, Jack (CBC Assignment); Blackburn, W. (Canadian Communications Foundation); Borrett, William (Canadian Communications Foundation); Botterill, Norm (Selkirk Collection); Boyle, Harry (CBC Assignment, National Archives); Bowman, Bob (Canadian Communications Foundation); Bowman, Charles (University of British Columbia Archives); Boyling, Sid (Canadian Communications Foundation); Bremner, Hugh (Canadian Communications Foundation); Brown, Murray (Canadian Communications Foundation); Browne, James H. (British Columbia Archives); Bushnell, Ernie (Canadian Communications Foundation); Caldwell, Spence (Selkirk Collection); Cannings, Bert (Selkirk Collection, Canadian Communications Foundation); Caple, Ken (British Columbia Archives); Cruickshank, "Doc" (CBC Assignment); Dales, Walter (Canadian Communications Foundation); Darling, Tom (Canadian Communications Foundation); Dawson, Jack (Canadian Communications Foundation); Deaville, Frank (Canadian Communications Foundation); Finlayson, Stuart (CBC Assignment); George, Vic (Canadian Communications Foundation); Gray, Jane (Canadian Communications Foundation); Hartford, Don (Selkirk Collection); Henderson, Eve (Canadian Communications Foundation); Hewitt, Foster (Canadian Communications Foundation); Hind-Smith, Michael (Canadian Communications Foundation); Hooper, Bert (Canadian Communications Foundation); Hyndman, Walter (Canadian Communications Foundation); Keeble, Gordon (Canadian Communications Foundation); Kope, Orv (Canadian Communications Foundation); Laws, Don (British Columbia Archives); Lees, Ramsay (Canadian Communications Foundation); Lombardi, Johnny (Canadian Communications Foundation); Love, Gordon (CBC Assignment); MacCurdy, H. T. (Canadian Communications Foundation); MacDonald, Finlay (Canadian Communications Foundation); Mackay, J. Stuart (Selkirk Collection); McCreath, Ross (Selkirk Collection); McDermott, Andy (Canadian Communications Foundation); Mills, Hugh (Canadian Communications Foundation); Montagnes, Jim (Canadian Communications Foundation); Morrow, Marianne (Canadian Communications Foundation); Murphy, A. A. (CBC Assignment); Parkin, Kay (Canadian Communications Foundation); Pelletier, Aurele (Canadian Communications Foundation); Potts, Lyman (Canadian Communications Foundation, National Archives); Purdy, Rai (Canadian

Communications Foundation); Rice, G. A. R. (CBC Assignment, Canadian Communications Foundation); Roberts, Herb (Canadian Communications Foundation); Robertson, T. C. (National Archives); Ross, Sam (Canadian Communications Foundation); Rowe, Melvin (Canadian Communications Foundation); Slaight, Allan (Canadian Communications Foundation); Soble, Ken (Ryerson); Speers, Bill (Canadian Communications Foundation); Stovin, Horace (CBC Assignment); Swabey, H. C. (Canadian Communications Foundation); Wedge, Pip (CTV); Weinthal, Arthur (CTV).

House of Commons

Parliamentary Committee Reports, 1932–2001
Parliamentary Committee Testimony, 1932–2001
Hansard, 1925–2001

Major Government Commissions and Task Forces

Royal Commission on Radio Broadcasting, Sir John Aird, 1929.
Survey of National Radio in Canada, Gladstone Murray, 1933.
Royal Commission on National Development in the Arts, Letters and Sciences, Vincent Massey, 1951.
Royal Commission on Broadcasting, Robert Fowler, 1957.
Advisory Committee on Broadcasting, Robert Fowler, 1965.
White Paper on Broadcasting, 1966.
Special Senate Committee on Mass Media, Sen. Keith Davey, 1970.
Royal Commission on Government Organization, Grant Glassco, 1963.
Federal Cultural Policy Review Committee, Louis Applebaum and Jacques Hébert, 1982.
Task Force on Broadcasting Policy, Gerald Caplan and Florian Sauvageau, 1986.
Mandate Review Committee CBC, NFB, Telefilm, Pierre Juneau, Dr. Catherine Murray, and Peter Herrndorf, 1996.

Miscellaneous Documents

Allard, T. J., Various Speeches, Statements, Letters, and Interviews, 1942–1980

Ashcroft, Ralph, Various Speeches and Statements

Asper, Izzy, Various Speeches, Statements, and Interviews

BBG, Annual and Other Reports, 1958–68

Bennett, R. B., Private Papers, National Archives of Canada, Ottawa

Black, A. J., Chronology of Network Broadcasting in Canada, 1901–1961

Blakely, Stewart W., "Canadian Private Broadcasters and Establishment of a Private Broadcasting Network." Ph.D. Thesis, 1979

Bowman, Charles, Private Papers, National Archives of Canada, Ottawa

Bushnell, Ernie, Various Speeches, Statements, and Interviews and Private Papers, National Archives of Canada, Ottawa

Canadian Association of Broadcasters, Various Documents, 1926–2000

CanWest Global, Annual Reports, 1999–2000

CBC, Annual Reports, 1933–2000

CBC, Responses to CRTC, 1968–2000

CFQC Saskatchewan, *Action, Achievement, Modern, 1923–1949*

CHML Hamilton, Ontario, Golden Anniversary, 1977

CHUMCITY, Annual Reports, 1999–2000

Coopers & Lybrand, Specialty Services: Background and Business Analysis, 1998

CRBC, Annual Reports, 1933–36

CRBC, Minutes, 1933–36

CRTC, Annual and Other Reports, 1968–2000

CTV, Annual Reports, 1990–2000

Dulmage, William G., Radio and TV Station History, 1998

Economic Council of Canada, Canadian Television Broadcasting Structure, 1979

Fecan, Ivan, Various Speeches, Statements

Forsey, Eugene, Various Letters, Statements, and Interviews

Friends of Canadian Broadcasting, Various Documents

Frequence, La Radio Diffusion, 1922–1997

Hind-Smith, Michael. "High Wire." (unpublished book outline), 1990

Hoskins and McFayden Study, 1980

Johnson, Al, "Touchstone for the CBC," 1977, Various Speeches and Statements

Juneau, Pierre, "Let's Do It!" 1985, Various Speeches and Statements

Malone, William, Ph.D. Thesis, Harvard, Boston, 1962

McCabe, Michael, Various Speeches, Statements, and Interviews

McKay, Bruce. "The CBC and the Public." Stanford University, Stanford, California, Ph.D. Thesis, 1976

Morrison, Ian, Various Speeches, Statements, and Interviews

Murray, Gladstone, Private Papers, National Archives of Canada, Ottawa

Nolan, Michael. "An Infant Industry: Canadian Private Radio 1919–36." *Canadian Historical Review*, 1989

O'Brien, Rev. John. "A History of the Canadian Radio League 1930–36." University of Southern California, Los Angeles, Ph.D. Thesis, 1964

Pagè, Prof. Pierre C., L'Origine des stations XWA (1915) et CFCF (1922) de Marconi Wireless Telegraph

Peladeau, Pierre-Karl, Various Speeches, Statements, and Interviews

Pickering, Edward A. "Failure of a Dream." (unpublished memoir notes), 1993

Plaunt, Alan, Private Papers, University of British Columbia Special Collections, Vancouver, B.C.

Potts, Lyman, Various Papers, Documents, and Memorabilia

Rabinovitch, Robert, Various Speeches, Statements, and Interviews

Reynolds, George F., "Early Wireless and Radio in Manitoba, 1909–1924," History and Scientific Society of Manitoba

Rickwood, Roger. "Canadian Broadcasting Policy and Private Broadcasters." University of Toronto, Toronto, Ph.D. Thesis, 1976

Rogers Communications, Inc., Annual Reports, 1990–2000

Rogers, Ted, Various Speeches, Statements, and Interviews

Sedgwick, Harry, Various Speeches and Statements

Sedgwick, Joe, Various Speeches and Statements

Shaw, J. R., Various Speeches, Statements, and Interviews

Spry, Graham, Various Speeches, Statements, Interviews, and Private Papers, National Archives of Canada, Ottawa

Task Force on Implementation of Digital Television

Secondary Sources

Magazines and Newspapers

Broadcaster, and *Canadian Broadcaster*, from 1942
Canadian Forum, from 1931
Canadian Historical Review
Canadian Magazine, 1929
CBC Times, from 1948
Chatelaine, from 1934
Financial Post, from 1932
Gazette, Montreal
Globe, Toronto, 1934
Globe and Mail, Toronto
Hamilton Spectator
Journal, Edmonton
La Presse, Montreal, 1922
Le Devoir
Liberty
Marketing
Maclean's, from 1922
Mail and Empire, Toronto
Montreal Herald
Montreal Star, from 1919
National Post
Ottawa Citizen, from 1920
Ottawa Journal
Ottawa Sun
Playback Toronto
Queen's Quarterly
Regina Leader, 1922
Regina Leader-Post
Saturday Night
Telegram, Toronto, from 1913
The Times, London, 1958
Toronto Star, from 1922
Vancouver Sun

Vancouver Province
Variety
Windsor Star
Winnipeg Free Press, 1922
Winnipeg Tribune, 1922

Books

Allen, Ralph. *The Chartered Libertine*. Toronto: Macmillan of Canada, 1954.
Allard, T. J. *Straight Up*. Ottawa: Canadian Communications Foundation, 1979.
——— *The CAB Story, 1926–76: Private Broadcasting in Canada*. Ottawa: Canadian Association of Broadcasters, 1976.
Anderson, Robert, and Gruneau, Richard, and Heyer, Paul. "TVTV The Debate." Vancouver: Canadian Journal of Communication, 1998.
Anthony, Ian A. *Radio Wizard, Edward Samuel Rogers and the Revolution of Communications*. Toronto: Gage Publishing, 2000.
Audley, Paul. *Canada's Cultural Industries: Broadcasting, Publishing, Records and Film*. Toronto: James Lorimer & Co., 1983.
Bird, Roger. *Documents of Canadian Broadcasting*. Ottawa: Carleton University Press, 1988.
Black, A. J. *Chronology of Network Broadcasting in Canada 1901–1961*. Ottawa: CBC, 1961.
Bothwell, Robert, and Kilbourn, William. *C. D. Howe*. Toronto: McClelland & Stewart, 1979.
Bowman, Charles A. *Ottawa Editor*. Sidney, B.C.: Gray's Publishing, 1966.
Boyle, Harry. *Mostly in Clover*. Toronto: Holt, Rinehart and Winston, 1973.
Braddon, Russell. *Roy Thomson of Fleet Street*. London, Toronto: Collins, 1965.
Carney, Pat. *Trade Secrets*. Toronto: Key Porter Books, 2000.
Charlesworth, Hector. *I'm Telling You: Being the Further Candid Chronicles of Hector Charlesworth*. Toronto: Macmillan of Canada, 1937.
Conrad, Margaret. *George Nowlan: Maritime Conservative in National Politics*. Toronto: University of Toronto Press, 1986.

Crothers, Tom. *Out of Thin Air*. Charlottetown: Applecross Press, 1985.

Dales, Walter. "A Light-Hearted Look at Radio Broadcasting in Canada" (unpublished).

Diefenbaker, John. *One Canada*. Vols. 1–3, Toronto: Macmillan of Canada, 1976.

Easton, Ken. *Building an Industry: A History of Cable Television and Its Development in Canada*. Lawrencetown Beach, N.S.: Pottersfield Press, 2000.

Ellis, David. *Evolution of the Canadian Broadcasting System 1928–68*. Ottawa: Department of Communications, 1979.

——— *Split Screen, Home Entertainment and New Technologies*. Toronto: Friends of Canadian Broadcasting, 1992.

English, John. *Arthur Meighen*. Don Mills, Ontario: Fitzhenry and Whiteside, 1977.

Forsey, Eugene. *A Life at the Fringe*. Toronto: Oxford University Press, 1990.

Foster, Frank. *Broadcasting Policy Development*. Ottawa: Franfost Communications Ltd., 1982.

Fraser, Matthew. *Free-for-All: The Struggle for Dominance on the Digital Frontier*. Toronto: Stoddart Publishing Co. Ltd., 1999.

Gittins, Susan. *CTV: The Television Wars*. Toronto: Stoddart Publishing Co. Ltd., 1999.

Goldenberg, Susan. *The Thomson Empire*. Toronto: Methuen, 1984.

Goodman, Eddie. *Life of the Party*. Toronto: Key Porter Books, 1988.

Gwyn, Richard. *Smallwood: The Unlikely Revolutionary*. Toronto: McClelland & Stewart, 1968.

Hallman, Eugene. *Broadcasting in Canada*. Toronto: General Publishing, 1977.

Hardin, Herschel. *Closed Circuits: The Sellout of Canadian Television*. Vancouver: Douglas & McIntyre, 1984.

Havill, Adrian. *The Last Mogul: An Unauthorized Biography of Jack Kent Cooke*. New York: St. Martin's Press, 1992.

Hewitt, Foster. *His Own Story*. Toronto: Ryerson Press, 1967.

Hindley, H. *Broadcasting in Canada*. Toronto: General Publishing, 1977.

Hull, William H. N. *Canadian Television Policy and the Board of Broadcast Governors, 1958–1968*. Edmonton: University of Alberta Press, 1994.

Jack, Donald. *Sinc, Betty and the Morning Man.* Toronto: Macmillan Canada, 1977.

Jamieson, Don. *The Troubled Air.* Fredericton, New Brunswick: Brunswick Press, 1968.

LaMarsh, Judy. *Memoirs of a Bird in a Gilded Cage.* Toronto: McClelland & Stewart, 1969.

Large, Betty Rogers. *Out of Thin Air.* Charlottetown: Applecross Press, 1985.

Levine, Allan. *The CanWest Global Story: The First Twenty Years.* Toronto: CanWest Global Communications, Co., 1997.

Meighen, Arthur. *Unrevised and Unrepentant: Debating Speeches and Others.* Toronto: Clarke, Irwin & Co., 1949.

McDougall, Bruce. *Ted Rogers.* Toronto: Burgher Books, 1995.

McIntyre, Ian. *The Expense of Glory: A Life of John Reith.* London: HarperCollins, 1993.

McNeil, Bill. *Signing On: The Birth of Radio in Canada.* Toronto: Doubleday Canada Ltd., 1982.

Nash, Knowlton. *Prime Time at Ten.* Toronto: McClelland & Stewart, 1987.

———— *The Microphone Wars.* Toronto: McClelland & Stewart, 1994.

———— *Cue the Elephant!: Backstage Tales at the CBC.* Toronto: McClelland & Stewart, 1996.

Newman, Peter C. *Titans: How the New Canadian Establishment Seized Power.* Toronto: Viking, Penguin Books Canada Ltd., 1998.

Nolan, Michael. *Foundations: Alan Plaunt and the Early Days of CBC Radio.* Toronto: CBC Enterprises, 1986.

———— *Walter Blackburn: A Man for All Media.* Toronto: Macmillan of Canada, 1989.

O'Malley, Martin and Pungente, SJ, John J. *More Than Meets the Eye.* Toronto: McClelland & Stewart, 1999.

Pearson, Lester B. *Mike: The Memoirs of the Right Honourable Lester B. Pearson.* Vols. 1–3, Toronto: University of Toronto Press, 1972–73.

Peers, Frank W. *The Politics of Canadian Broadcasting 1920–51.* Toronto: University of Toronto Press, 1969.

———— *The Public Eye: Television and the Politics of Canadian Broadcasting 1952–68.* Toronto: University of Toronto Press, 1979.

Pickersgill, J. W. *My Years with Louis St. Laurent.* Toronto: University of Toronto Press, 1975.

———— *The Mackenzie King Record*. Toronto: University of Toronto Press, 1960–1970.

Potvin, Rose. *Passion and Conviction: The Letters of Graham Spry*. Regina: Canadian Plains Research Centre, 1992.

Rutherford, Paul. *Prime Time Canada*. Toronto: University of Toronto Press, 1990.

———— *The Making of the Canadian Media*. Toronto: McGraw Hill Ryerson Ltd., 1978.

Raboy, Marc. *Missed Opportunities: The Story of Canada's Broadcast Policy*. Montreal: McGill-Queen's University Press, 1990.

Ruby, Ormand. *Radio's First Voice: The Story of Reginald Fessenden*. Toronto: Macmillan of Canada, 1970.

Santerre, Roger. *History of Telecommunications 1820–1987*. Ottawa: CBC Enterprises, 1987.

Shea, Albert A. *Broadcasting the Canadian Way*. Montreal: Harvest House, 1963.

Siegal, Arthur. *Politics and the Media in Canada*. Toronto: McGraw-Hill Ryerson Ltd., 1983.

Siggins, Maggie. *Bassett*. Toronto: James Lorimer & Co., 1979.

Schmaltz, Wayne. *On Air: Radio in Saskatchewan*. Regina: Coteau Books, 1990.

Smith, Denis. *Rogue Tory: The Life and Legend of John G. Diefenbaker*. Toronto: Macfarlane, Walter & Ross, 1995.

Stewart, Andrew. *Canadian Television Policy and the Board of Broadcast Governors 1958–1968*. Edmonton: University of Alberta Press, 1994.

Stewart, Sandy. *A Pictorial History of Radio in Canada*. Toronto: Gage Publishing Ltd., 1975.

———— *From Coast to Coast*. Toronto: CBC Enterprises, 1985.

———— *Here's Looking at Us*. Toronto: CBC Enterprises, 1986.

Stursburg, Peter. *Mr. Broadcasting: The Ernie Bushnell Story*. Toronto: Peter Martin Associates Ltd., 1971.

Thomas, Stan. *Cable: A Vision of the Pioneers*. Delta, B.C.: Guiness Enterprises, 1982.

Troyer, Warner. *The Sound and the Fury*. Rexdale, Ontario: John Wiley and Sons, Canada, 1980.

Van Dusen, Tommy. *The Chief*. New York: McGraw-Hill, 1968.

Vipond, Mary. *The First Decade of Canadian Broadcasting, 1922–32*. Montreal: McGill-Queen's University Press, 1992.

Weir, Austin. *The Struggle for National Broadcasting in Canada*. Toronto: McClelland & Stewart, 1965.

Wolfe, Morris. *Jolts: The TV Wasteland and the Canadian Oasis*. Toronto: James Lorimer & Co., 1985.

——— *Signing On: The Birth of Radio in Canada*. Toronto: Doubleday Canada Ltd., 1982.

Zimmerman, Arthur Eric. *In the Shadow of the Shield*. Kingston, Ontario: A. E. Zimmerman, 1991.

Index

Committee, 76; on Massey, 143; on Massey report, 149; on Plaunt, 99; on political use of public broadcasting, 187; on politics in licensing, 161-62; on private broadcasters' philosophical differences, 136; on radio's impact in West, 53; on social unacceptability of radio, 243; on Taylor, Pearson, Carson, 138; ousted from CAB leadership, 217; plan to infiltrate Radio League, 164, 199; relationship with Diefenbaker, 170, 196; responsible for private broadcasters' comeback, 176, 209, 275; revitalizes CAB, 15, 134, 137; sets up *Report from Parliament Hill*, 118-19; soulmate of Dales, 120, 123, 219
All-Canada Radio and Television, 138, 161, 227
Alliance party, 270
Allison, Carlyle, 179, 181
American Broadcasting Company (ABC), 191
Argus Corporation, 128
Arthur, Jack, 92
Ashcroft, Ralph W.: establishes Trans-Canada Broadcasting, 74; heads Dominion Broadcasters Association, 79; on Aird report, 68-69, 73; on Broadcasting Act, 97; on Canadian content, 148; on CRBC failure, 99; station bought out by CRBC, 82; testifies to Aird commission, 66
As It Happens (radio), 221
Asper, Izzy: achieves national network for Global, 235; and internal wrangling at Global, 236-37; background, 248; business and life style, 249-50; buys Southam newspapers, 258-59;

career path, 240, 249-51; holds TV future in his hands, 259; on availability of Canadian talent, 266; on broadcasting today, 277; on cable, 228-29; on Canadian content, 262; on CBC's future, 270; on diminishing of regulations, 267; on importance of programming, 261; on mergers, 241-42; political aspirations, 248; takes over Global, 236-38; wealth, 15, 244, 247, 250
Asper, Leonard, 238-39, 242, 251
Association of Canadian Advertisers, 69, 101, 132, 154
Association of Canadian Clubs, 58, 70
Astral Media, 240-41
AT&T, 253
Atkinson, Joseph, 32
Autry, Gene, 92
Avison, John, 46
Aylesworth, Merlin, 72

Baird, John, 149-50
Baker, Bill, 40, 93
Bambrick, Kenneth, 53
Bankhart, Donald, 26
Bannerman, Glen, 101-2, 113, 115-16, 128-29, 134
Baptist Church, 40, 49, 62
Barenaked Ladies, 217
Barnaby, Jack, 96
Barris, Alex, 141
Bartlett, Geoffrey, 44
Bassett, Douglas: hires Fecan, 247, 263; on budget cuts to CBC, 224; on CBC's future, 271; on his father, 161, 189, 211-12, 215; on need for CBC, 271; on need for CRTC, 268; pursues CTV control, 212, 233
Bassett, John: and Canadian content rules, 214-15, 227; battles with

Johnston, Alexander, 56, 62
Johnston, Gaston "Gee," 50
Journal (TV), 223, 225
Juneau, Pierre: and Canadian content, 215-16; cuts CBC commercial time, 221-22; friendship with Bassett, 214-15; heads CRTC, 209, 214; licenses cable companies, 231; on role of CBC, 272
Just Mary (radio), 34

KCND Pembina, North Dakota (TV), 227, 249
KDKA Pittsburgh (radio), 23-24, 34
Keeble, Gordon, 211-12
Keith, Irving, 154
Kelly, Barbara, 38
Kelly, Hal, 140
Kelvin Radio Club, 28
Kennedy, John, 191
Kenney, Mart, 36, 89, 107, 216
Kids in the Hall (TV), 247
King, William Lyon Mackenzie: 1921 election win, 48, 59; 1930 election loss, 69; 1935 election win, 99-100; advisers, 116; Aird commission, 63-64, 69; appoints Dunton to head CBC, 129; first hears radio, 25, 59; hears pleas for public radio, 58-59, 62; leaves politics, 135, 142, 145; policies dismissed by Jamieson, 203; political skills, 208; supported by *Star*, 62; supports CBC, 107, 117, 133; supports public radio, 14, 59-60, 71, 75, 101, 103, 105, 121, 176; uses CBC, 109, 112
KOA Denver (radio), 56
Kotcheff, Tom, 212
KSL Salt Lake City (radio), 56
KVOS Bellingham, Washington (TV), 227

LaFlèche, Leo R., 112, 117
Lalonde, Marc, 204
Lalonde, Phil, 130
Lamarre, Daniel, 263
LaMarsh, Judy, 207-9
Landscape Entertainment, 261
Lane, Abby, 90
LaPierre, Laurier, 206
La Presse, 18-19, 68-69, 83
Laurendeau, André, 144
Lawler, Jack, 88
Laws, Don, 52
Lees, Ramsay, 89
Lévesque, René, 173
Lewis, Richard: alarmed by BBG licensing of CBC stations, 188; excellent editor, 113; on BBG, 181; on Bushnell's return to private broadcasting, 187; on CBC advertising rates, 163; on CBC dilution, 192; on Fowler's recommendations, 205; on lust for money versus lust for power, 186; wants CAB to be more aggressive, 128
Liba, Peter, 249
Liberal party: 1930 election loss, 73; 1935 election win, 99; 1949 election win, 144; 1953 election win, 159-60; 1963 election win, 197-99; 1965 election win, 206; 1967 Broadcast Act, 209; agrees with Fowler report, 170; and CBC politicking, 170, 178; Asper's aspirations, 248; CAB lobbies, 205; CBC politicking, 112; cuts CBC budget, 225; discontent in ranks about TV policy, 114, 134, 144, 154-55, 159, 163, 201; fears cost of public TV, 151; growing discontent with CBC, 164; licence politicking, 161-62, 200, 207-8; lone holdout against 1932 bill, 77; Massey's

Neill, Malcolm, 167, 172, 176, 180, 182
Nelvana, 241
New Brunswick Lumberjacks, 89
New Canada Movement, 80
Newcap, 240
New Democratic Party, 196
Newman, Peter C., 211, 239, 255
Niosi, Bert, 107
Noble, Percy, 220
Nolles, Ferne, 90
Northern Electric Company, 19
Noseworthy, Joe, 153
Nowlan, George: helps set up BBG, 178, 180; interference with CBC, 185; on Canadian content, 181; prepares broadcast policy for Diefenbaker, 172-73, 175; TV licensing, 171, 188; wards off hard proposals for CBC, 196

Osborne, Ron, 254
Ottawa Citizen, 25, 58-61, 69
Ouelette, Andre, 220
Ouimet, J. Alphonse: admired by Pearson, 197; appointed president of CBC, 180; experiments with TV, 150-51; on advertising on CBC, 222; on CAB, 168; on CBC and CTV, 195; pay and position restored by Pearson, 199-200; problems inside CBC, 184-85; *Seven Days* controversy, 207; studies broadcasting policy for Pearson, 203; urges industry review, 197

Parade of the Provinces (radio), 84
Parker, Pete, 42
Parkin, Kay, 88
PBS, funding campaign forerunners, 81
Pearl, Bert, 87, 107
Pearson, Hugh, 137-38

Pearson, Lester: 1963 election win, 197-98, 203; 1965 election win, 206; and *Seven Days* controversy, 206; cannot save Fowler recommendations, 208; on Diefenbaker's broadcast policy changes, 175; political style, 179; restores Ouimet's pay and position, 199-200; supports public broadcasting, 71, 201-2, 204
Peers, Frank, 179, 203
Péladeau, Erik, 244
Péladeau, Pierre, 239
Péladeau, Pierre-Karl, 239-40, 244, 259, 271
Pelletier, Gérard, 144
Periodical Press Association, 112
Perley, Sir George, 98
Peterson, David, 255
Peters, Ray, 15, 211-13
Phil the Greek, 96-97
Philpott, Elmore, 111
Picard, Laurent, 221
Pickering, Edward, 100, 103-4
Pickersgill, Jack: advises BBG on cable TV, 230; criticizes CBC-TV Edmonton station, 188; delays Canadian arrival of pay-TV, 230; in Pearson cabinet, 200-203, 205, 207-9; link with Jamieson, 154, 160; link with Plaunt, 99; warms to idea of private network, 193
Pigeon, Louis-Joseph, 144
Plaunt, Alan: and CRBC demise, 99; attitude to broadcasting, 97, 120-22, 124, 126; behind-the-scenes promotion of CBC, 107; blamed for CRBC's demise, 104; death, 110-11; establishes Canadian Radio League, 120-21; Jamieson's view of, 201; lobbies for public radio, 15, 70-72, 74-78, 121, 126, 143, 176; on advertising in

Vaughan, Denny, 216
Veilleux, Gérard, 246-47
Vidéotron, 230, 239, 254
Vipond, Mary, 74, 79
VOCM St. John's (radio), 41
VOWR St. John's (radio), 41

Wallace, Claire, 90, 92
Wallin, Pamela, 228
Waters, Allan, 165, 168, 171, 207-8, 258
Watson, Patrick, 206
Way It Is (TV), 257
Weir, E. Austin, 85
Wells, Jack, 88
Western Association of Broadcasters, 136
Western International Communications (WIC), 234-35, 237-38, 266
West Richards, Hermina, 46
White, Nancy, 246
WIC. *See* Western International Communications (WIC)
William Nielsen, 74
Willis, J. Frank, 93
Wilson, Don, 44
Wilson, Woodrow, 21
Windsor Star, 268
Winnipeg Free Press, 53-54, 98, 116, 193
Winnipeg Tribune, 35, 53-54, 193
Wintermeyer, John, 154
Wireless Association of Canada, 26

Witney, C. H., 168
Wolfe, Morris, 231
Woodhouse and Hawkins, 88, 90
Woodill, Wilf, 86
Woodsworth, J. S., 62
Worden, H. R., 66
WWJ Detroit (radio), 60

XEY Winnipeg (radio), 28
XWA Montreal (radio, later CFCF): 1920s programming, 25, 32, 59; first radio station in Canada, 14, 18, 24-25; interviews Dempsey, 27; loses Coats, 39

Young, Alan, 107
Young Bloods of Beaver Bend (radio), 83-84
Young, E. J., 77

Znaimer, Moses: background, 255-56; business and life style, 256, 259; career path, 256-58; champions localism, 232; hires Fecan, 246; holds TV future in his hands, 259; on cable, 228; on CBC's future, 270; on future of broadcasting, 261-62; on importance of programming, 261; on mergers, 242; tough reputation, 247